Quantum Computational Number Theory

Song Y. Yan

Quantum Computational Number Theory

Song Y. Yan

Song Y. Yan
Wuhan University
Wuhan, China

ISBN 978-3-319-79846-2   ISBN 978-3-319-25823-2   (eBook)
DOI 10.1007/978-3-319-25823-2

Springer Cham Heidelberg New York Dordrecht London
© Springer International Publishing Switzerland 2015
Softcover reprint of the hardcover 1st edition 2015

Printed on acid-free paper

Springer International Publishing AG Switzerland is part of Springer Science+Business Media (www.
springer.com)

Preface

Imagination is more important than knowledge. Knowledge is limited. Imagination encircles the world.

ALBERT EINSTEIN (1879–1955)
The 1921 Nobel Laureate in Physics

Quantum computational number theory is a new interdisciplinary subject of number theory, computation theory, and quantum computing together. The aim of quantum computational number theory is to use the new quantum computing techniques to solve the intractable computational problems in number theory and number-theoretic cryptography. Indeed, the most famous quantum algorithm, namely, Shor's quantum factoring algorithm, is for solving the integer factorization problem and for breaking the RSA cryptographic system.

The book consists of six chapters. In Chapter 1, we try to answer briefly what is computational number theory and what is quantum computational number theory. Chapter 2 presents some basic concepts and results in classical and quantum computation. Chapter 3 gives an account of classical and quantum algorithms for the integer factorization problem (IFP). Chapter 4 discusses classical and quantum algorithms for the discrete logarithm problems (DLP), whereas Chapter 5 deals with classical and quantum algorithms for elliptic curve discrete logarithm problems (ECDLP). Since all classical algorithms are not powerful enough to solve IFP, DLP, and ECDLP in polynomial-time, all IFP-, DLP-, and ECDLP-based cryptographic system is secure, provided that they are constructed and used properly. However, if a practical quantum computer can be built, then the quantum algorithms discussed can be used to break all the IFP-, DLP-, and ECDLP-based cryptographic systems. Of course, we cannot expect quantum algorithms or more generally quantum computers to break all the cryptographic systems, since quantum computers use a different paradigm for computation, and they are not faster version of classical computers; for some computational problems such as IFP and DLP, they can exponentially (more specifically superpolynomially) speed up the computation, but for other problems such as any $\mathcal{NP}$-complete problem, e.g., the traveling salesman problem (TSP), they will not be able to speed up the computation at all. Thus, there exist cryptographic systems that quantum computers cannot break; these types of cryptographic systems are called quantum-resistant cryptographic systems. Finally, in Chapter 6, we shall discuss some more quantum algorithms for other number-theoretic and algebraic problems.

The monograph can be regarded as a new version of the author's earlier book *Quantum Attacks on Public-Key Cryptosystems*, with an emphasis on quantum attacking for both the IFP, DLP, and ECDLP problems and the IFP-, DLP-, and ECDLP-based cryptography. It is self-contained and can be used as a basic reference for computer scientists, mathematicians, electrical engineers, and physicists, interested in quantum computational number theory. It can also be used as an advanced text for final year undergraduates or first-year graduates in the field.

Acknowledgments

The book was written while I worked in Computer School of Wuhan University as a specially appointed professor. The research related to the topics of the book was supported in part by the Royal Academy of Engineering London, the Royal Society London, Massachusetts Institute of Technology, Harvard University, and Wuhan University (Fund No: SKLSE-2015-A-02) over the past 10 years or so. I would like to thank my Ph.D. student Ya-Hui Wang for reading the draft version of the book and for providing some computational examples.

Wuhan, China
August 2015

Song Y. Yan

Contents

Chapter 1
Introduction

God used beautiful mathematics in creating the world.

PAUL DIRAC (1902–1984)
The 1933 Nobel Laureate in Physics

Number theory is one of the oldest subjects in mathematics. Traditionally, number theory is the purest of the pure mathematical discipline. But with the advent of modern computers, it becomes more and more computation involved, giving to the birth of computational number theory, and even the quantum computational number theory, just as analytic number theory and algebraic number theory, where analysis and algebra play an important role. This chapter provides an introduction to the basic ideas and concepts, as well as some important open problems in number theory and computational number theory and quantum computational number theory. More specifically, we shall give a descriptive answer to the following three questions:

1. What is number theory?
2. What is computational number theory?
3. What is quantum computational number theory?

1.1 What is Number Theory

Number theory, or the theory of numbers, is concerned mainly with the study of the properties of the integers

$$\mathbb{Z} = \{\cdots, -3, -2, -1, 0, 1, 2, 3, \cdots\},$$

particularly the positive integers

$$\mathbb{Z}^+ = \{1, 2, 3, \cdots\}.$$

© Springer International Publishing Switzerland 2015
S.Y. Yan, *Quantum Computational Number Theory*,
DOI 10.1007/978-3-319-25823-2_1

For example, by the divisibility property, all positive integers may be classified into three categories:

1. Unit: 1.
2. Prime numbers: $2, 3, 5, 7, 11, 13, 17, 19, 23, \cdots$.
3. Composite numbers: $4, 6, 8, 9, 10, 12, 14, 15, 16, 18, 20, 21, 22, \cdots$.

Recall that a positive integer $n > 1$ is called a prime number, if its only divisors are 1 and n, otherwise, it is a composite number. 1 is neither prime number nor composite number. Prime numbers play a central role in number theory, as any positive integer $n > 1$ can be written uniquely into the following standard prime factorization form:

$$n = p_1^{\alpha_1} p_2^{\alpha_2} \cdots p_k^{\alpha_k},$$

where $p_1 < p_2 < \cdots < p_k$ are primes and $\alpha_1, \alpha_2, \cdots, \alpha_k$ positive integers. Although prime numbers have been studied for more than 2000 years, there are still many open problems about the distribution of prime numbers. Let us investigate some of the most interesting problems about prime numbers.

1. The distribution of prime numbers.

   Euclid proved 2000 years ago in his *Elements* that there were infinitely many prime numbers. That is, the sequence of prime numbers

$$2, 3, 5, 7, 11, 13, 17, 19, \cdots$$

is endless. For example, $2, 3, 5$ are the first three prime numbers, whereas $2^{57885161} - 1$ is the largest prime number, as of August 2015, it has 17425170 digits, it was discovered on 25 January 2013. Let $\pi(x)$ denote the number of prime numbers up to x (Table 1.1 gives some values of $\pi(x)$ for some large x), then Euclid's theorem of infinitude of primes actually says that

$$\pi(x) \to \infty, \quad \text{as } x \to \infty.$$

A much better result about the distribution of prime numbers is the Prime Number Theorem, stating that

$$\pi(x) \sim x / \log x.$$

In other words,

$$\lim_{x \to \infty} \frac{\pi(x)}{x / \log x} = 1.$$

Table 1.1 $\pi(x)$ for some large x

x	$\pi(x)$	$\pi(x) - x/\log x$
10	4	-0.3
10^2	25	3.3
10^3	168	23
10^4	1229	143
10^5	9592	906
10^6	78498	6116
10^7	664579	44158
10^8	5761455	332774
10^9	50847534	2592592
10^{10}	455052511	20758029
10^{11}	4118054813	169923159
10^{12}	37607912018	1416705193
10^{13}	346065536839	11992858452
10^{14}	3204941750802	102838308636
10^{15}	29844570422669	891604962452
10^{16}	279238341033925	7804289844393
10^{17}	2623557157654233	68883734693281
10^{18}	24739954287740860	612483070893536
10^{19}	234057667276344607	5481624169369960
10^{20}	2220819602560918840	49347193044659701
10^{21}	21127269486018731928	446579871578168707
10^{22}	201467286689315906290	4060704006019620994
10^{23}	1925320391606803968923	37083513766578631309
10^{24}	18435599767349200867866	339996354713708049069
10^{25}	176846309399143769411680	3128516637843038351228
10^{26}	1699246750872437141327603	28883358936853188823261

Note that the log is the natural logarithm $\log_e$ (normally denoted by ln), where $e = 2.7182818 \cdots$. However, if the Riemann hypothesis [8] is true, then there is a refinement of the Prime Number Theorem

$$\pi(x) = \int_2^x \frac{dt}{\log t} + \mathcal{O}\left(x e^{-c\sqrt{\log x}}\right)$$

to the effect that

$$\pi(x) = \int_2^x \frac{dt}{\log t} + \mathcal{O}\left(\sqrt{x}\log x\right).$$

Of course we do not know if the Riemann hypothesis is true. Whether or not the Riemann hypothesis is true is one of the most important open problems in mathematics, and in fact it is one of the seven Millennium Prize Problems proposed by the Clay Mathematics Institute in Boston in 2000, each with one million US dollars (see [8, 9, 17, 58]). The Riemann hypothesis states that all the nontrivial (complex) zeros ρ of the ζ function

$$\zeta(s) = \sum_{n=1}^{\infty} \frac{1}{n^s}, \quad s = \sigma + it, \ \{\sigma, t\} \in \mathbb{R}, \ i = \sqrt{-1}$$

lying in the critical strip $0 < \mathrm{Re}(s) < 1$ must lie on the critical line $\mathrm{Re}(s) = \frac{1}{2}$, that is, $\rho = \frac{1}{2} + it$, where ρ denotes a nontrivial zero of $\zeta(s)$. Riemann calculated the first five non-trivial zeros of $\zeta(s)$ and found that they all lie on the critical line (see Figure 1.1), he then conjectured that all the non-trivial zeros of $\zeta(s)$ are on the critical line.

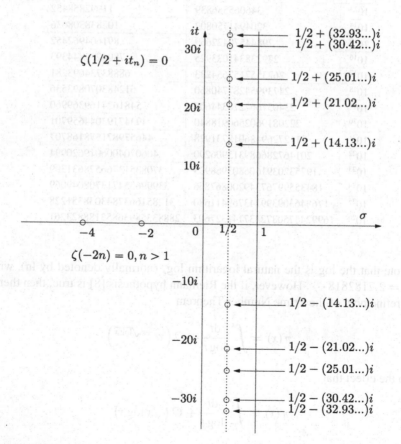

Figure 1.1 Riemann's hypothesis

Table 1.2 Twenty large twin prime pairs

Rank	Twin primes	Digits	Time
1	$3756801695685 \cdot 2^{666669} \pm 1$	200700	Dec 2011
2	$65516468355 \cdot 2^{333333} \pm 1$	100355	Aug 2009
3	$4884940623 \cdot 2^{198800} \pm 1$	59855	July 2015
4	$2003663613 \cdot 2^{195000} \pm 1$	58711	Jan 2007
5	$38529154785 \cdot 2^{173250} \pm 1$	52165	July 2014
6	$194772106074315 \cdot 2^{171960} \pm 1$	51780	Jun 2007
7	$100314512544015 \cdot 2^{171960} \pm 1$	51780	Jun 2006
8	$16869987339975 \cdot 2^{171960} \pm 1$	51779	Sep 2005
9	$33218925 \cdot 2^{169690} \pm 1$	51090	Sep 2002
10	$22835841624 \cdot 7^{54321} \pm 1$	45917	Nov 2010
11	$1679081223 \cdot 2^{151618} \pm 1$	45651	Feb 2012
12	$9606632571 \cdot 2^{151515} \pm 1$	45621	Jul 2014
13	$84966861 \cdot 2^{140219} \pm 1$	42219	Apr 2012
14	$12378188145 \cdot 2^{140002} \pm 1$	42155	Dec 2010
15	$23272426305 \cdot 2^{140001} \pm 1$	42155	Dec 2010
16	$8151728061 \cdot 2^{125987} \pm 1$	37936	May 2010
17	$598899 \cdot 2^{118987} \pm 1$	35825	Apr 2010
18	$307259241 \cdot 2^{115599} \pm 1$	34808	Jan 2009
19	$60194061 \cdot 2^{114689} \pm 1$	34533	Nov 2002
20	$5558745 \cdot 10^{33334} \pm 1$	33341	Apr 2011

2. The distribution of twin prime numbers.

Twin prime numbers are of the form $n \pm 1$, where both numbers are prime. For example, $(3, 5), (5, 7), (11, 13)$ are the first three smallest twin prime pairs, whereas the largest twin primes so far are $65516468355 \cdot 2^{333333} \pm 1$, discovered in August 2009, both numbers having 100355 digits. Table 1.2 gives 20 large twin prime pairs. Let $\pi_2(x)$ be the number of twin primes up to x (Table 1.3 gives some values of $\pi_2(x)$ for different x), then the twin prime conjecture states that

$$\pi_2(x) \to \infty, \text{ as } x \to \infty.$$

If the probability of a random integer x and the integer $x + 2$ being prime were statistically independent, then it would follow from the Prime Number Theorem that

$$\pi_2(x) \sim \frac{x}{(\log x)^2},$$

or more precisely,

$$\pi_2(x) \sim c \frac{x}{(\log x)^2},$$

with

$$c = 2 \prod_{p \geq 3} \left(1 - \frac{1}{(p-1)^2}\right).$$

As these probabilities are not independent, so Hardy and Littlewood conjectured that

$$\pi_2(x) = 2 \prod_{p \geq 3} \frac{p(p-2)}{(p-1)^2} \int_2^x \frac{dt}{(\log t)^2}$$

$$\approx 1.320323632 \int_2^x \frac{dt}{(\log t)^2}.$$

The infinite product in the above formula is the twin prime constant; this constant was estimated to be approximately $0.66016181584686957392\cdots$, so $2c \approx 1.3203236316937391478$. The conjectured values of $\pi_2(x)$ for various x is also given in Table 1.3 (see the information in the right most column of the table). Using very complicated arguments based on sieve methods in his work on the Goldbach conjecture, the Chinese mathematician Chen [10] showed that *there are infinitely many pairs of integers $(n, n + 2)$, with n prime and $n + 2$ a product of at most two primes*. More recently, Zhang [62] showed that

$$\liminf_{n \to \infty}(P_{n+1} - P_n) < N, \quad \text{with} \quad N < 7 \cdot 10^7,$$

Table 1.3 $\pi_2(x)$ for some values x

x	Actual values for $\pi_2(x)$	Conjectured values for $\pi_2(x)$
10	2	4
10^2	8	13
10^3	34	45
10^4	205	214
10^5	1224	1248
10^6	8169	8248
10^7	58980	58753
10^8	440312	440367
10^9	3424506	3425308
10^{10}	27412679	27411416
10^{11}	224376048	224368864
10^{12}	1870585220	1870559866
10^{13}	15834664872	15834598305
10^{14}	135780321665	135780264894
10^{15}	1177209242304	1177208491860
10^{16}	10304195697298	10304192554495

where P_n is the nth prime, which is a major improvement on the Goldston-Graham-Pintz-Yildrim result [27]:

$$\liminf_{n \to \infty} \frac{P_{n+1} - P_n}{\log P_n} = 0.$$

Notice that the value of N in Zhang's result has been reduced to 246, by a group of people in the Polymath Project. A similar and equivalent problem to the twin prime number conjecture is the Goldbach conjecture, which states that *every even number greater than 4 is the sum of two odd prime numbers.* It was conjectured by Goldbach in a letter to Euler in 1742. It remains unsolved to this day. The best result for this conjecture is the due to Chen, who announced it in 1966 but the full proof was not given until 1973 [10], due to the chaotic Culture Revolution, that *every sufficiently large even number is the sum of one prime number and the product of at most two prime numbers*, i.e., $E = p_1 + p_2 p_3$, where E is a sufficiently large even number and p_1, p_2, p_3 are prime numbers. As a consequence, there are infinitely many such twin numbers ($p_1, p_1 + 2 = p_2 p_3$). Extensions relating to the twin prime numbers have also been considered. For example, are there infinitely many triplet primes (p, q, r) with $q = p + 2$ and $r = p+6$? The first five triplets of this form are as follows: $(5, 7, 11)$, $(11, 13, 17)$, $(17, 19, 23)$, $(41, 43, 47)$, $(101, 103, 107)$. The triplet prime problem is much harder than the twin prime problem. It is amusing to notice that there is only one triplet primes (p, q, r) with $q = p + 2$ and $r = p + 4$. That is, $(3, 5, 7)$. The Riemann hypothesis, the twin prime problem and the Goldbach conjecture form the famous Hilbert's 8th Problem.

3. The distribution of arithmetic progressions of prime numbers.
An arithmetic progression of prime numbers is defined to be the sequence of primes satisfying:

$$p, p + d, p + 2d, \cdots, p + (k - 1)d,$$

where p is the first term, d the common difference, and $p + (k - 1)d$ the last term of the sequence. For example, the following are some sequences of the arithmetic progression of primes:

$$3 \quad 5 \quad 7,$$

$$5 \quad 11 \quad 17 \quad 23,$$

$$5 \quad 11 \quad 17 \quad 23 \quad 29.$$

The longest arithmetic progression of primes is the following sequence with 23 terms: $56211383760397 + k \cdot 44546738095860$ with $k = 0, 1, \cdots, 22$. Thanks to Green and Tao [29] who proved in 2007 that *there are arbitrary long arithmetic progressions of primes* (i.e., k can be any arbitrary large natural number), which enabled, among others, Tao to receive a Field Prize in 2006, an equivalent Nobel Prize for Mathematics. However, their result is not about consecutive primes; we still do not know if there are arbitrary long arithmetic progressions of consecutive primes, although Chowa proved in 1944 that there exists an infinity of three consecutive primes of arithmetic progressions. Note that an arithmetic progression of consecutive primes is a sequence of consecutive primes in the progression. In 1967, Jones, Lal and Blundon found an arithmetic progression of five consecutive primes $10^{10} + 24493 + 30k$ with $k = 0, 1, 2, 3, 4$. In the same year, Lander and Parkin discovered six in an arithmetic progression $121174811 + 30k$ with $k = 0, 1, 2, 3, 4, 5$. The longest arithmetic progression of consecutive primes, discovered by Manfred Toplic in 1998, is

$$507618446770482 \cdot 193\# + x77 + 210k,$$

where

$$\begin{cases} 193\# \text{ is the product of all primes } \leq 193, \\ x77 \text{ is the following 77 digit number} \\ \quad 5453824168388758266818970359011065905786593476460487384 \\ \quad 0781923513421103495579, \\ k = 0, 1, 2, \cdots, 9. \end{cases}$$

It should be noted that problems in number theory are easy to state because they are mainly concerned with integers which we are very familiar, but often very hard to solve!

Problems for Section 1.1

1. Show that there are infinitely many prime numbers.
2. Prove or disprove that there are infinitely many twin prime numbers.
3. Are there infinitely many triple prime numbers of the form $p, p+2, p+4$, where $p, p+2, p+4$ are all prime numbers? For example, 3, 5, 7 are such triple prime numbers.
4. Are there infinitely many triple prime numbers of the form $p, p+2, p+6$, where $p, p+2, p+6$ are all prime numbers? For example, 5, 7, 11 are such triple prime numbers.
5. (Prime Number Theorem) Show that

$$\lim_{x \to \infty} \frac{\pi(x)}{x/\log x} = 1.$$

6. (Twin Prime Number Conjecture) Show that

$$\lim_{x \to \infty} \frac{\pi_2(x)}{x/(\log x)^2} = 1.$$

7. (Hardy-Littlewood's Conjecture of Twin Prime Numbers) Show that

$$\pi_2(x) = 2 \prod_{p \geq 3} \frac{p(p-2)}{(p-1)^2} \int_2^x \frac{dt}{(\log t)^2}$$

$$\approx 1.320323632 \int_2^x \frac{dt}{(\log t)^2}.$$

8. The Riemann ζ-function is defined as follows:

$$\zeta(s) = \sum_{n=1}^{\infty} \frac{1}{n^s},$$

where $s = \sigma + it$ is a complex number. Riemann conjectured that all zeroes of the $\zeta(s)$ in the critical strip $0 \leq \sigma \leq 1$ must lie on the critical line $\sigma = \frac{1}{2}$. That is,

$$\zeta\left(\frac{1}{2} + it\right) = 0.$$

Prove or disprove the Riemann hypothesis.

9. Andrew Beal in 1993 conjectured that the equation $x^a + y^b = z^c$ has no positive integer solutions in x, y, z, a, b, c, where $a, b, c \geq 3$ and $\gcd(x, y) = \gcd(y, z) = \gcd(x, z) = 1$. Beal has offered \$100,000 for a proof or a disproof of this conjecture.

10. Prove or disprove the Goldbach conjecture that any even number greater than 6 is the sum of two odd prime numbers.

11. A positive integer n is perfect if $\sigma(n) = 2n$, where $\sigma(n)$ is the sum of all divisors of n. For example, 6 is perfect since $\sigma(6) = 1 + 2 + 3 + 6 = 2 \cdot 6 = 12$. Show that n is perfect if and only if $n = 2^{p-1}(2^p - 1)$, where $2^p - 1$ is a Mersenne prime.

12. All known perfect numbers are even perfect. Recent research shows that if there exists an odd perfect number, it must be greater than 10^{300} and must have at least 29 prime factors (not necessarily distinct). Prove or disprove that there exists at least one odd perfect number.

13. Show that there are arbitrary long arithmetic progressions of primes numbers

$$p, p + d, p + 2d, \cdots, p + (k-1)d,$$

where p is the first term, d the common difference and $p + (k-1)d$ the last term of the sequence, furthermore, all the terms in the sequence are prime numbers and k can be any arbitrary large positive integer.

14. Prove or disprove that there are arbitrary long arithmetic progressions of consecutive prime numbers.

1.2 What is Computational Number Theory

Computational number theory, as its name suggested, may be regarded as a combined subject of number theory and computation theory. That is,

Computational Number Theory := Number Theory $\oplus$ Computation Theory.

Basically, any topic in number theory where computation plays a central role can be regarded as a topic in computational number theory. Computational number theory aims at either using computing techniques to solve number-theoretic problems, or using number theoretic techniques to solve computer science problems. We concentrate in this book on using computing techniques to solve number theoretic problems that have connections and applications in modern public-key cryptography. Typical questions or problems in this category of computational number theory include:

1. **Primality Testing Problem (PTP).** PTP can be formally defined as follows:

$$\text{PTP} \stackrel{\text{def}}{=} \begin{cases} \text{Input}: & n > 1, \\ \text{Output}: & \begin{cases} \text{Yes}: n \in \text{Primes}, \\ \text{No}: \text{Otherwise}. \end{cases} \end{cases}$$

Theoretically speaking, PTP can be solved in polynomial-time, i.e., PTP can be solved efficiently on a computer. However, it may still be difficult to decide whether or not a large number is prime. Call a number a Mersenne prime if it is of the form

$$M_p = 2^p - 1,$$

where p is prime and $2^p - 1$ is also prime. Up to date, only 47 such p have been found (see Table 1.4); the first four were found 2500 years ago. Note that $2^{43112609} - 1$ is not only the largest known Mersenne prime, but also the largest known prime in the world to date. The search for the largest Mersenne prime and/or the largest prime has always been a hot topic in computational number theory. EFF (Electronic Frontier Foundation) has offered in total 550,000 US dollars to the first individual or organization who find the following large primes:

Prizes	Conditions for the new primes
$50,000	at least 1000000 digits
$100,000	at least 10000000 digits
$150,000	at least 100000000 digits
$250,000	at least 1000000000 digits

Table 1.4 The 47 known Mersenne primes $M_p = 2^p - 1$

No	p	Digits (M_p)	Time	No	p	Digits (M_p)	Time
1	2	1	–	2	3	1	–
3	5	2	–	4	7	3	–
5	13	4	1461	6	17	6	1588
7	19	6	1588	8	31	10	1750
9	61	19	1883	10	89	27	1911
11	107	33	1913	12	127	39	1876
13	521	157	1952	14	607	183	1952
15	1279	386	1952	16	2203	664	1952
17	2281	687	1952	18	3217	969	1957
19	4253	1281	1961	20	4423	1332	1961
21	9689	2917	1963	22	9941	2993	1963
23	11213	3376	1963	24	19937	6002	1971
25	21701	6533	1978	26	23209	6987	1979
27	44497	13395	1979	28	86243	25962	1982
29	110503	33265	1988	30	132049	39751	1983
31	216091	65050	1985	32	756839	227832	1992
33	859433	258716	1994	34	1257787	378632	1996
35	1398269	420921	1996	36	2976221	895932	1997
37	3021377	909526	1998	38	6972593	2098960	1999
39	13466917	4053946	2001	40	20996011	6320430	2003
41	24036583	7235733	2004	42	25964951	7816230	2005
43	30402457	9152052	2005	44	32582657	9808358	2006
45	37156667	11185272	2008	46	42643801	12837064	2009
47	43112609	12978189	2008	48	?	?	?

The first prize was claimed by Nayan Hajratwala in Michigan in 1996, who found the 38th Mersenne prime $2^{6972593} - 1$ with 2098960 digits, the second prize was claimed by Edson Smith at UCLA in 2008, who found the 46th Mersenne prime $2^{42643801} - 1$ with 12837064 digits. The remaining two prizes remain unclaimed. Of course, we still do not know if there are infinitely many Mersenne primes.

2. **Integer Factorization Problem (IFP).** IFP can be formally defined as follows:

$$\text{IFP} \stackrel{\text{def}}{=} \begin{cases} \text{Input}: & n > 1, \\ \text{Output}: a \mid n, & 1 < a < n. \end{cases}$$

The IFP assumption is that given the positive integer $n > 1$, it is hard to find its non-trivial factor(s), i.e.,

$$\{n = ab\} \stackrel{\text{hard}}{\longrightarrow} \{a, \ 1 < a < n\}.$$

Note that in IFP, we aim at finding just one non-trivial factor a (not necessarily prime factor) of n. The Fundamental Theorem of Arithmetic asserts that any

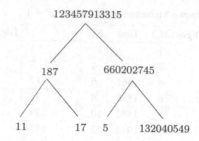

Figure 1.2 Prime factorization of 123457913315

positive integer $n > 1$ can be uniquely written into the following standard prime factorization form:

$$n = p_1^{\alpha_1} p_2^{\alpha_2} \cdots p_k^{\alpha_k},$$

where $p_1 < p_2 < \cdots < p_k$ are primes and $\alpha_1, \alpha_2, \cdots, \alpha_k$ positive integers. Clearly, recursively performing the operations of primality testing and integer factorization, n can be eventually written in its standard prime factorization form, say, if we wish to factor 123457913315, the recursive process can be shown in Figure 1.2. So, if we define the Prime Factorization Problem (PFP) as follows:

$$\text{PFP} \stackrel{\text{def}}{=} \begin{cases} \text{Input}: & n > 1, \\ \text{Output}: & p_1^{\alpha_1}, p_2^{\alpha_2}, \cdots, p_k^{\alpha_k}, \end{cases}$$

then

$$\text{PFP} \stackrel{\text{def}}{=} \text{PTP} \oplus \text{IFP}.$$

Although PTP can be solved efficiently in polynomial-time, IFP cannot be solved in polynomial-time. Finding polynomial-time factoring algorithm is one of the most important research topics in computational number theory. At present, no polynomial-time algorithm for factoring has been found and no-one yet has proved that no such an algorithm exists. The current world record for integer factorization is the RSA-768 (a number with 768 bits and 232 digits):

1230186684530117755130494958384962720772853569595334792197322452151726400507263657518745202199786469389956474942774063845925192557326303453731548268507917026122142913461670429214311602221240479274737794080665351419597459856902143413

=

334780716989568987860441698482126908177047949837137685689124313889828883793878700228761471165253174308773781446799948

×

367460436667995904282446337799627952632279158164343087642676032

283815739666511279 233373417143396810270092798736308917.

It was factored on 9 Dec 2009 [35]. The factoring process requires about 10^{20} operations and would need about 2000 years of computation on a single core 2.2 GHz AMD Opteron.

3. **Discrete Logarithm Problem (DLP)**. According to historical records, logarithms over the set of real numbers $\mathbb{R}$ were first invented in the sixteenth century by the Scottish mathematician John Napier (1550–1617). We define k to be the logarithm to the base x of y

$$k = \log_x y,$$

if and only if

$$x^k = y.$$

So the Logarithm Problem (LP) over $\mathbb{R}$ may be defined as follows:

$$\text{LP} \overset{\text{def}}{=} \begin{cases} \text{Input}: & x, y, \\ \text{Output}: & k \text{ such that } y = x^k. \end{cases}$$

For example, $\log_3 19683 = 9$, since $3^9 = 19683$. LP over $\mathbb{R}$ is easy to solve, since

$$\log_x y = \frac{\ln y}{\ln x},$$

where the natural logarithms can be calculated efficiently by the following formula (of course, depending on the accuracy):

$$\ln x = \sum_{n=1}^{\infty} (-1)^{n+1} \frac{(x-1)^n}{n}.$$

For example,

$$\log_2 5 = \frac{\ln 5}{\ln 2} \approx \frac{1.609437912}{0.692147106} \approx 2.321928095.$$

We can always get a result at certain level of accuracy. The Discrete Logarithm Problem over the multiplicative group $\mathbb{Z}_n^*$, discussed in this book, is completely different from the traditional one we just mentioned. Let

$$\mathbb{Z}_n^* = \{a : 1 \leq a \leq n, \ a \in \mathbb{Z}_{n>0}, \ \gcd(a, n) = 1\}.$$

DLP may be defined as follows:

$$\text{DLP} \stackrel{\text{def}}{=} \begin{cases} \text{Input}: \quad x, n, y, \\ \text{Output}: k \text{ such that } y \equiv x^k \pmod{n}. \end{cases}$$

The DLP assumption is that

$$\{x, n, y \equiv x^k \pmod{n}\} \stackrel{\text{hard}}{\longrightarrow} \{k\}.$$

The following are some small and simple examples of DLP:

$$\log_3 57 \equiv k \pmod{1009} \implies k \text{ does not exist;}$$
$$\log_{11} 57 \equiv k \pmod{1009} \implies k = 375;$$
$$\log_3 20 \equiv k \pmod{1009} \implies k = \{165, 333, 501, 669, 837, 1005\}.$$

As can be seen, in the first example, the required discrete logarithm does not exist, whereas in the last example, the required discrete logarithms are not unique. In what follows, we give a little bit large example of DLP: Let

$$p = (739 \cdot 7^{149} - 736)/3,$$
$$7^a \equiv 127402180119973946824269244334322849749382042586931621654$$
$$5577352903229146790959986818609788130465951664554581 44280$$
$$588076766033781 \pmod{p},$$
$$7^b \equiv 180162285287453102444782834836799895015967046695346697313$$
$$025121734059953772058475958176910625380692101651848662362$$
$$137934026803049 \pmod{p}.$$

Find 7^{ab}. To compute 7^{ab}, we need either to find a from $7^a \bmod p$ or b from $7^b \bmod p$, so that we can calculate $7^{ab} = (7^a)^b = (7^b)^a$. This problem was proposed by McCurley in 1990 [40] and solved by Weber in 1998 [55].

4. **Elliptic Curve Discrete Logarithm Problem (ECDLP).** Elliptic Curve Discrete Logarithm Problem (ECDLP) is a very natural generalization of the Discrete Logarithm Problem (DLP) from multiplication group $\mathbb{Z}_n^*$ to the elliptic curve groups $E(\mathbb{Q})$, $E(\mathbb{Z}_n)$ or $E(\mathbb{F}_p)$. Let E be an elliptic curve

$$E : y^2 = x^3 + ax + b$$

over a field $\mathcal{K}$, denoted by $E \backslash \mathcal{K}$. A straight line (non-vertical) L connecting points P and Q intersects the elliptic curve E at a third point R, and the point $P \oplus Q$ is the reflection of R in the X-axis. That is, if $R = (x_3, y_3)$, then $P \oplus Q = (x_3, -y_3)$ is the reflection of R in the X-axis. Note that a vertical line, such as L' or L'', meets the curve at two points (not necessarily distinct), and also at the point at infinity $\mathcal{O}_E$ (we may think of the point at infinity as lying far off in the direction of the Y-axis). The line at infinity meets the curve at the point $\mathcal{O}_E$ three times. Of course, the non-vertical line meets the curve in three points in the XY plane. Thus, every line meets the curve in three points. The algebraic formula for computing $P_3(x_3, y_3) = P_1(x_1, y_1) + P_2(x_2, y_2)$ on E is as follows:

$$(x_3, y_3) = (\lambda^2 - x_1 - x_2, \ \lambda(x_1 - x_3) - y_1),$$

where

$$\lambda = \begin{cases} \dfrac{3x_1^2 + a}{2y_1} & \text{if } P_1 = P_2, \\[2ex] \dfrac{y_2 - y_1}{x_2 - x_1} & \text{otherwise.} \end{cases}$$

Given E and $P \in E$, it is easy to find $Q = kP$, which is of course also in E. For example, to compute $Q = 105P$, we first let

$$k = 105 = (1101001)_2,$$

then perform the operations as follows:

1: $Q \leftarrow P + 2Q \Rightarrow Q \leftarrow P$		$\Rightarrow Q = P$
1: $Q \leftarrow P + 2Q \Rightarrow Q \leftarrow P + 2P$		$\Rightarrow Q = 3P$
0: $Q \leftarrow 2Q \qquad \Rightarrow Q \leftarrow 2(P + 2P)$		$\Rightarrow Q = 6P$
1: $Q \leftarrow P + 2Q \Rightarrow Q \leftarrow P + 2(2(P + 2P))$		$\Rightarrow Q = 13P$
0: $Q \leftarrow 2Q \qquad \rightarrow Q \leftarrow 2(P + 2(2(P + 2P)))$		$\Rightarrow Q = 26P$
0: $Q \leftarrow 2Q \qquad \Rightarrow Q \leftarrow 2(2(P + 2(2(P + 2P))))$		$\Rightarrow Q = 52P$
1: $Q \leftarrow P + 2Q \Rightarrow Q \leftarrow P + 2(2(2(P + 2(2(P + 2P)))))$		$\Rightarrow Q = 105P.$

This gives the required result $Q = P + 2(2(2(P + 2(2(P + 2P))))) = 105P$.

As can be seen, given $(E \backslash \mathcal{K}, k, P)$ it is easy to compute

$$Q = kP.$$

However, it is hard to find k given $(E \backslash \mathcal{K}, P, Q)$. This is the Elliptic Curve Discrete Logarithm Problem (ECDLP), which may be formally defined as follows (let E be an elliptic curve over finite field $\mathbb{F}_p$):

$$\text{ECDLP} \stackrel{\text{def}}{=} \begin{cases} \text{Input}: \ E \backslash \mathbb{F}_p, (P, Q) \in E(\mathbb{F}_p), \\ \text{Output}: \ k > 1 \text{ such that } Q \equiv kP \pmod{p}. \end{cases}$$

The ECDLP assumption asserts that

$$\{(P, Q \equiv kP \pmod{p}) \in E(\mathbb{F}_p)\} \stackrel{\text{hard}}{\longrightarrow} \{k\}.$$

Suppose that we are given

$$(190, 271) \equiv k(1, 237) \pmod{1009},$$

with

$$E: \ y^2 \equiv x^3 + 71x + 602 \pmod{1009},$$

then it is easy to find

$$k = 419,$$

since the finite field $\mathbb{F}_p$ is small. However, when the finite field is large, such as

$$Q(x_Q, y_Q) \equiv kP(x_P, y_P) \pmod{p}$$

on $E\backslash\mathbb{F}_p$, where

$p = 155003179783434785924857641481313994 2411,$

$a = 139926757373635788158779052359711153316710,$

$b = 100929654219153246407626036752581629 3976,$

$x_P = 131795376323959588846552414558987269 5690,$

$y_P = 434829348619031278460656303481105428081,$

$x_Q = 1247392211317907151303247721489640699240,$

$y_Q = 2075348584420904521939995710263159 95117.$

In this case, it is very hard to find the k. Certicom Canada offered 20,000 US dollars to the first individual or organization who first got the correct value of the k. More Certicom prize problems along with this line may be found in Table 1.5 (the above mentioned \$20,000 prize curve corresponds to ECCp-131, as p has 131 bits in this example).

Table 1.5 Some certicom ECDLP challenge problems

Curves	Bits	Operations	Prizes (US dollars)	Status
ECCp-97	97	$3.0 \cdot 10^{14}$	\$5,000	1998
ECCp-109	109	$2.1 \cdot 10^{16}$	\$10,000	2002
ECCp-131	131	3.5×10^{19}	\$20,000	?
ECCp-163	163	2.4×10^{24}	\$30,000	?
ECCp-191	191	4.9×10^{28}	\$40,000	?
ECCp-239	239	8.2×10^{35}	\$50,000	?
ECCp-359	359	9.6×10^{53}	\$100,000	?

5. **The Root Finding Problem (RFP)**. The k-th Root Finding Problem (RFP), or RFP Problem for short, may be defined as follows:

$$k\mathrm{RFP} \overset{\mathrm{def}}{=} \{k, N, y \equiv x^k \ (\mathrm{mod} \ N)\} \xrightarrow{\text{find}} \{x \equiv \sqrt[k]{y} \ (\mathrm{mod} \ N)\}.$$

If the prime factorization of N is known, one can compute the Euler function $\phi(N)$ and solve the linear Diophantine equation $ku - \phi(N)v = 1$ in u and v, and the computation $x \equiv y^u \ (\mathrm{mod} \ N)$ gives the required value. Thus, if IFP can be solved in polynomial-time, then RFP can also be solved in polynomial-time:

$$\mathrm{IFP} \overset{\mathcal{P}}{\Longrightarrow} \mathrm{RFP}.$$

The security of RSA relies on the intractability of IFP, and also on RFP; if any one of the problems can be solved in polynomial-time, RSA can be broken in polynomial-time.

6. **The SQuare RooT Problem (SQRT)**. Let $y \in \mathrm{QR}_N$, where QR_N denotes the set of quadratic residues modulo N, which should be introduced later. The SQRT is to find an x such that

$$x^2 \equiv y \ (\mathrm{mod} \ N) \ \text{ or } \ x \equiv \sqrt{y} \ (\mathrm{mod} \ N).$$

That is,

$$\mathrm{SQRT} \overset{\mathrm{def}}{=} \{N \in \mathbb{Z}_{>1}^{+}, y \in \mathrm{QR}_n, y \equiv x^2 \ (\mathrm{mod} \ N)\} \xrightarrow{\text{find}} \{x\}.$$

When N is prime, the *SQRT problem* can be solved in polynomial-time. However, when N is composite one needs to factor N first. Thus, if IFP can be solved in polynomial-time, SQRT can also be solved in polynomial-time:

$$\mathrm{IFP} \overset{\mathcal{P}}{\Longrightarrow} \mathrm{QRP}.$$

On the other hand, if SQRT can be solved in polynomial-time, IFP can also be solved in polynomial-time:

$$\mathrm{SQRT} \overset{\mathcal{P}}{\Longrightarrow} \mathrm{IFP}.$$

That is,

$$\mathrm{SQRT} \overset{\mathcal{P}}{\Longleftrightarrow} \mathrm{IFP}.$$

It is precisely this intractability of SQRT that Rabin used to construct his cryptosystem in 1979 [46].

7. **Modular Polynomial Root Finding Problem (MPRFP)**. It is easy to compute the integer roots of a polynomial in one variable over $\mathbb{Z}$:

$$p(x) = 0,$$

but the following modular polynomial root finding problem (MPRFP), or the MPRFP problem for short, can be hard:

$$p(x) \equiv 0 \ (\text{mod } N),$$

which aims at finding integer roots (solutions) of the modular polynomial in one variable. This problem can, of course, be extended to find integer roots (solutions) of the modular polynomial in several variables as follows:

$$p(x, y, \cdots) \equiv 0 \ (\text{mod } N).$$

Coppersmith in 1997 [18] developed a powerful method to find all small solutions x_0 of the modular polynomial equations in one or two variables of degree δ using the lattice reduction algorithm LLL [37]. Of course, for LLL to be run in reasonably amount of time in finding such x_0's, the values of δ cannot be big.

8. **The Quadratic Residuosity Problem (QRP)**. Let $N \in \mathbb{Z}_{>1}^{+}$, $\gcd(y, N) = 1$. Then y is a quadratic residue modulo N, denoted by $y \in QR_N$, if the quadratic congruence

$$x^2 \equiv y \ (\text{mod } N)$$

has a solution in x. If the congruence has no solution in x, then y is a quadratic nonresidue modulo N, denoted by $y \in \overline{QR_N}$. The Quadratic Residuosity Problem (QRP), or the *QRP Problem* for short, is to decide whether or not $y \in QR_N$:

$$QRP \stackrel{\text{def}}{=} \{N \in \mathbb{Z}_{>1}^{+}, x^2 \equiv y \ (\text{mod } N)\} \xrightarrow{\text{decide}} \{y \in QR_N\}.$$

If N is prime, or the prime factorization of N is known, then QRP can be solved simply by evaluating the Legendre symbol $L(y, N)$. If N is not a prime then one evaluates the Jacobi symbol $J(y, N)$ which, unfortunately, does not reveal if $y \in QR_N$, i.e., $J(y, N) = 1$ does not imply $y \in QR_N$ (it does if N is prime). For example, $L(15, 17) = 1$, so $x^2 \equiv 15 \ (\text{mod } 17)$ is soluble, with $x = \pm 21$ being the two solutions. However, although $J(17, 21) = 1$ there is no solution for $x^2 \equiv 17 \ (\text{mod } 21)$. Thus, when N is composite, the only way to decide whether or not $y \in QR_N$ is to factor N. Thus, if IFP can be solved in polynomial-time, QRP can also be solved in polynomial-time:

$$IFP \stackrel{\mathcal{P}}{\Longrightarrow} QRP.$$

The security of the Goldwasser-Micali probabilistic encryption scheme [28] is based on the intractability of QRP.

9. **Shortest Vector Problem (SVP)**. Problems related to lattices are also often hard to solve. Let $\mathbb{R}^n$ denote the space of n-dimensional real vectors $a = \{a_1, a_2, \cdots, a_n\}$ with usual dot product $a \cdot b$ and Euclidean Norm or length $||a|| = (a \cdot a)^{1/2}$. $\mathbb{Z}^n$ is the set of vectors in $\mathbb{R}^n$ with integer coordinates. If $A = \{a_1, a_2, \cdots, a_n\}$ is a set of linear independent vectors in $\mathbb{R}^n$, then the set of vectors

$$\left\{ \sum_{i=1}^{n} k_i a_i \ : \ k_1, k_2, \cdots, k_n \in \mathbb{Z} \right\}$$

is a lattice in $\mathbb{R}^n$, denoted by $L(A)$ or $L(a_1, a_2, \cdots, a_n)$. A is called a basis of the lattice. A set of vectors in $\mathbb{R}^n$ is a n-dimensional lattice if there is a basis V of n linear independent vectors such that $L = L(V)$. If $A = \{a_1, a_2, \cdots, a_n\}$ is a set of vectors in a lattice L, then the length of the set A is defined by $\max(||a_i||)$. A fundamental theorem, due to Minkowski, is as follows.

Theorem 1.1 (Minkowski). *There is a universal constant γ, such that for any lattice L of dimension n, $\exists v \in L$, $v \neq 0$, such that*

$$||v|| = \gamma \sqrt{n} \det (L)^{1/n}.$$

The determinant $\det(L)$ of a lattice is the volume of the n-dimensional fundamental parallelepiped, and the absolute constant γ is known as Hermite's constant.

A natural problem concerned with lattices is the *shortest vector problem (SVP)*, or the *SVP problem* for short:

Find the shortest non-zero vector in a high dimensional lattice.

Minkowski's theorem is just an existence-type theorem and offers no clue on how to find a short or the shortest vector non-zero vector in a high dimensional lattice. There is no efficient algorithm for finding the shortest non-zero vector, or finding an approximate short non-zero vector. The lattice reduction algorithm LLL [37] can be used to find short vectors, but it is not effective in finding short vectors when the dimension n is large, say, for example, $n \geq 100$. This allows lattices to be used in the design of cryptographic systems and in fact, several cryptographic systems, such as NTRU [33] and the Ajtai-Dwork system [2], are based on the intractability of finding the shortest non-zero vector in a high dimensional lattice.

In this book, we shall be more interested in those number theoretic problems that are computationally intractable, since the security of modern public-key cryptography relies on the intractability of these problems. A problem is computationally intractable if it cannot be solved in polynomial-time. Thus, from a computational

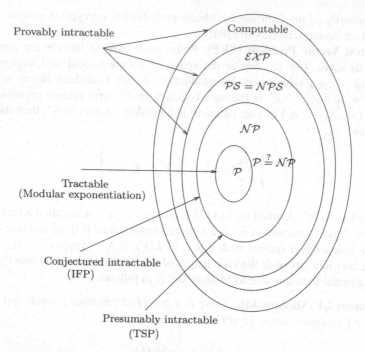

Figure 1.3 Tractable and intractable problems

complexity point of view, any problem beyond $\mathcal{P}$ is intractable. There are, however, different types of intractable problems (see Figure 1.3).

1. Provably intractable problems: Problems that are Turing computable but can be shown in $\mathcal{PS}$ ($\mathcal{P}$-$\mathcal{S}$pace), $\mathcal{NPS}$ ($\mathcal{NP}$-$\mathcal{S}$pace), $\mathcal{EXP}$ (exponential-time) etc., of course outside $\mathcal{NP}$, are provably and certainly intractable. Note that although we do not know if $\mathcal{P} = \mathcal{NPS}$, we know $\mathcal{PS} = \mathcal{NPS}$.
2. Presumably intractable problems: Problems in $\mathcal{NP}$ but outside of $\mathcal{P}$, particularly those problem in $\mathcal{NPC}$ ($\mathcal{NP}$-Complete) such as the Travelling Salesman Problem, the Knapsack Problem, and the satisfiability problem, are presumably intractable, since we do not know whether or not $\mathcal{P} = \mathcal{NP}$. If $\mathcal{P} = \mathcal{NP}$, then all problems in $\mathcal{NP}$ will no longer be intractable. However, it is more likely that $\mathcal{P} \neq \mathcal{NP}$. From a cryptographic point of view, it would be nice if encryption schemes can be designed to be based on some $\mathcal{NP}$-Complete problems, since these types of schemes can be difficult to break. Experience, however, tells us that very few encryption schemes are based on $\mathcal{NP}$-Complete problems.
3. Conjectured intractable problems: By conjectured intractable problems we mean that the problems are currently in $\mathcal{NP}$-Complete, but no-one can prove they must be in $\mathcal{NP}$-Complete; they may be in $\mathcal{P}$ if efficient algorithms are invented for solving these problems. Typical problems in this category include the Integer Factorization Problem, the Discrete Logarithm Problem and the Elliptic Curve

Discrete Logarithm Problem. Again, from a cryptographic point of view, we are more interested in this type of intractable problems, and in fact, IFP, DLP and ECDLP are essentially the only three intractable problems that are practical and widely used in commercial cryptography. For example, the most famous and widely used RSA cryptographic system relies its security on the intractability of the IFP problem.

The difference between the presumably intractable problems and the conjectured intractable problems is important and should not be confused. For example, both TSP and IFP are intractable, but the difference between TSP and IFP is that TSP has been proved to be $\mathcal{NP}$-Complete whereas IFP is only *conjectured* to be $\mathcal{NP}$-Complete. IFP may be $\mathcal{NP}$-Complete, but also may not be $\mathcal{NP}$-Complete.

Finally, we present a complexity measure of number-theoretic problems in big-$\mathcal{O}$ notation.

Definition 1.1. Let

$$f, g : \mathbb{Z}^+ \to \mathbb{R}.$$

Define

$$f = \mathcal{O}(g),$$

if there exists $c \in \mathbb{R}_{>0}$ with

$$|f(n)| \leq cg(n), \text{ for all } n.$$

Definition 1.2. Let

$$L_n(\alpha, c) = \exp(c(\log n)^\alpha (\log \log n)^{1-\alpha}),$$

where $\alpha \in [0, 1], c \in \mathbb{R}_{>0}$.

(1) If a problem can be solved by an algorithm in expected running time

$$T(n) = \mathcal{O}(L_n(0, c)),$$

then the algorithm is polynomial-time algorithm (or efficient algorithm), and the corresponding problem is easy problem (i.e., the problem can be solved easily). It is also often to use $\mathcal{O}((\log n)^k)$ with k constant to represent polynomial-time complexity. For example, the multiplication of two $\log n$ bit numbers by ordinary method takes time in $\mathcal{O}((\log n)^2)$, the fastest known multiplication method has a running time of

$$\mathcal{O}(\log n \log \log n \log \log \log n) = \mathcal{O}((\log n)^{1+\epsilon}).$$

(2) If a problem can be solved by an algorithm in expected running time

$$T(n) = \mathcal{O}(L_n(1, c)),$$

then the algorithm is exponential-time algorithm (or inefficient algorithm), and the corresponding problem is a hard problem (i.e., the problem is hard to solve). Note that since $\log n$ is the length of input, $\mathcal{O}((\log n)^{12})$ is polynomial-time complexity, whereas $\mathcal{O}((n)^{0.1})$ is not, since $\mathcal{O}((n)^{0.1}) = \mathcal{O}(2^{0.1 \log n})$, an exponential complexity.

(3) An algorithm is of subexponential-time complexity if

$$T(n) = \mathcal{O}(L_n(\alpha, c)), \quad 0 < \alpha < 1.$$

Subexponential-time complexity is an important and interesting class between the two extremes, and in fact, many of the number-theoretic algorithms discussed in this book, such as the algorithms for integer factorization and discrete logarithms, fall into this special class, which is slower than polynomial-time but faster than exponential-time. For example, the best algorithms for IFP and DLP run in subexponential-time. For ECDLP, we even do not have a subexponential-time algorithm.

Problems for Section 1.2

1. Prove or disprove that

   (1) there are infinitely many Mersenne prime numbers;
   (2) there are infinitely many Mersenne composite numbers.

   Find the 48th Mersenne prime.
2. What is the difference between the Integer Factorization Problem and the Prime Factorization Problem?
3. What is the difference between the Discrete Logarithm Problem and the Elliptic Discrete Logarithm Problem?
4. Show that solving the Square Root Problem is equivalent to that of the Integer Factorization Problem.
5. Show that solving the Quadratic Residuosity Problem is equivalent to that of the Integer Factorization Problem.
6. Find all the prime factors of the following numbers:

   (1) 11111111111 (the number consisting of eleven 1)
   (2) 111111111111 (the number consisting of twelve 1)
   (3) 1111111111111 (the number consisting of thirteen 1)
   (4) 11111111111111 (the number consisting of fourteen 1)
   (5) 111111111111111 (the number consisting of fifteen 1)

(6) 1111111111111111 (the number consisting of sixteen 1)

(7) 11111111111111111 (the number consisting of seventeen 1)

(8) Can you find any pattern for the prime factorization of the above numbers?

7. Do you think the Integer Factorization Problem, or more generally the Prime Factorization Problem are hard to solve? Justify your answer.

8. Can you find some problems that have the similar properties or difficulty of the Integer Factorization Problem (we shall explain this in detail in the next section).

9. Find the discrete logarithm k

$$k \equiv \log_2 3 \pmod{11}$$

such that

$$2^k \equiv 3 \pmod{11},$$

and the discrete logarithm k

$$k \equiv \log_{123456789} 962 \pmod{9876543211}$$

such that

$$123456789^k \equiv 962 \pmod{9876543211}.$$

10. Find the square root y

$$y \equiv \sqrt{3} \pmod{11}$$

such that

$$y^2 \equiv 3 \pmod{11},$$

and the square root y

$$y \equiv \sqrt{123456789} \pmod{987654321}$$

such that

$$y^2 \equiv 123456789 \pmod{987654321}.$$

1.3   What is Quantum Computational Number Theory

Just the same as computational number theory, quantum computational number theory, as its name suggested, may be regarded as a combined subject of computational number theory and quantum computing. That is,

$$\text{Quantum Computational Number Theory} :=$$

$$\text{Computational Number Theory} \oplus \text{Quantum Computing}.$$

The aim of quantum computational number theory is to use the quantum computational techniques to solve number-theoretic problems, that are hard, more precisely, intractable for classical computers. The main research goals in the area is to build practical and large scale quantum computers and to discover new and polynomial-time quantum algorithms to solve the intractable, hopefully, $\mathcal{NP}$-Complete problems in number theory.

Generally speaking, there are three categories of problems that quantum computers may have a play:

1. Algorithms related to determine the functional periodicity. Algorithms in this category include:

   (1) Simon's algorithm for distinguishing different functions (see [51, 52]).
   (2) Shor's algorithms for IFP, DLP and ECDLP (see [44, 47, 48]).
   (3) Hallgren's algorithm for solving Pell's equation $x^2 - dy^2 = 1$ for a given positive integer d.

2. Algorithms related to information retrieval, such as Grover's quantum algorithm for search.
3. Algorithms related to simulations and computations in quantum mechanics, say e.g., Feynman's simulation of quantum physics.

In computational number theory, we are interested in the first two categories of the quantum algorithms, as they are directly related to problems in number theory.

It has been known for some times that some number-theoretic problems cannot be solved in polynomial-time by classical computers but can by quantum computers, provided that a practical quantum computer can be built. Problems in this category include:

1. The Integer Factorization Problems (IFP): It is well-known that IFP is intractable for computers, which is exactly the security basis of the RSA (Rivest-Shamir-Adleman) cryptography. The fastest algorithm, namely, the Number Field Sieve, runs in subexponential-time

$$\mathcal{O}(\exp(c(\log n)^{1/3}(\log \log n)^{2/3})),$$

where $c = (\frac{64}{9})^{1/3} \approx 1.5$ for special numbers and $c = (\frac{32}{9})^{1/3} \approx 1.9$ for general numbers. Surprisingly, Shor in 1994 (see [47, 48]) proposed a quantum algorithm which can be used to solve IFP in polynomial-time

$$\mathcal{O}((\log n)^{2+\epsilon}),$$

provided that a practical quantum computer is available.

2. The Discrete Logarithm Problem (DLP): Just the same as IFP, DLP is also an intractable computational problem, for which no polynomial-time algorithm has been found so far. The security of the famous DHM (Diffie-Hellman-Merkle) key-exchange scheme and DSA (US government's Digital Signature Algorithm) relies on the intractability of DLP. In the classical computing world, the fastest algorithm for DLP, namely, NFS, runs in subexponential-time

$$\mathcal{O}(\exp(c(\log Q)^{1/3}(\log \log Q)^{2/3})),$$

where Q is the size of a finite field, as the DLP problem we are interested in (particularly in the cryptographic setting) is normally over a large finite field $Q = \mathbb{Z}_p^*$. However, for finite fields with small characteristic, there is a slightly faster algorithm, namely, FFS (Functional Field Sieve) runs in time proportion to

$$\mathcal{O}(\exp(c(\log Q)^{1/3}(\log \log Q)^{2/3})),$$

where

$$c = \left(\frac{4}{9}\right)^{1/3}.$$

There is even faster algorithm, again for some finite fields with small characteristic, runs in time

$$\mathcal{O}(\exp(c(\log Q)^{1/4}(\log \log Q)^{3/4})),$$

for some small constant c. Remarkably, Shor's quantum algorithm can also be used to solve DLP in polynomial-time

$$\mathcal{O}((\log n)^{2+\epsilon}),$$

as the same as IFP.

3. The Elliptic Curve Discrete Logarithm Problem (ECDLP): Recall that the general DLP problem may defined over a multiplicative group $\mathbb{Z}_n$ (when n is replaced by p^k, then $\mathbb{Z}_{p^k}$ is a finite field, also denoted by $\mathbb{F}_{p^k}$, or $GF(p^k)$). If we replace the multiplicative group $\mathbb{Z}_{p^k}$ with an elliptic curve group $E(\mathcal{Q})$, the DLP problem over $E(\mathcal{Q})$ is the Elliptic Curve Discrete Logarithm Problem (ECDLP), which may be defined as follows: Let P, Q be two points of the elliptic curve

$E : y^2 = x^3 + ax + b$ over the rational field Q, then the problem to find the integer k such that $P = kQ$ is the ECDLP problem. Although there are many algorithms to solve ECDLP, but none of them can run in polynomial-time, Again, Surprisingly, Shor's quantum algorithm for DLP can be used to solve the ECDLP problem in polynomial-time.

4. Pell's Equation: A Pell's equation (see [31, 38, 59]) is a quadratic Diophantine equation in any one of the following three forms

$$x^2 - dy^2 = 1,$$

$$x^2 - dy^2 = -1,$$

$$x^2 - dy^2 = n,$$

where d is a positive integer other than a perfect square, and n a positive integer greater than 1. For simplicity, we only consider the following Pell's equation:

$$x^2 - dy^2 = 1.$$

In this type of Pell's equation, we are interested in finding positive integer solution x, y, for a given d. Clearly, if we can find the first (i.e., the smallest possible or the fundamental) solution x_1, y_1, the nth solution x_n, y_n can be written in terms of the first one as follows:

$$x_n + y_n \sqrt{d} = (x_1 + y_1 \sqrt{d})^n.$$

For example, given Pell's equation

$$x^2 - 73y^2 = 1,$$

one may find $\{x_1, y_1\} = \{2281249, 267000\}$, that is,

$$2281249^2 - 73 \cdot 267000^2 = 1.$$

The fastest method to solve Pell's equation is the smooth number method, similar to NFS for IFP or DLP, runs in subexponential-time

$$\mathcal{O}(\exp(c(\log d)^{1/3}(\log \log d)^{2/3})),$$

where $\log d$ is the input size and $c < 1$ is a small real constant. Hallgren in 2002 discovered a quantum algorithm for solving Pell's equation, which run in polynomial-time

$$\mathcal{O}(\text{poly}(\log d)), \quad \text{with the probability } 1/\text{poly}(\log d),$$

where $\mathcal{O}(\text{poly}(\log d))$ is the polynomial-time complexity

$$\mathcal{O}((\log d)^k), \quad \text{some constant } k.$$

5. Function Distinguishing: Let us first define the function distinguishing problem (or Simon's problem in short). Suppose we are given a function $f : \{0, 1\}^n \to \{0, 1\}^m$ with $m \geq n$, satisfying the property that f is 1-to-1 or there exists a nontrivial s such that

$$\forall x \neq x' (f(x) = f(x') \Longleftrightarrow x' = x \oplus s),$$

where $\oplus$ denotes bitwise condition exclusive-or. We are asked to determine which of these conditions holds for f, and in the second case, to find s. In 1994 Simon (see [51, 52]) proposed a quantum algorithm that solves the function distinguishing problem exponentially faster than any (deterministic or probabilistic) classical algorithm. Although the problem and the solution themselves are of little practical value it is interesting because it provides an exponential speedup over any classical algorithm. Moreover, it was also the inspiration for Shor to develop his quantum factoring algorithm. Note that both the factoring problem and Simon's problem are special cases of the abelian hidden subgroup problem, which is now known to have efficient quantum algorithms.

It is helpful to make a remark about the power of quantum computation by saying that quantum computers not just faster versions of classical computers, but use a different paradigm for computation; they may provide an exponential speedup over any existing classical algorithm for some computational problems such as IFP, DLP and ECDLP, but for other hard computational problems, such as the $\mathcal{N}P$-Complete problems (e.g., the famous travelling salesman problem), they do not provide any speedup at all. For quantum computers to be useful, we would expect them to solve the $\mathcal{N}P$-Complete problems.

Problems for Section 1.3

1. Explain why for some computational problems quantum computers can provide exponentially fast speedup, but for other problems not at all.
2. Explain why Shor's factoring algorithm (see [47, 48]) can factor integers in polynomial-time.
3. Explain why Shor's quantum factoring algorithm for IFP can be extended to DLP and ECDLP.
4. Pell's equation can be solved by using the continued fractions which can be implemented by the efficient Euclid's algorithm. Explain why Pell's equation cannot be solved efficiently in polynomial-time by any classical algorithm (see [38]).

5. Explain why Pell's equation can be solved in polynomial-time by a quantum algorithm (see [31]).
6. (Hard research problem) All problems currently solvable by a quantum computer are not $\mathcal{N}P$-Complete. Can a quantum computer solve an $\mathcal{N}P$-Complete problem? If so, give an example.

1.4 Chapter Notes and Further Reading

In this beginning chapter of the book, we have provided an introduction and overview of the basic concepts and problems in number theory, computation theory, computational number theory and quantum computational number theory. In the rest of the chapters of the book, we shall concentrate on quantum computational number theory.

The theory of numbers is one of the oldest branches in mathematics, and of course the basis for quantum computational number theory. There are many established and classical books and references in the field. Readers are strongly suggested to consult the following books by Baker [3, 4], Davenport [21] , Hardy, Wright and Wiles [32], Niven, Zuckerman and Montgomery [43].

Computational number theory, a combined subject of number theory and computer science, more specifically, the theory of computation, is an active, lively and young subject of study in both mathematics and computer science, the following books are somewhat the standard references in the field: [14, 20, 36, 45, 59].

Quantum computing in general and quantum computational number theory in particular are the main topics of the present book. Readers are suggested to consult the following references before moving on to the rest chapters of the book in order to get some more background information: [1, 5–7, 11, 22–24, 30, 41, 42, 47–50, 56, 57] and [60, 61].

Computation is the main ingredient of both computational number theory and quantum computational number theory. Although historically computation is as old as mathematics, the modern theory of computation may started its life just in the 1930s by the work of Turing [54], Church [12, 13], and some others. We shall discuss in detail the theory of computation, both classical and quantum, in the next chapter, but readers may consult the following references before moving on to the read of the next chapter: [15–17, 19, 25, 26, 34, 36, 39, 53].

References

1. L.M. Adleman, J. DeMarrais, M.-D.A. Huang, Quantum computability. SIAM J. Comput. **26**(5), 1524–1540 (1996)
2. M. Ajtai, C. Dwork, A public-key cryptosystem with worst-case/average-case equivalence. *Proceedings of Annual ACM Symposium on Theory of Computing* (1997), pp. 284–293

3. A. Baker, *A Concise Introduction to the Theory of Numbers* (Cambridge University Press, Cambridge, 2008)
4. A. Baker, *A Comprehensive Course in Number Theory* (Cambridge University Press, Cambridge, 2012)
5. P. Benioff, The computer as a physical system – a microscopic quantum mechanical hamiltonian model of computers as represented by Turing machines. J. Stat. Phys. **22**(5), 563–591 (1980)
6. C.H. Bennett, Strengths and weakness of quantum computing. SIAM J. Comput. **26**(5), 1510–1523 (1997)
7. C.H. Bennett, D.P. DiVincenzo, Quantum information and computation. Nature **404**(6775), 247–255 (2000)
8. E. Bombieri, *The Riemann Hypothesis*, in The Millennium Prize Problems, ed. by J. Carlson, A. Jaffe, A. Wiles (Clay Mathematics Institute/American Mathematical Society, Providence, 2006), pp. 107–152
9. J. Carlson, A. Jaffe, A. Wiles (eds.), *The Millennium Prize Problems* (Clay Mathematics Institute/American Mathematical Society, Providence, 2006)
10. J.R. Chen, On the representation of a large even integer as the sum of a prime and the product of at most two primes. Sci. China Math. **16**(2), 157–176 (1973)
11. I.L Change, R. Laflamme, P. Shor, W.H. Zurek, Quantum computers, factoring, and decoherence. Science **270**(5242), 1633–1635 (1995)
12. A. Church, An unsolved problem of elementary number theory. Am. J. Math. **58**(2), 345–363 (1936)
13. A. Church, Book review: on computable numbers, with an application to the entscheidungsproblem by Turing. J. Symb. Log. **2**(1), 42–43 (1937)
14. H. Cohen, *A Course in Computational Algebraic Number Theory*. Graduate Texts in Mathematics, vol.138 (Springer, New York, 1993)
15. S. Cook, The complexity of theorem-proving procedures, in *Proceedings of the 3rd Annual ACM Symposium on the Theory of Computing*, New York (1971), pp. 151–158
16. S. Cook, The importance of the P versus NP question. J. ACM **50**(1), 27–29 (2003)
17. S. Cook, *The P versus NP problem*, in The Millennium Prize Problems, ed. by J. Carlson, A. Jaffe, A. Wiles (Clay Mathematics Institute/American Mathematical Society, Providence, 2006), pp. 87–106
18. D. Coppersmith, Small solutions to polynomial equations, and low exponent RSA vulnerabilities. J. Cryptol. **10**(4), 233–260 (1997)
19. T.H. Cormen, C.E. Ceiserson, R.L. Rivest, *Introduction to Algorithms*, 3rd edn. (MIT Press, New York, 2009)
20. R. Crandall, C. Pomerance, *Prime Numbers – A Computational Perspective*, 2nd edn. (Springer, New York, 2005)
21. H. Davenport, *Higher Arithmetic: An Introduction to the Theory of Numbers*, 7th edn. (Cambridge University Press, Cambridge, 1999)
22. D. Deutsch, Quantum theory, the Church–Turing principle and the universal quantum computer. Proc. R. Soc. Lond. **A-400**(1818), 96–117 (1985)
23. R.P. Feynman, Simulating physics with computers. Int. J. Theor. Phys. **21**(6), 467–488 (1982)
24. R.P. Feynman, *Feynman Lectures on Computation*, ed. by A.J.G. Hey, R.W. Allen (Addison-Wesley, New York, 1996)
25. M.R. Garey, D.S. Johnson, *Computers and Intractability – A Guide to the Theory of NP-Completeness* (W.H. Freeman and Company, New York, 1979)
26. O. Goldreich, *P, NP, and NP-Completeness*, (Cambridge University Press, Cambridge, 2010)
27. D.A. Goldston, S.W. Graham, J. Pintz, C.Y. Yildirim, Small gaps between primes or almost prime. Trans. Am. Math. Soc. **361**(10), 5285–5330 (2009)
28. S. Goldwasser, S. Micali, Probabilistic encryption. J. Comput. Syst. Sci. **28**(2), 270–299 (1984)
29. B. Green, T. Tao, The primes contain arbitrarily long arithmetic progressions. Ann. Math. **167**(2), 481–547 (2008)
30. J. Grustka, *Quantum Computing* (McGraw-Hill, New York, 1999)

31. S. Hallgren, Polynomial-time quantum algorithms for Pell's equation and the principal ideal problem. J. ACM **54**(1), Article 4, 19 p. (2007)
32. G.H. Hardy, E.M. Wright, A. Wiles, *An Introduction to the Theory of Numbers*, 6th edn. (Oxford University Press, Oxford, 2008)
33. J. Hoffstein, N. Howgrave-Graham, J. Pipher et al., NTRUEncrypt and NTRUSign: efficient public key algorithms for a post-quantum world, in *Proceedings of the International Workshop on Post-quantum Cryptography*, 23–26 May 2006, pp. 71–77
34. J. Hopcroft, R. Motwani, J. Ullman, *Introduction to Automata Theory, Languages, and Computation*, 3rd edn. (Addison-Wesley, New York, 2007)
35. T. Kleinjung, K. Aoki, J. Franke et al., Factorization of a 768-Bit RSA modulus, in *Advances in Cryptology – Crypto 2010*. Lecture Notes in Computer Science, vol. 6223 (Springer, New York, 2010), pp. 333–350
36. D.E. Knuth, *The Art of Computer Programming II – Seminumerical Algorithms*, 3rd edn. (Addison-Wesley, New York, 1998)
37. A.K. Lenstra, H.W. Lenstra, L. Lovász, Factoring polynomials with rational coefficients. Math. Ann. **261**(4), 515–534 (1982)
38. H.W. Lenstra Jr., Solving the Pell equation. Not. AMS **49**(2), 182–192 (2002)
39. H.R. Lewis, C.H. Papadimitrou, *Elements of the Theory of Computation* (Prentice-Hall, Englewood Cliffs, 1998)
40. K.S. McCurley, The discrete logarithm problem, in *Cryptology and Computational Number Theory*, ed. by C. Pomerance. Proceedings of Symposia in Applied Mathematics, vol. 42 (American Mathematics Society, Providence, 1990), pp. 49–74
41. N.D. Mermin, *Quantum Computer Science* (Cambridge University Press, Cambridge, 2007)
42. M.A. Nielson, I.L. Chuang, *Quantum Computation and Quantum Information*, 10th anniversary edition (Cambridge University Press, Cambridge, 2010)
43. I. Niven, H.S. Zuckman, H.L. Montgomery, *An Introduction to the Theory of Numbers*, 5th edn. (Wiley, New York, 1991)
44. J. Proos, C. Zalka, Shor's discrete logarithm algorithm for elliptic curves. Quantum Inf. Comput. **3**(4), 317–344 (2003)
45. H. Riesel, *Prime Numbers and Computer Methods for Factorization* (Birkhäuser, Boston, 1990)
46. M.O. Rabin, *Digitalized Signatures and Public-Key Functions as Intractable as Factorization* (MIT Laboratory for Computer Science, Cambridge, MA, 1979)
47. P. Shor, Algorithms for quantum computation: discrete logarithms and factoring, in *Proceedings of 35th Annual Symposium on Foundations of Computer Science* (IEEE Computer Society Press, New York, 1994), pp. 124–134
48. P. Shor, Polynomial-time algorithms for prime factorization and discrete logarithms on a quantum computer. SIAM J. Comput. **26**(5), 1411–1473 (1997)
49. P. Shor, Introduction to quantum algorithms, in *AMS Proceedings of Symposium in Applied Mathematics*, vol. 58 (2002), pp. 143–159
50. P. Shor, Why haven't more quantum algorithms been found? J. ACM **50**(1), 87–90 (2003)
51. D.R. Simon, On the power of quantum computation, in *Proceedings of the 35 Annual Symposium on Foundations of Computer Science* (IEEE Computer Society Press, New York, 1994), pp. 116–123
52. D.R. Simon, On the power of quantum computation. SIAM J. Comput. **25**(5), 1474–1483 (1997)
53. M. Sipser, *Introduction to the Theory of Computation*, 2nd edn. (Thomson, Toronto, 2006)
54. A. Turing, On computable numbers, with an application to the entscheidungsproblem. Proc. Lond. Math. Soc. **S2-42**(1), 230–265 (1937)
55. D. Weber, T.F. Denny, The solution of McCurley's discrete log challenge, in *Advances in Cryptology – CRYPTO 1998*. Lecture Notes in Computer Science, vol. 1462 (1998), Springer, New York, pp. 458–471
56. C.P. Williams, S.H. Clearwater, *Explorations in Quantum Computation*. The Electronic Library of Science (TELOS) (Springer, New York, 1998)

57. C.P. Williams, *Explorations in Quantum Computation*, 2nd edn. (Springer, New York, 2011)
58. A. Wiles, *The Birch and Swinnerton-Dyer conjecture*, in The Millennium Prize Problems, ed. by J. Carlson, A. Jaffe, A. Wiles (Clay Mathematics Institute/American Mathematical Society, Providence, 2006), pp. 31–44
59. S.Y. Yan, *Number Theory for Computing*, 2nd edn. (Springer, New York, 2002)
60. N.S. Yanofsky, M.A. Mannucci, *Quantum Computing for Computer Scientists* (Cambridge University Press, Cambridge, 2008)
61. A. Yao, Classical physics and the Church-Turing thesis. J. ACM **50**(1), 100–105 (2003)
62. Y.T. Zhang, Bounded gaps between primes. Ann. Math. **179**(3), 1121–1174 (2014)

Chapter 2
Classical and Quantum Computation

*If quantum mechanics hasn't profoundly shocked you, you
haven't understood it yet.*

NIELS BOHR (1885–1962)
The 1922 Nobel Laureate in Physics

Computation has long been deriving force in the development of mathematics in
general and in number theory in particular. Many of the great theorems such as
the Prime Number Theorem and conjectures such as the Riemann hypothesis and
the BSD (Birch and Swinnerton-Dyer) conjecture, are rooted and motivated from the
computational experiments. So computation is the main ingredient and component
of both computational number theory and quantum computational number theory.
In this chapter, we shall give an account of the basic concepts and results in both
classical and quantum computation theories, that will be used in the rest of the
book. More specifically, we shall try to answer the following questions related to
computation:

1. What is computation/quantum computation?
2. What computers can/cannot do?
3. What a quantum computer can/cannot do?

2.1 Classical Computability Theory

Computability studies what a computer can do and what a computer cannot do.
As a Turing machine can do everything that a real computer can do, our study of
computability will be within the theoretical framework of Turing machines.

© Springer International Publishing Switzerland 2015
S.Y. Yan, *Quantum Computational Number Theory*,
DOI 10.1007/978-3-319-25823-2_2

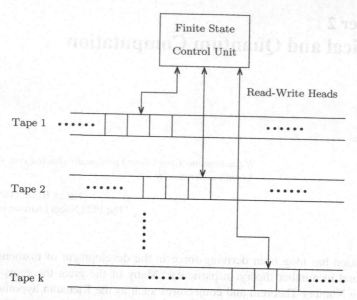

Figure 2.1 *k*-tape ($k \geq 1$) Turing machine

2.1.1 *Turing Machines*

The idea and the theory of Turing machines were first proposed and studied by the great English logician and mathematician Alan Turing (1912–1954) in his seminal paper [45] published in 1936. First of all, we shall present a formal definition of the Turing machine.

Definition 2.1. A standard multitape *Turing machine*, M (see Figure 2.1), is an algebraic system defined by

$$M = (Q, \Sigma, \Gamma, \delta, q_0, \Box, F)$$

where

1. Q is a finite set of *internal states*;
2. Σ is a finite set of symbols called the *input alphabet*. We assume that $\Sigma \subseteq \Gamma - \{\Box\}$;
3. Γ is a finite set of symbols called the *tape alphabet*;
4. δ is the transition function, which is defined by

   (1) if M is a Deterministic Turing Machine (DTM), then

   $$\delta : Q \times \Gamma^k \to Q \times \Gamma^k \times \{L, R\}^k,$$

(2) if M is a Non-Deterministic Turing Machine (NDTM), then

$$\delta : Q \times \Gamma^k \to 2^{Q \times \Gamma^k \times \{L,R\}^k},$$

where L and R specify the movement of the read-write head *left* or *right*. When $k = 1$, it is just a standard one-tape Turing machine;

5. $\square \in \Gamma$ is a special symbol called the *blank*;
6. $q_0 \in Q$ is the *initial state*;
7. $F \subseteq Q$ is the set of *final states*.

Turing machines, although simple and abstract, provide us with a most suitable model of computation for modern *digital* and even *quantum* computers.

Example 2.1. Given two positive integers x and y, design a Turing machine that computes $x + y$. First, we have to choose some convention for representing positive integers. For simplicity, we will use unary notation in which any positive integer x is represented by $w(x) \in \{1\}^+$, such that $|w(x)| = x$. Thus in this notation, 4 will be represented by 1111. We must also decide how x and y are placed on the tape initially and how their sum is to appear at the end of the computation. It is assumed that $w(x)$ and $w(y)$ are on the tape in unary notation, separated by a single 0, with the read-write head on the leftmost symbol of $w(x)$. After the computation, $w(x + y)$ will be on the tape followed by a single 0, and the read-write head will be positioned at the left end of the result. We therefore want to design a Turing machine for performing the computation

$$q_0 w(x) 0 w(y) \overset{*}{\vdash} q_f w(x + y) 0,$$

where $q_f \in F$ is a final state, and $\overset{*}{\vdash}$ indicates an unspecified number of steps as follows:

$$q_0 w(x) 0 w(y) \vdash \cdots \vdash q_f w(x + y) 0.$$

Constructing a program for this is relatively simple. All we need to do is to move the separating 0 to the right end of $w(y)$, so that the addition amounts to nothing more than the coalition of the two strings. To achieve this, we construct

$$M = (Q, \Sigma, \Gamma, \delta, q_0, \square, F),$$

with

$$Q = \{q_0, q_1, q_2, q_3, q_4\},$$
$$F = \{q_4\},$$
$$\delta(q_0, 1) = (q_0, 1, R),$$
$$\delta(q_0, 0) = (q_1, 1, R),$$

$$\delta(q_1, 1) = (q_1, 1, R),$$

$$\delta(q_1, \square) = (q_2, \square, L),$$

$$\delta(q_2, 1) = (q_3, 0, L),$$

$$\delta(q_3, 1) = (q_3, 1, L).$$

Note that in moving the 0 right we temporarily create an extra 1, a fact that is remembered by putting the machine into state q_1. The transition $\delta(q_2, 1) = (q_3, 0, L)$ is needed to remove this at the end of the computation. This can be seen from the sequence of instantaneous descriptions for adding 111 to 11:

$$q_0 1110011 \vdash 1q_0 110011$$

$$\vdash 11q_0 1011$$

$$\vdash 111q_0 011$$

$$\vdash 1111q_1 11$$

$$\vdash 11111q_1 1$$

$$\vdash 11111q_1 1$$

$$\vdash 111111q_1$$

$$\vdash 11111q_2 1$$

$$\vdash 1111q_3 10$$

$$\vdots$$

$$\vdash q_3 \square 111110$$

$$\vdash q_4 111110,$$

or, briefly as follows:

$$q_0 1110011 \overset{*}{\vdash} q_4 111110.$$

2.1.2 The Church-Turing Thesis

Any *effectively* computable function can be computed by a Turing machine, and there is no effective procedure that a Turing machine cannot perform. This leads naturally to the following famous Church-Turing thesis, named after Alonzo Church and Alan Turing:

The Church-Turing thesis. Any effectively computable function can be computed by a Turing machine.

The Church-Turing thesis thus provides us with a powerful tool to distinguish what is computation and what is not computation, what function is computable and what function is not computable, and more generally, what computers can do and what computers cannot do.

It must be noted that the Church-Turing thesis is not a mathematical theorem, and hence it cannot be proved formally, since, to prove the Church-Turing thesis, we need to formalize what is effectively computable, which is impossible. However, many computational evidences support the thesis and in fact no counterexample has been found yet.

Remark 2.1. Church in his famous 1936 paper [7] proposed the important concept of λ-definable and later in his book review [8] on Turing's 1936 paper, he said that *all effective procedures are in fact Turing equivalent.* This is what we call now the Church-Turing thesis. It is interesting to note that Church was the Ph.D. advisor of Alan Turing (1938), Michael Rabin (1957) and Dana Scott (1958), all at Princeton; Rabin and Scott were also the 1976 Turing Award Recipients, a Prize considered as an equivalent Nobel Prize in Computer Science.

2.1.3 Decidability and Computability

Although a Turing machine can do everything that a real computer can do, there are, however, many problems that Turing machines cannot do; the simplest one is actually related the Turing machine itself, the so-called *Turing machine halting problem.*

Definition 2.2. A language is *Turing-acceptable* if there exists a Turing machine that accepts the language. A Turing-acceptable language is also called a *recursively enumerable language.*

When a Turing machine starts on an input, there are three possible outcomes: accept, reject or loop (i.e., the machine falls into an infinite loop without any output). If a machine can always make a decision to accept or reject a language, then the machine is said to decide the language.

Definition 2.3. A language is *Turing-decidable* if there exists a Turing machine that decides the language, otherwise, it is *Turing-undecidable.* A Turing-decidable language is also called *recursive language.*

Definition 2.4. The Turing Machine Halting Problem may be defined as follows:

$$L_{\text{TM}} = \{(M, w) \mid M \text{ is a Turing machine and } M \text{ accepts } w\}.$$

Theorem 2.1. L_{TM} *is undecidable.*

Turing machines that always halt are good model of an *algorithm*, a well-defined sequence of steps that always finishes and produces an answer. If an algorithm

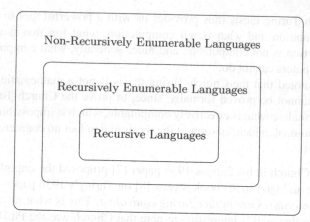

Figure 2.2   Relationships among recursive-related languages/problems

for a given problem exists, then the problem is *decidable*. Let the language L be a *problem*, then L is decidable if it is recursive language, and it is undecidable if it is not recursive language. From a practical point of view, the existence or non-existence of an algorithm to solve a problem is of more important than the existence or non-existence of a Turing machine to solve the problem. So, to distinguish problems or languages between decidable or undecidable is of more important than that between recursively enumerable and non-recursively enumerable. Figure 2.2 shows the relationships among the three classes of problems/languages.

Problems for Section 2.1

1. Explain
   (1) why a Turing machine can do everything that a real computer can do.
   (2) why any computable function can be computed by a Turing machine.
2. Explain why Church-Turing thesis cannot be proved rigorously.
3. Explain why all different types of Turing machines such single tape Turing machines and multiple tape Turing machines are equivalent.
4. Show that there is a language that is recursively enumerable but not recursive [29].
5. Hilbert's tenth problem [30] states that given a Diophantine equation with any number of unknown quantities and with rational integral numerical coefficients: To devise a process according to which it can be determined in a finite number of operations whether the equation is solvable in rational integers. Show that Hilbert's tenth problem is undecidable.
6. Show that the Turing Machine Halting Problem is undecidable. Give some more examples (problems) that is are undecidable [24].

2.2 Classical Complexity Theory

Computability is only concerned with what computer can do, but ignores the computing resources such as the time and space required for completing a computation task. Computational complexity, on the other hand, fills this gap by considering mainly the computing resources such as the time and space required for completing a computation task. Thus a theoretically computable problem may be practically uncomputable if it required too much time such as 50 million years or too much space. In this section, we shall study mainly the time complexity of computational problems.

2.2.1 Complexity Classes

First of all, we shall present a series of formal definitions for some common computational complexity classes based on Turing machines. To do so, we need a definition for probabilistic or randomized Turing machines.

Definition 2.5. A Probabilistic Turing Machine (PTM) is a type of nondeterministic Turing machine with distinct states called *coin-tossing states*. For each coin-tossing state, the finite control unit specifies two possible legal next states. The computation of a probabilistic Turing machine is deterministic except that in coin-tossing states the machine tosses an unbiased coin to decide between the two *possible legal* next states.

A probabilistic Turing machine can be viewed as a Randomized Turing Machine [24], as described in Figure 2.3. The first tape, holding input, is just the same as conventional multitape Turing machine. The second tape is referred to as random tape, containing randomly and independently chosen bits, with probability $1/2$ of a 0 and the same probability $1/2$ of a 1. The third and subsequent tapes are used, if needed, as scratch tapes by the Turing machine.

Definition 2.6. $\mathcal{P}$ is the class of problems solvable in polynomial-time by a Deterministic Turing Machine (DTM). Problems in this class are classified to be tractable (feasible) and easy to solve on a computer. For example, additions of any two integers, no matter how big they are, can be performed in polynomial-time, and hence it is in $\mathcal{P}$.

Definition 2.7. $\mathcal{NP}$ is the class of problems solvable in polynomial-time on a Non-Deterministic Turing Machine (NDTM). Problems in this class are classified to be intractable (infeasible) and hard to solve on a computer. For example, the Traveling Salesman Problem (TSP) is in $\mathcal{NP}$, and hence it is hard to solve.

In terms of formal languages, we may also say that $\mathcal{P}$ is the class of languages where the membership in the class can be decided in polynomial-time, whereas $\mathcal{NP}$ is the class of languages where the membership in the class can be verified

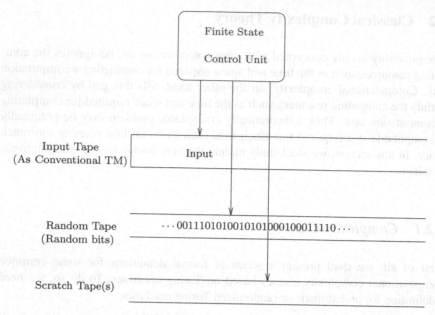

Figure 2.3 Randomized Turing machine

in polynomial-time [43]. It seems that the power of polynomial-time verifiable is greater than that of polynomial-time decidable, but no proof has been given to support this statement (see Figure 2.4). The question of whether or not $\mathcal{P} = \mathcal{NP}$ is one of the greatest unsolved problems in computer science and mathematics, and in fact it is one of the seven Millennium Prize Problems proposed by the Clay Mathematics Institute in Boston in 2000, each with one-million US dollars [12].

Definition 2.8. $\mathcal{EXP}$ is the class of problems solvable by a deterministic Turing machine in time bounded by 2^{n^i}.

Definition 2.9. A function f is polynomial-time computable if for any input w, $f(w)$ will halt on a Turing machine in polynomial-time. A language A is polynomial-time reducible to a language B, denoted by $A \leq_{\mathcal{P}} B$, if there exists a polynomial-time computable function such that for every input w,

$$w \in A \iff f(w) \in B.$$

The function f is called the polynomial-time reduction of A to B.

Definition 2.10. A language/problem L is $\mathcal{NP}$-Completeness if it satisfies the following two conditions:

1. $L \in \mathcal{NP}$,
2. $\forall A \in \mathcal{NP}$, $A \leq_{\mathcal{P}} L$.

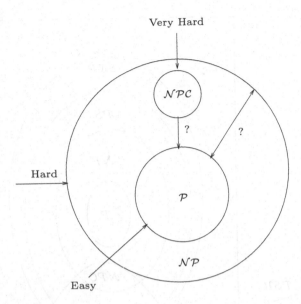

Figure 2.4 The $\mathcal{P}$ versus $\mathcal{NP}$ problem

Definition 2.11. A problem D is $\mathcal{NP}$-Hard if it satisfies the following condition:

$$\forall A \in \mathcal{NP}, \ A \leq_P D$$

where D may be in $\mathcal{NP}$, or may not be in $\mathcal{NP}$. Thus, $\mathcal{NP}$-Hard means *at least as hard as any $\mathcal{NP}$-problem*, although it might, in fact, be harder.

Similarly, one can define the class of problems of $\mathcal{P}$-Space, $\mathcal{P}$-Space Complete, and $\mathcal{P}$-Space Hard. We shall use $\mathcal{NPC}$ to denote the set of $\mathcal{NP}$-Complete problems, $\mathcal{PSC}$ the set of $\mathcal{P}$-Space Complete problems, $\mathcal{NPH}$ the set of $\mathcal{NP}$-Hard problems, and $\mathcal{PSH}$ the set of $\mathcal{P}$-Space Hard problems. The relationships among the classes $\mathcal{P}, \mathcal{NP}, \mathcal{NPC}, \mathcal{PSC}, \mathcal{NPH}, \mathcal{PSH}$ and $\mathcal{EXP}$ may be described in Figure 2.5.

Definition 2.12. $\mathcal{RP}$ is the class of problems solvable in expected polynomial-time with *one-sided error* by a probabilistic (randomized) Turing machine. By "one-sided error" we mean that the machine will answer "yes" when the answer is "yes" with a probability of error $< 1/2$, and will answer "no" when the answer is "no" with zero probability of error.

Definition 2.13. $\mathcal{ZPP}$ is the class of problems solvable in expected polynomial-time with *zero error* on a probabilistic Turing machine. It is defined by $\mathcal{ZPP} = \mathcal{RP} \cap \text{co-}\mathcal{RP}$, where co-$\mathcal{RP}$ is the complementary language of $\mathcal{RP}$, i.e., co-$\mathcal{RP} = \{L : \bar{L} \in \mathcal{RP}\}$. By "zero error" we mean that the machine will answer "yes" when the answer is "yes" (with zero probability of error), and will answer "no" when the answer is "no" (also with zero probability of error). But note that the machine may also answer "?", which means that the machine does not know the answer is "yes"

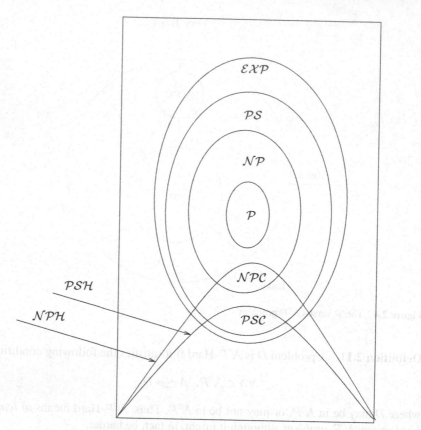

Figure 2.5 Conjectured relationships among classes $\mathcal{P}$, $\mathcal{NP}$ and $\mathcal{NPC}$, etc.

or "no". However, it is guaranteed that at most half of simulation cases the machine will answer "?". $\mathcal{ZPP}$ is usually referred to an *elite class*, because it also equals to the class of problems that can be solved by randomized algorithms that always give the correct answer and run in expected polynomial-time.

Definition 2.14. $\mathcal{BPP}$ is the class of problems solvable in expected polynomial-time with *two sided error* on a probabilistic Turing machine, in which the answer always has probability at least $\frac{1}{2} + \delta$, for some fixed $\delta > 0$ of being correct. The "$\mathcal{B}$" in $\mathcal{BPP}$ stands for "bounded away the error probability from $\frac{1}{2}$"; for example, the error probability could be $\frac{1}{3}$.

The space complexity classes $\mathcal{P}$-SPACE and $\mathcal{NP}$-SPACE can be defined analogously as $\mathcal{P}$ and $\mathcal{NP}$. It is clear that a time class is included in the corresponding space class since one unit is needed to the space by one square. Although it is not known whether or not $\mathcal{P} = \mathcal{NP}$, it is known that $\mathcal{P}$-SPACE $= \mathcal{NP}$-SPACE. It is generally believed that

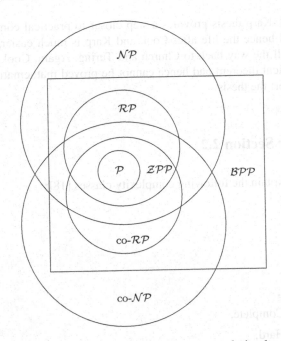

Figure 2.6 Conjectured relationships among some common complexity classes

$$\mathcal{P} \subseteq \mathcal{ZPP} \subseteq \mathcal{RP} \subseteq \binom{\mathcal{BPP}}{\mathcal{NP}} \subseteq \mathcal{P}\text{-SPACE} \subseteq \mathcal{EXP}.$$

Besides the proper inclusion $\mathcal{P} \subset \mathcal{EXP}$, it is not known whether any of the other inclusions in the above hierarchy is proper. Note that the relationship of $\mathcal{BPP}$ and $\mathcal{NP}$ is not known, although it is believed that $\mathcal{NP} \not\subseteq \mathcal{BPP}$. Figure 2.6 shows the relationships among the various common complexity classes.

2.2.2 The Cook-Karp Thesis

It is widely believed, although no proof has been given, that problems in $\mathcal{P}$ are computationally tractable (or feasible, easy), whereas problems not in (i.e., beyond) $\mathcal{P}$ are computationally intractable (or infeasible, hard, difficult). This is the famous *Cook-Karp thesis*, named after Stephen Cook, who first studied the $\mathcal{P}$-$\mathcal{NP}$ problem and Richard Karp, who proposed a list of the $\mathcal{NP}$-Complete problems.

The Cook-Karp thesis. Any computationally tractable problem can be computed by a Turing machine in deterministic polynomial-time.

Thus, problems in $\mathcal{P}$ are tractable whereas problems in $\mathcal{NP}$ are intractable. However, there is not a clear cut between the two types of problems. This is exactly the hard $\mathcal{P}$ versus $\mathcal{NP}$ problem, mentioned earlier. Compared to the Church-Turing thesis, the Cook-Karp thesis provides a step closer to practical computability and complexity, and hence the life after Cook and Karp is much easier, since there is no need to go all the way back to Church and Turing. Again, Cook-Karp thesis is not a mathematical theorem and hence cannot be proved mathematically, however evidences support the thesis.

Problems for Section 2.2

1. Define and explain the following complexity classes [18]:

$$\mathcal{P},$$
$$\mathcal{NP},$$
$$\mathcal{RP},$$
$$\mathcal{BPP},$$
$$\mathcal{ZPP},$$
$$\mathcal{NP}\text{-Complete},$$
$$\mathcal{NP}\text{-Hard},$$
$$\mathcal{P}^{\#\mathcal{P}},$$
$$\mathcal{P}\text{-Space},$$
$$\mathcal{NP}\text{-Space},$$
$$\mathcal{EXP}.$$

2. Show that $\mathcal{P} \subset \mathcal{RP}$.
3. Let SAT denote the *SATisfiability problem*. Show that

$$\text{SAT} \in \mathcal{NP},$$

and

$$\text{SAT} \in \mathcal{NP}\text{-Complete}.$$

4. Let HPP denote the *Hamiltonian Path Problem*. Show that

$$\text{HPP} \in \mathcal{NP},$$

and

$$\text{HPP} \in \mathcal{NP}\text{-Complete}.$$

5. Show that HPP is polynomial-time reducible to TSP.
6. Prove or disprove $\mathcal{P} \neq \mathcal{NP}$.

7. Just the same as that it is not known if $\mathcal{P} \neq \mathcal{NP}$, it is also currently not known if $\mathcal{BPP} \neq \mathcal{P}$-Space, and proving or disproving this would be a major breakthrough in computational complexity theory. Prove or disprove

$$\mathcal{BPP} \neq \mathcal{P}\text{-Space.}$$

2.3 Quantum Information and Computation

The idea that computers can be viewed as physical objects and computations as physical processes is revolutionary; it was conceived by several scientists, most notably Richard Feynman (1918–1988) and David Deutsch (Born 1953). For example, Feynman published posthumously a book *Feynman Lectures on Computation* [17] in 1996, where he introduced the theory of reversible computation, quantum mechanical computers and quantum aspects of computation in great detail, whereas Deutsch in 1985 published a paper [15] explaining the basic idea of quantum Turing machine and the universal quantum computer.

Quantum computers are machines that rely on characteristically quantum phenomena, such as quantum interference and quantum entanglement, in order to perform computation, whereas the classical theory of computation usually refers not to physics but to purely mathematical subjects. A conventional digital computer operates with bits (we may call them *Shannon bits*, since Shannon was the first to use bits to represent information)—the Boolean states 0 and 1—and after each computation step the computer has a definite, exactly measurable state, that is, all bits are in the form 0 or 1 but not both. A quantum computer, a quantum analogue of a digital computer, operates with *quantum bits* (the quantum version of Shannon bit) involving quantum states. The state of a quantum computer is described as a *basis vector* in a *Hilbert space*,[1] named after the German mathematician David Hilbert (1862–1943). More formally, we have:

Definition 2.15. A *qubit* is a quantum state $|\Psi\rangle$ of the form

$$|\Psi\rangle = \alpha |0\rangle + \beta |1\rangle,$$

where the amplitudes $\alpha, \beta \in \mathbb{C}$, such that $||\alpha||^2 + ||\beta||^2 = 1$, $|0\rangle$ and $|1\rangle$ are *basis vectors* of the Hilbert space.

Note that state vectors are written in a special angular bracket notation called a "ket vector" $|\Psi\rangle$, an expression coined by Paul Dirac who wanted a shorthand

---

[1]Hilbert space is defined to be a complete inner-product space. The set of all sequences $x = (x_1, x_2, \cdots)$ of complex numbers (where $\sum_{i=1}^{\infty} |x_i|^2$ is finite) is a good example of a Hilbert space, where the sum $x + y$ is defined as $(x_1 + y_1, x_2 + y_2, \cdots)$, the product ax as $(ax_1, ax_2, \cdots)$, and the inner product as $(x, y) = \sum_{i=1}^{\infty} \bar{x}_i y_i$, where $\bar{x}_i$ is the complex conjugate of x_i, $x = (x_1, x_2, \cdots)$ and $y = (y_1, y_2, \cdots)$. In modern quantum mechanics all possible physical states of a system are considered to correspond to space vectors in a Hilbert space.

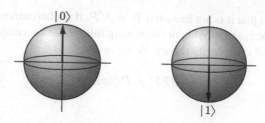

Figure 2.7 A qubit for the binary values 0 and 1

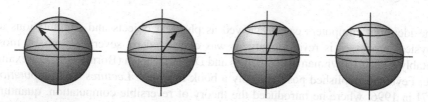

Figure 2.8 *Each sphere* represents a qubit with the same proportions of the $|0\rangle$ and $|1\rangle$

notation for writing formulae that arise in quantum mechanics. In a quantum computer, each qubit could be represented by the state of a simple 2-state quantum system such as the spin state of a spin-$\frac{1}{2}$ particle. The spin of such a particle, when measured, is always found to exist in one of two possible states $\left|+\frac{1}{2}\right\rangle$ (spin-up) and $\left|-\frac{1}{2}\right\rangle$ (spin-down). This *discreteness* is called *quantization*. Clearly, the two states can then be used to represent the binary value 1 and 0 (see Figure 2.7; by courtesy of Williams and Clearwater [49]). The main difference between qubits and classical bits is that a bit can only be set to either 0 and 1, while a qubit $|\Psi\rangle$ can take any (uncountable) quantum superposition of $|0\rangle$ and $|1\rangle$ (see Figure 2.8; by courtesy of Williams and Clearwater [49]). That is, a qubit in a simple 2-state system can have two states rather than just one allowed at a time as the classical Shannon bit. Moreover, if a 2-state quantum system can exist in any one of the states $|0\rangle$ and $|1\rangle$, it can also exist in the *superposed* state

$$|\Psi\rangle = \alpha_1 |0\rangle + \alpha_2 |1\rangle.$$

This is known as the *principle of superposition*. More generally, if a k-state quantum system can exist in any one of the following k eigenstates $|c_1\rangle, |c_1\rangle, \cdots, |c_k\rangle$, it can also exist in the *superposed* state

$$|\Psi\rangle = \sum_{i=0}^{2^k-1} \alpha_i |c_i\rangle,$$

where the amplitudes $\alpha_i \in \mathbb{C}$, such that $\sum_i ||\alpha_i||^2 = 1$, and each $|c_i\rangle$ is a basis vector of the Hilbert space. Once we can encode the binary values 0 and 1 in the states of a physical system, we can make a complete memory of register out of a chain of such systems.

Definition 2.16. A *quantum register*, or more generally, a *quantum computer*, is an ordered set of a finite number of qubits.

In order to use a physical system to do computation, we must be able to change the state of the system; this is achieved by applying a sequence of unitary transformations to the state vector $|\Psi\rangle$ via a unitary matrix (a unitary matrix is one whose conjugate transpose is equal to its inverse). Suppose now a computation is performed on a one-bit quantum computer, then the superposition will be

$$|\Psi\rangle = \alpha|0\rangle + \beta|1\rangle,$$

where $\alpha, \beta \in \mathbb{C}$, such that $||\alpha||^2 + ||\beta||^2 = 1$. The different possible states are $|0\rangle = \begin{pmatrix} 1 \\ 0 \end{pmatrix}$ and $|1\rangle = \begin{pmatrix} 0 \\ 1 \end{pmatrix}$. Let the unitary matrix M be

$$M = \frac{1}{\sqrt{2}} \begin{pmatrix} 1 & 1 \\ -1 & 1 \end{pmatrix}.$$

Then the quantum operations on a qubit can be written as follows:

$$M|0\rangle = \frac{1}{\sqrt{2}} \begin{pmatrix} 1 & 1 \\ -1 & 1 \end{pmatrix} \begin{pmatrix} 1 \\ 0 \end{pmatrix} = \frac{1}{\sqrt{2}}|0\rangle - \frac{1}{\sqrt{2}}|1\rangle,$$

$$M|1\rangle = \frac{1}{\sqrt{2}} \begin{pmatrix} 1 & 1 \\ -1 & 1 \end{pmatrix} \begin{pmatrix} 0 \\ 1 \end{pmatrix} = \frac{1}{\sqrt{2}}|0\rangle + \frac{1}{\sqrt{2}}|1\rangle,$$

which is actually the quantum gate (analogous to the classical logic gate):

$$|0\rangle \rightarrow \frac{1}{\sqrt{2}}|0\rangle - \frac{1}{\sqrt{2}}|1\rangle,$$

$$|1\rangle \rightarrow \frac{1}{\sqrt{2}}|0\rangle + \frac{1}{\sqrt{2}}|1\rangle.$$

Logic gates can be regarded as logic operators. The NOT operator defined as

$$\text{NOT} = \begin{pmatrix} 0 & 1 \\ 1 & 0 \end{pmatrix},$$

changes the state of its input as follows:

$$\text{NOT}|0\rangle = \begin{pmatrix} 0 & 1 \\ 1 & 0 \end{pmatrix} \begin{pmatrix} 1 \\ 0 \end{pmatrix} = \begin{pmatrix} 0 \\ 1 \end{pmatrix} = |1\rangle,$$

$$\text{NOT}|1\rangle = \begin{pmatrix} 0 & 1 \\ 1 & 0 \end{pmatrix} \begin{pmatrix} 0 \\ 1 \end{pmatrix} = \begin{pmatrix} 1 \\ 0 \end{pmatrix} = |0\rangle.$$

Similarly, we can define the quantum gate of two bits as follows:

$$|00\rangle \rightarrow |00\rangle,$$

$$|01\rangle \rightarrow |01\rangle,$$

$$|10\rangle \rightarrow \frac{1}{\sqrt{2}}|10\rangle + \frac{1}{\sqrt{2}}|11\rangle,$$

$$|11\rangle \rightarrow \frac{1}{\sqrt{2}}|10\rangle - \frac{1}{\sqrt{2}}|11\rangle,$$

or equivalently by giving the unitary matrix of the quantum operation:

$$M = \begin{pmatrix} 1 & 0 & 0 & 0 \\ 0 & 1 & 0 & 0 \\ 0 & 0 & \dfrac{1}{\sqrt{2}} & \dfrac{1}{\sqrt{2}} \\ 0 & 0 & \dfrac{1}{\sqrt{2}} & -\dfrac{1}{\sqrt{2}} \end{pmatrix}. \tag{2.1}$$

This matrix is actually the counterpart of the truth table of Boolean logic used for digital computers. Suppose now the computation is in the superposition of the states:

$$\frac{1}{\sqrt{2}}|10\rangle - \frac{1}{\sqrt{2}}|11\rangle,$$

or

$$\frac{1}{\sqrt{2}}|10\rangle + \frac{1}{\sqrt{2}}|11\rangle.$$

Then using the unitary transformations defined in (2.1), we have

$$\frac{1}{\sqrt{2}}|10\rangle - \frac{1}{\sqrt{2}}|11\rangle \rightarrow \frac{1}{\sqrt{2}}\left(\frac{1}{\sqrt{2}}|10\rangle + \frac{1}{\sqrt{2}}|11\rangle\right)$$

$$- \frac{1}{\sqrt{2}}\left(\frac{1}{\sqrt{2}}|10\rangle - \frac{1}{\sqrt{2}}|11\rangle\right)$$

$$= \frac{1}{2}(|10\rangle + |11\rangle) - \frac{1}{2}(|10\rangle - |11\rangle)$$

$$= |11\rangle,$$

$$\frac{1}{\sqrt{2}}|10\rangle + \frac{1}{\sqrt{2}}|11\rangle \rightarrow \frac{1}{2}(|10\rangle + |11\rangle) + \frac{1}{2}(|10\rangle - |11\rangle)$$

$$= |10\rangle.$$

Problems for Section 2.3

1. Let

$$\text{NOT} = \begin{pmatrix} 0 & 1 \\ 1 & 0 \end{pmatrix}, \quad |0\rangle = \begin{pmatrix} 1 \\ 0 \end{pmatrix}.$$

Show that

$$\text{NOT}\,|0\rangle = |1\rangle.$$

2. Let

$$\text{NOT} = \begin{pmatrix} 0 & 1 \\ 1 & 0 \end{pmatrix}, \quad |1\rangle = \begin{pmatrix} 0 \\ 1 \end{pmatrix}.$$

Show that

$$\text{NOT}\,|0\rangle = |0\rangle.$$

3. Let the action of the $\sqrt{\text{NOT}}$ gate as follows:

$$\sqrt{\text{NOT}} = \begin{pmatrix} \dfrac{1+i}{2} & \dfrac{1-i}{2} \\ \dfrac{1-i}{2} & \dfrac{1+i}{2} \end{pmatrix}.$$

Show that

$$\sqrt{\text{NOT}} \cdot \sqrt{\text{NOT}} = \begin{pmatrix} 0 & 1 \\ 1 & 0 \end{pmatrix}.$$

4. Let the conjugate transpose of $\sqrt{\text{NOT}}$, denoted by $(\sqrt{\text{NOT}})^{+}$, be as follows:

$$(\sqrt{\text{NOT}})^{+} = \begin{pmatrix} \dfrac{1-i}{2} & \dfrac{1+i}{2} \\ \dfrac{1+i}{2} & -\dfrac{1-i}{2} \end{pmatrix}.$$

Show that

$$\sqrt{\text{NOT}} \cdot (\sqrt{\text{NOT}})^{+} = \begin{pmatrix} 1 & 0 \\ 0 & 1 \end{pmatrix}.$$

5. Let

$$|+\rangle = \frac{1}{\sqrt{2}} (|0\rangle + |1\rangle),$$

$$|-\rangle = \frac{1}{\sqrt{2}} (|0\rangle - |1\rangle),$$

$$|i\rangle = \frac{1}{\sqrt{2}} (|0\rangle + i|1\rangle),$$

$$|-i\rangle = \frac{1}{\sqrt{2}} (|0\rangle - i|1\rangle).$$

Which pairs of expressions for quantum states represent the same state?

(1) $\frac{1}{\sqrt{2}} (|0\rangle + |1\rangle)$ and $\frac{1}{\sqrt{2}} (-|0\rangle + i|1\rangle)$.

(2) $\frac{1}{\sqrt{2}} (|0\rangle + e^{i\pi/4}|1\rangle)$ and $\frac{1}{\sqrt{2}} (e^{-i\pi/4}|0\rangle + |1\rangle)$.

6. Give the set of all values of γ such that following pairs of quantum states are equivalent state:

(1) $|1\rangle$ and $\frac{1}{\sqrt{2}} (|+\rangle + e^{i\gamma}|-\rangle)$.

(2) $\frac{1}{2}|0\rangle - \frac{\sqrt{3}}{2}|1\rangle$ and $e^{i\gamma} \left(\frac{1}{2}|0\rangle - \frac{\sqrt{3}}{2}|1\rangle \right)$.

2.4 Quantum Computability and Complexity

In this section, we shall give a brief introduction to some basic concepts of quantum computability and complexity within the theoretical framework of quantum Turing machines.

The first true quantum Turing machine was proposed in 1985 by Deutsch [15]. A *Quantum Turing Machine* (QTM) is a quantum mechanical generalization of a probabilistic Turing machine, in which each cell on the tape can hold a *qubit* (quantum bit) whose state is represented as an arrow contained in a sphere (see Figure 2.9). Let $\overline{\mathbb{C}}$ be the set consisting of $\alpha \in \mathbb{C}$ such that there is a deterministic Turing machine that computes the real and imaginary parts of α within 2^{-n} in time polynomial in n, then the quantum Turing machines can still be defined as an algebraic system

$$M = (Q, \Sigma, \Gamma, \delta, q_0, \Box, F),$$

where

$$\delta : Q \times \Gamma \to \overline{\mathbb{C}}^{Q \times \Gamma \times \{L,R\}},$$

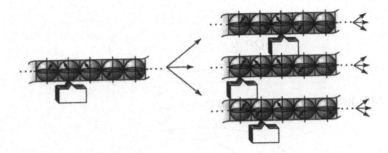

Figure 2.9 A quantum turing machine

and the rest remains the same as a probabilistic Turing machine. Readers are suggested to consult Bernstein and Vazirani [5] for a more detailed discussion of quantum Turing machines. Quantum Turing machines open a new way to model our universe which is quantum physical, and offer new features of computation. However, quantum Turing machines do not offer more computation power than classical Turing machines. This leads to the following quantitative version of the Church-Turing thesis for quantum computation (see [49]; by courtesy of Williams and Clearwater):

The Church-Turing thesis for quantum computation. Any physical (quantum) computing device can be simulated by a Turing machine in a number of steps polynomial in the resources used by the computing device.

That is, from a computability point of view, a *quantum* Turing machine has no more computation power than a *classical* Turing machine. However, from a computational complexity point of view, a quantum Turing machine may be more efficient than a classical Turing machine for certain type of computational intractable problems. For example, the Integer Factorization Problem and the Discrete Logarithm Problem are intractable on classical Turing machines (as everybody knows at present), but they are tractable on quantum Turing machines. More precisely, IFP and DLP cannot be solved in polynomial-time on a classical computer (classical Turing machine), but can be solved in polynomial-time on a quantum computer (quantum Turing machine).

Remark 2.2. Quantum computers are not just faster versions of classical computers, but use a different paradigm for computation. They would speed up the computation of some problems such as IFP and DLP by large factors, but other problems not at all. For quantum computers to be practically useful, we would expect they solve the $\mathcal{NP}$ problems in $\mathcal{P}$. But unfortunately, we do not know this yet. What we know is that quantum computers can solve e.g., IFP and DLP in $\mathcal{P}$, but IFP and DLP have not been proved in $\mathcal{NP}$.

Just as there are classical complexity classes, so are there quantum complexity classes. As quantum Turing machines are generalizations of probabilistic Turing machines, the quantum complexity classes resemble the probabilistic complexity classes. First, we gave the following quantum analog of classical $\mathcal{P}$:

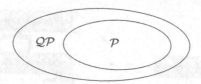

Figure 2.10   Relationship between $\mathcal{QP}$ and $\mathcal{P}$

Figure 2.11   Relationship between $\mathcal{ZQP}$ and $\mathcal{ZPP}$

Definition 2.17. $\mathcal{QP}$ (Quantum Analogue of $\mathcal{P}$) is the class of problems solvable, with certainty, in polynomial-time on a quantum Turing machine.

It can be shown that $\mathcal{P} \subset \mathcal{QP}$ (see Figure 2.10). That is, the quantum Turing machine can solve more problems *efficiently* in *worse-case* polynomial-time than a classical Turing machine.

Similarly, we have the following quantum analog of classical $\mathcal{ZPP}$.

Definition 2.18. $\mathcal{ZQP}$ (Quantum Analogue of $\mathcal{ZPP}$) is the class of problems solvable in expected polynomial-time with zero-error probability by a quantum Turing machine.

It is clear that $\mathcal{ZPP} \subset \mathcal{ZQP}$ (see Figure 2.11).

Definition 2.19. $\mathcal{BQP}$ (Quantum Analogue of $\mathcal{BPP}$) is the class of problems solvable in polynomial-time by a quantum Turing machine, possibly with a *bounded* probability $\epsilon < 1/3$ of error.

It is known that $\mathcal{P} \subseteq \mathcal{BPP} \subseteq \mathcal{BQP} \subseteq \mathcal{P}$-SPACE, and hence, it is not known whether quantum Turing machines are more powerful than probabilistic Turing machines. It is also not known the relationship between $\mathcal{BQP}$ and $\mathcal{NP}$. Figure 2.12 shows the suspected relationships of $\mathcal{BQP}$ to some other well-known classical computational classes.

Problems for Section 2.4

1. Explain the complexity classes in the following conjectured containment relationships involving classical and quantum computation in Figure 2.13:

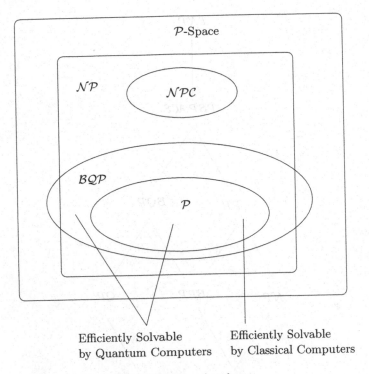

Figure 2.12 Suspected relationships of $\mathcal{BQP}$ to other classes

2. Show that

$$\mathcal{P} \subseteq \mathcal{QP} \subseteq \mathcal{BQP}.$$

3. One of the most significant results in quantum computational complexity is that $\mathcal{BQP} \subseteq \mathcal{P}\text{-Space}$. Show that

$$\mathcal{BPP} \subseteq \mathcal{BQP} \subseteq \mathcal{P}\text{-Space}.$$

4. Show that

$$\mathcal{BQP} \subseteq \mathcal{P}^{\#\mathcal{P}} \subseteq \mathcal{P}\text{-Space},$$

where $\mathcal{P}^{\#\mathcal{P}}$ be the set of problems which could be solved in polynomial-time if sums of exponentially many terms could be computed efficiently (where these sums must satisfy the requirement that each term is computable in polynomial-time).

5. Show that

$$\mathcal{IP} = \mathcal{P}\text{-Space}$$

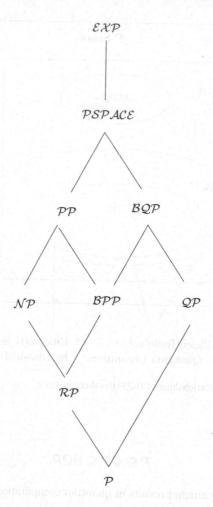

Figure 2.13 Suspected containment relationships of complexity classes

where $\mathcal{IP}$ is the set of problems having interactive systems, and

$$QIP = P\text{-Space}$$

where $\mathcal{QIP}$ is the set of problems having quantum interactive systems.

6. It is currently not known if a Quantum Turing Machine (QTM) has more computational power than a Probabilistic Turing Machine (PTM). Provide evidence to support the statement that quantum computers do not violate the Church-Turing Thesis—any algorithmic process can be simulated by a Turing machine.

7. The Church-Turing thesis (CT), from a computability point of view, can be interpreted as that if a function can be computed by an conceivable hardware system, then it can be computed by a Turing machine. The Extended Church-Turing

thesis (ECT), from a computational complexity point of view, makes the stronger assertion that the Turing machine is also as efficient as any computing device can be. That is, if a function can be computed by some hardware device in time $T(n)$ for input of size n, then it can be computed by a Turing machine in time $(T(n))^k$ for fixed k, depending on the problem. Do you think ECT is valid for quantum computers and for cloud computation?

2.5   Chapter Notes and Further Reading

The aim of quantum computational number theory is to use the quantum computational approach including e.g., quantum hardware–quantum computers and quantum software–quantum algorithms and programs, to solve the difficult number-theoretic problems that are hard to solve by classical computers and algorithms, thus quantum computation plays an important role in quantum computational number theory. This chapter presented the necessary background information for classical and quantum computation theories that will be used in the rest of the book.

Turing's seminal paper on computable numbers with application to decision problem was published in 1936 [45], it is in this paper, he proposed the famous Turing machine model. Church's seminal paper on an unsolved problem in elementary number theory was also published in 1936 [7]. So, 1936 is a great year for theoretical computer science. Church also wrote a rather length review paper [8] on Turing paper [45]. The famous Church-Turing thesis was proposed and formulated basically in these three papers. The Cook-Karp thesis was basically proposed and formulated in Cook's 1971 paper [10] and Karp's 1972 paper [25]. These papers, among others, are the founding papers of modern theory of computability and computational complexity. There are a huge number of papers and books devoted to the theories of computability and complexity, including, e.g., Cook's paper on the $\mathcal{P}$ versus $\mathcal{NP}$ problem [11] and Yao's paper on the Church-Turing thesis and the Extended Church-Turing thesis [53]. The standard references in the field include Hopcroft, Motwani and Ullman's classical book [24] (now in its 3rd edition), and Garey and Johnson's book on computational intractability [18]. Other excellent and comprehensive books include Lewis and Papadimitrou [28], Linz [29], Papadimitrou [33] and Sipser [53] in Chapter 1. More information on number-theoretic computation may be found in [9, 13, 14, 19–21, 35] and many others.

Quantum computation is a new paradigm of computation. Quantum computers would speed up some problems by large factors, but not for all problems. In fact, as far as we know at present, quantum computation does not violate the Church-Turing thesis and quantum computers do not offer more computational power than classical computers. The first person to systematically study quantum computation is possibly the 1965 Nobel Laureate Richard Feynman (see Feynman [16, 17]). The following references provide more information on quantum computing, including quantum computability and quantum complexity: [2, 4, 6, 22, 23, 26, 27, 31, 32, 34, 36–41, 44, 46–48, 50–52].

There is a special section on quantum computation in SIAM Journal, Volume 26, Number 5, October 1997, with some of the classical papers in the field by Bernstein and Vazirani [5] on quantum complexity theory, Simon [42] on the power of quantum computation, Shor [37] on polynomial-time quantum algorithms for IFP and DLP, Bennett [3] on strengths and weaknesses of quantum computing, and Adleman et al. [1] on quantum computability, etc.

References

1. L.M. Adleman, J. DeMarrais, M.-D.A. Huang, Quantum computability. SIAM J. Comput. **26**(5), 1524–1540 (1996)
2. P. Benioff, The computer as a physical system – a microscopic quantum mechanical hamiltonian model of computers as represented by Turing machines. J. Stat. Phys. **22**(5), 563–591 (1980)
3. C.H. Bennett, Strengths and weakness of quantum computing. SIAM J. Comput. **26**(5), 1510–1523 (1997)
4. C.H. Bennett, D.P. DiVincenzo, Quantum information and computation. Nature **404**(6775), 247–255 (2000)
5. E. Bernstein, U. Vazirani, Quantum complexity theory. SIAM J. Comput. **26**(5), 1411–1473 (1997)
6. I.L. Change, R. Laflamme, P. Shor, W.H. Zurek, Quantum computers, factoring, and decoherence. Science **270**(5242), 1633–1635 (1995)
7. A. Church, An unsolved problem of elementary number theory. Am. J. Math. **58**(2), 345–363 (1936)
8. A. Church, Book review: on computable numbers, with an application to the Entscheidungsproblem by Turing. J. Symb. Log. **2**(1), 42–43 (1937)
9. H. Cohen, *A Course in Computational Algebraic Number Theory*. Graduate Texts in Mathematics, vol. 138 (Springer, New York, 1993)
10. S. Cook, The complexity of theorem-proving procedures, in *Proceedings of the 3rd Annual ACM Symposium on the Theory of Computing*, New York (1971), pp. 151–158
11. S. Cook, The importance of the P versus NP question. J. ACM **50**(1), 27–29 (2003)
12. S. Cook, *The P versus NP problem*, in The Millennium Prize Problems, ed. by J. Carlson, A. Jaffe, A. Wiles (Clay Mathematics Institute and American Mathematical Society, Providence, 2006), pp. 87–104
13. T.H. Cormen, C.E. Ceiserson, R.L. Rivest, *Introduction to Algorithms*, 3rd edn. (MIT, Cambridge, 2009)
14. R. Crandall, C. Pomerance, *Prime Numbers – A Computational Perspective*, 2nd edn. (Springer, New York, 2005)
15. D. Deutsch, Quantum Theory, the Church–Turing principle and the universal quantum computer. Proc. R. Soc. Lond. Ser. A **400**(1818), 96–117 (1985)
16. R.P. Feynman, Simulating physics with computers. Int. J. Theor. Phys. **21**(6), 467–488 (1982)
17. R.P. Feynman, *Feynman Lectures on Computation*, ed. by A.J.G. Hey, R.W. Allen (Addison-Wesley, Reading, 1996)
18. M.R. Garey, D.S. Johnson, *Computers and Intractability – A Guide to the Theory of NP-Completeness* (W.H. Freeman, San Francisco, 1979)
19. O. Goldreich, *Foundations of Cryptography: Basic Tools* (Cambridge University Press, Cambridge, 2001)

20. O. Goldreich, *Foundations of Cryptography: Basic Applications* (Cambridge University Press, Cambridge, 2004)
21. O. Goldreich, *P, NP, and NP-Completeness* (Cambridge University Press, Cambridge, 2010)
22. J. Grustka, *Quantum Computing* (McGraw-Hill, London, 1999)
23. M. Hirvensalo, *Quantum Computing*, 2nd edn. (Springer, New York, 2004)
24. J. Hopcroft, R. Motwani, J. Ullman, *Introduction to Automata Theory, Languages, and Computation*, 3rd edn. (Addison-Wesley, Reading, 2007)
25. R. Karp, Reducibility among combinatorial problems, in *Complexity of Computer Computations*, ed. by R.E. Miller, J.W. Thatcher (Plenum, New York, 1972), pp. 85–103
26. D.E. Knuth, *The Art of Computer Programming II – Seminumerical Algorithms*, 3rd edn. (Addison-Wesley, Reading, 1998)
27. M. LeBellac, *A Short Introduction to Quantum Information and Quantum Computation* (Cambridge University Press, Cambridge, 2005)
28. H.R. Lewis, C.H. Papadimitrou, *Elements of the Theory of Computation* (Prentice-Hall, Englewood, 1998)
29. P. Linz, *An Introduction to Formal Languages and Automata*, 5th edn. (Jones and Bartlett, Boston, 2011)
30. Y.V. Matiyasevich, *Hilbert's Tenth Problem* (MIT, Cambridge, 1993)
31. N.D. Mermin, *Quantum Computer Science* (Cambridge University Press, Cambridge, 2007)
32. M.A. Nielson, I.L. Chuang, *Quantum Computation and Quantum Information*, 10th anniversary edition (Cambridge University Press, Cambridge, 2010)
33. C.H. Papadimitrou, *Computational Complexity* (Addison Wesley, Reading, 1994)
34. E. Rieffel, W. Polak, *Quantum Computing: A Gentle Introduction* (MIT, Cambridge, 2011)
35. H. Riesel, *Prime Numbers and Computer Methods for Factorization* (Birkhäuser, Boston, 1990)
36. P. Shor, Algorithms for quantum computation: discrete logarithms and factoring, in *Proceedings of 35th Annual Symposium on Foundations of Computer Science* (IEEE Computer Society, Los Alamitos, 1994), pp. 124–134
37. P. Shor, Polynomial-time algorithms for prime factorization and discrete logarithms on a quantum computer. SIAM J. Comput. **26**(5), 1411–1473 (1997)
38. P. Shor, Quantum computing. Doc. Math. Extra Volume ICM I, 467–486 (1998)
39. P. Shor, Introduction to quantum algorithms. AMS Proc. Symp. Appl. Math. **58**, 143–159 (2002)
40. P. Shor, Why haven't more quantum algorithms been found? J. ACM **50**(1), 87–90 (2003)
41. D.R. Simon, On the power of quantum computation, in *Proceedings of the 35 Annual Symposium on Foundations of Computer Science* (IEEE Computer Society, Los Alamitos, 1994), pp. 116–123
42. D.R. Simon, On the power of quantum computation. SIAM J. Comput. **25**(5), 1474–1483 (1997)
43. M. Sipser, *Introduction to the Theory of Computation*, 2nd edn. (Thomson, Boston, 2006)
44. W. Trappe, L. Washington, *Introduction to Cryptography with Coding Theory*, 2nd edn. (Pearson Prentice-Hall, Upper Saddle River, 2006)
45. A. Turing, On computable numbers, with an application to the Entscheidungsproblem. Proc. Lond. Math. Soc. **S2-42**(1), 230–265 (1937)
46. U.V. Vazirani, On the power of quantum computation. Philos. Trans. R. Soc. Lond. **A356** (1743), 1759–1768 (1998)
47. U.V. Vazirani, Fourier transforms and quantum computation, in *Proceedings of Theoretical Aspects of Computer Science*. Lecture Notes in Computer Science, vol. 2292 (Springer, New York, 2000), pp. 208–220
48. U.V. Vazirani, A survey of quantum complexity theory. AMS Proc. Symp. Appl. Math. **58**, 193–220 (2002)
49. C.P. Williams, S.H. Clearwater, *Explorations in Quantum Computation*. The Electronic Library of Science (Springer, New York, 1998)

50. J. Watrous, Quantum computational complexity, in *Encyclopedia of Complexity and System Science* (Springer, New York, 2009), pp. 7174–7201
51. C.P. Williams, *Explorations in Quantum Computation*, 2nd edn. (Springer, New York, 2011)
52. N.S. Yanofsky, M.A. Mannucci, *Quantum Computing for Computer Scientists* (Cambridge University Press, Cambridge, 2008)
53. A. Yao, Classical physics and the Church-Turing thesis. J. ACM **50**(1), 100–105 (2003)

Chapter 3
Quantum Algorithms for Integer Factorization

Anything one man can imagine, other men can make real.

JULES VERNE (1828–1905)
French Novelist, Father of Science Fiction

It is well-known that the most famous and widely used cryptographic system RSA relies its security on the intractability of the integer Factorization Problem (IFP), for which the inventor of RSA received the year 2002 Turing award, consider as the equivalent Nobel Prize in Computer Science. If IFP can be solved in polynomial-time, then RSA and many other cryptographic systems can be broken completely and efficiently. Surprisingly, in 1994, Shor proposed a quantum algorithm, which can solve IPF in polynomial-time. In this chapter, we shall discuss the following topics related to quantum factoring:

1. Classical algorithms for integer factorization;
2. Factoring based cryptography;
3. Shor's quantum factoring algorithm;
4. Variations (compiled and improved versions) of Shor's algorithm.

3.1 Classical Algorithms for Integer Factorization

3.1.1 Basic Concepts

There are many methods and algorithms for factoring integers. If we are concerned with the determinism of the algorithms, then there are two types of factoring algorithms:

1. Deterministic factoring algorithms;
2. Probabilistic factoring algorithms.

However, if we are more concerned with the form and the property of the integers to be factored, then there are two types factoring methods or algorithms:

© Springer International Publishing Switzerland 2015
S.Y. Yan, *Quantum Computational Number Theory*,
DOI 10.1007/978-3-319-25823-2_3

1. General purpose factoring algorithms: the running time depends mainly on the size of n, the number to be factored, and is not strongly dependent on the size of the factor p found. Examples are:

    (1) *Lehman's method* [48], which has a rigorous worst-case running time bound $\mathcal{O}\left(n^{1/3+\epsilon}\right)$.
    (2) *Euler's factoring method* [57], which has deterministic running time $\mathcal{O}\left(n^{1/3+\epsilon}\right)$.
    (3) *Shanks' SQUare FOrm Factorization method* (SQUFOF) [79], which has expected running time $\mathcal{O}\left(n^{1/4}\right)$.
    (4) *The FFT-based factoring methods of Pollard and Strassen* (see [69, 88]) which have deterministic running time $\mathcal{O}\left(n^{1/4+\epsilon}\right)$.
    (5) *The lattice-based factoring methods of Coppersmith* [19], which has deterministic running time $\mathcal{O}\left(n^{1/4+\epsilon}\right)$.
    (6) *Shanks' class group method* [78], which has running time $\mathcal{O}\left(n^{1/5+\epsilon}\right)$, assuming the ERH (Extended Riemann's Hypothesis).
    (7) *Continued FRACtion method* (CFRAC) [63], which under plausible assumptions has expected running time

    $$\mathcal{O}\left(\exp\left(c\sqrt{\log n \log\log n}\right)\right) = \mathcal{O}\left(n^{c\sqrt{\log\log n/\log n}}\right),$$

    where c is a constant (depending on the details of the algorithm); usually $c = \sqrt{2} \approx 1.414213562$.
    (8) *Quadratic Sieve/Multiple Polynomial Quadratic Sieve* (QS/MPQS) [71], which under plausible assumptions has expected running time

    $$\mathcal{O}\left(\exp\left(c\sqrt{\log n \log\log n}\right)\right) = \mathcal{O}\left(n^{c\sqrt{\log\log n/\log n}}\right),$$

    where c is a constant (depending on the details of the algorithm); usually $c = \dfrac{3}{2\sqrt{2}} \approx 1.060660172$.
    (9) *Number Field Sieve* (NFS) [50], which under plausible assumptions has the expected running time

    $$\mathcal{O}\left(\exp\left(c\sqrt[3]{\log n}\sqrt[3]{(\log\log n)^2}\right)\right),$$

    where $c = (64/9)^{1/3} \approx 1.922999427$ if GNFS (a general version of NFS) is used to factor an arbitrary integer n, whereas $c = (32/9)^{1/3} \approx 1.526285657$ if SNFS (a special version of NFS) is used to factor a special integer n such as $n = r^e \pm s$, where r and s are small, $r > 1$ and e is large. This is substantially and asymptotically faster than any other currently known factoring method.

2. Special purpose factoring algorithms: The running time depends mainly on the size of p (the factor found) of n. (We can assume that $p \le \sqrt{n}$.) Examples are:

(1) *Trial division* [46], which has running time $\mathcal{O}\left(p(\log n)^2\right)$.
(2) *Pollard's ρ-method* (see [11, 70]) (also known as Pollard's "rho" algorithm), which under plausible assumptions has expected running time $\mathcal{O}\left(p^{1/2}(\log n)^2\right)$.
(3) *Pollard's $p-1$ method* [69], which runs in $\mathcal{O}(B \log B(\log n)^2)$, where B is the smooth bound; larger values of B make it run more slowly, but are more likely to produce a factor of n.
(4) *Lenstra's Elliptic Curve Method* (ECM) [49], which under plausible assumptions has expected running time

$$\mathcal{O}\left(\exp\left(c\sqrt{\log p \log \log p}\right) \cdot (\log n)^2\right),$$

where $c \approx 2$ is a constant (depending on the details of the algorithm).

The term $\mathcal{O}\left((\log n)^2\right)$ is for the cost of performing arithmetic operations on numbers which are $\mathcal{O}(\log n)$ or $\mathcal{O}\left((\log n)^2\right)$ bits long; the second can be theoretically replaced by $\mathcal{O}\left((\log n)^{1+\epsilon}\right)$ for any $\epsilon > 0$.

3.1.2 Number Field Sieve Factoring

A fundamental idea of many modern general-purpose algorithms for factoring n is to find a suitable pair (x, y) such that

$$x^2 \equiv y^2 \pmod{n} \quad \text{but} \quad x \not\equiv \pm y \pmod{n},$$

then there is a good chance to factor n:

$$\text{Prob}(\gcd(x \pm y, n) = (f_1, f_2), \ 1 < f_1, f_2 < n) > \frac{1}{2}.$$

In practice, the asymptotically fastest general-purpose factoring algorithm is the Number Field Sieve, and runs in expect subexponential-time

$$\mathcal{O}(\exp(c(\log n)^{1/3}(\log \log n)^{2/3})).$$

Definition 3.1. A complex number α is an *algebraic number* if it is a root of a polynomial

$$f(x) = a_0 x^k + a_1 x^{k-1} + a_2 x^{k-2} + \cdots + a_k = 0 \qquad (3.1)$$

where $a_0, a_1, a_2, \ldots, a_k \in \mathbb{Q}$ and $a_0 \neq 0$. If $f(x)$ is irreducible over $\mathbb{Q}$ and $a_0 \neq 0$, then k is the degree of x.

Example 3.1. Two examples of algebraic numbers are as follows:

1. Rational numbers, which are the algebraic numbers of degree 1.
2. $\sqrt{2}$, which is of degree 2 because we can take $f(x) = x^2 - 2 = 0$ ($\sqrt{2}$ is irrational).

Any complex number that is not algebraic is said to be *transcendental* such as π and e.

Definition 3.2. A complex number β is an *algebraic integer* if it is a root of a monic polynomial

$$x^k + b_1 x^{k-1} + b_2 x^{k-2} + \cdots + b_k = 0 \tag{3.2}$$

where $b_0, b_1, b_2, \ldots, b_k \in \mathbb{Z}$.

Remark 3.1. A quadratic integer is an algebraic integer satisfying a monic quadratic equation with integer coefficients. A cubic integer is an algebraic integer satisfying a monic cubic equation with integer coefficients.

Example 3.2. Some examples of algebraic integers are as follows:

1. Ordinary (rational) integers, which are the algebraic integers of degree 1. i.e., they satisfy the monic equations $x - a = 0$ for $a \in \mathbb{Z}$.
2. $\sqrt[3]{2}$ and $\sqrt[5]{3}$, because they satisfy the monic equations $x^3 - 2 = 0$ and $x^3 - 5 = 0$, respectively.
3. $(-1 + \sqrt{-3})/2$, because it satisfies $x^2 + x + 1 = 0$.
4. Gaussian integer $a + b\sqrt{-1}$, with $a, b \in \mathbb{Z}$.

Clearly, every algebraic integer is an algebraic number, but the converse is not true.

Proposition 3.1. *A rational number* $r \in \mathbb{Q}$ *is an algebraic integer if and only if* $r \in \mathbb{Z}$.

Proof. If $r \in \mathbb{Z}$, then r is a root of $x - r = 0$. Thus r is an algebraic integer. Now suppose that $r \in \mathbb{Q}$ and r is an algebraic integer (i.e., $r = c/d$ is a root of (3.2), where $c, d \in \mathbb{Z}$; we may assume $\gcd(c, d) = 1$). Substituting c/d into (3.2) and multiplying both sides by d^n, we get

$$c^k + b_1 c^{k-1} d + b_2 c^{k-2} d^2 \cdots + b_k d^k = 0.$$

It follows that $d \mid c^k$ and $d \mid c$ (since $\gcd(c, d) = 1$). Again since $\gcd(c, d) = 1$, it follows that $d = \pm 1$. Hence $r = c/d \in \mathbb{Z}$. It follows, for example, that $2/5$ is an algebraic number but not an algebraic integer.   □

Remark 3.2. The elements of $\mathbb{Z}$ are the only rational numbers that are algebraic integers. We shall refer to the elements of $\mathbb{Z}$ as *rational integers* when we need to distinguish them from other algebraic integers that are not rational. For example, $\sqrt{2}$ is an algebraic integer but not a rational integer.

The most interesting results concerned with the algebraic numbers and algebraic integers are the following theorem.

Theorem 3.1. *The set of algebraic numbers forms a field, and the set of algebraic integers forms a ring.*

Proof. See pp. 67–68 of Ireland and Rosen [42]. □

Lemma 3.1. *Let $f(x)$ is an irreducible monic polynomial of degree d over integers and m an integer such that $f(m) \equiv 0 \pmod{n}$. Let α be a complex root of $f(x)$ and $\mathbb{Z}[\alpha]$ the set of all polynomials in α with integer coefficients. Then there exists a unique mapping $\Phi : \mathbb{Z}[\alpha] \mapsto \mathbb{Z}_n$ satisfying:*

1. $\Phi(ab) = \Phi(a)\Phi(b), \quad \forall a, b \in \mathbb{Z}[\alpha];$
2. $\Phi(a+b) = \Phi(a) + \Phi(b), \quad \forall a, b \in \mathbb{Z}[\alpha];$
3. $\Phi(za) = z\Phi(a), \quad \forall a \in \mathbb{Z}[\alpha], z \in \mathbb{Z};$
4. $\Phi(1) = 1;$
5. $\Phi(\alpha) = m \pmod{n}.$

Now we are in a position to introduce the Number Field Sieve (NFS). Note that there are two main types of NFS: NFS (general NFS) for general numbers and SNFS (special NFS) for numbers with special forms. The idea, however, behind the GNFS and SNFS are the same:

[1] Find a monic irreducible polynomial $f(x)$ of degree d in $\mathbb{Z}[x]$, and an integer m such that $f(m) \equiv 0 \pmod{n}$.
[2] Let $\alpha \in \mathbb{C}$ be an algebraic number that is the root of $f(x)$, and denote the set of polynomials in α with integer coefficients as $\mathbb{Z}[\alpha]$.
[3] Define the mapping (ring homomorphism): $\Phi : \mathbb{Z}[\alpha] \mapsto \mathbb{Z}_n$ via $\Phi(\alpha) = m$ which ensures that for any $f(x) \in \mathbb{Z}[x]$, we have $\Phi(f(\alpha)) \equiv f(m) \pmod{n}$.
[4] Find a finite set U of coprime integers (a, b) such that

$$\prod_{(a,b)\in U} (a - b\alpha) = \beta^2, \quad \prod_{(a,b)\in U} (a - bm) = y^2$$

for $\beta \in \mathbb{Z}[\alpha]$ and $y \in \mathbb{Z}$. Let $x = \Phi(\beta)$. Then

$$x^2 \equiv \Phi(\beta)\Phi(\beta)$$

$$\equiv \Phi(\beta^2)$$

$$\equiv \Phi\left(\prod_{(a,b)\in U} (a - b\alpha)\right)$$

$$\equiv \prod_{(a,b)\in U} \Phi(a - b\alpha)$$

$$\equiv \prod_{(a,b)\in U} (a - bm)$$

$$\equiv y^2 \qquad (\bmod\ n),$$

which is of the required form of the factoring congruence, and hopefully, a factor of n can be found by calculating $\gcd(x \pm y, n)$.

There are many ways to implement the above idea, all of which follow the same pattern as we discussed previously in CFRAC and QS/MPQS: by a sieving process one first tries to find congruences modulo n by working over a factor base, and then do a Gaussian elimination over $\mathbb{Z}/2\mathbb{Z}$ to obtain a congruence of squares $x^2 \equiv y^2 \pmod{n}$. We give in the following a brief description of the NFS algorithm [62].

Algorithm 3.1. Given an odd positive integer n, the NFS algorithm has the following four main steps in factoring n:

[1] (Polynomials selection) Select two irreducible polynomials $f(x)$ and $g(x)$ with small integer coefficients for which there exists an integer m such that

$$f(m) \equiv g(m) \equiv 0 \pmod{n}.$$

The polynomials should not have a common factor over $\mathbb{Q}$.

[2] (Sieving) Let α be a complex root of f and β a complex root of g. Find pairs (a, b) with $\gcd(a, b) = 1$ such that the integral norms of $a - b\alpha$ and $a - b\beta$:

$$N(a - b\alpha) = b^{\deg(f)} f(a/b), \qquad N(a - b\beta) = b^{\deg(g)} g(a/b)$$

are smooth with respect to a chosen factor base. (The principal ideals $a - b\alpha$ and $a - b\beta$ factor into products of prime ideals in the number field $\mathbb{Q}(\alpha)$ and $\mathbb{Q}(\beta)$, respectively.)

[3] (Linear algebra) Use techniques of linear algebra to find a set $U = \{a_i, b_i\}$ of indices such that the two products

$$\prod_U (a_i - b_i \alpha), \qquad \prod_U (a_i - b_i \beta) \tag{3.3}$$

are both squares of products of prime ideals.

[4] (Square root) Use the set S in (3.3) to find an algebraic numbers $\alpha' \in \mathbb{Q}(\alpha)$ and $\beta' \in \mathbb{Q}(\beta)$ such that

$$(\alpha')^2 = \prod_U (a_i - b_i \alpha), \qquad (\beta')^2 = \prod_U (a_i - b_i \beta). \tag{3.4}$$

Define $\Phi_\alpha : \mathbb{Q}(\alpha) \to \mathbb{Z}_n$ and $\Phi_\beta : \mathbb{Q}(\beta) \to \mathbb{Z}_n$ via $\Phi_\alpha(\alpha) = \Phi_\beta(\beta) = m$, where m is the common root of both f and g. Then

$$x^2 \equiv \Phi_\alpha(\alpha')\Phi_\alpha(\alpha')$$

$$\equiv \Phi_\alpha((\alpha')^2)$$

$$\equiv \Phi_\alpha\left(\prod_{i \in U}(a_i - b_i\alpha)\right)$$

$$\equiv \prod_U \Phi_\alpha(a_i - b_i\alpha)$$

$$\equiv \prod_U (a_i - b_i m)$$

$$\equiv \Phi_\beta(\beta')^2$$

$$\equiv y^2 \qquad (mod\ n),$$

which is of the required form of the factoring congruence, and hopefully, a factor of n can be found by calculating $\gcd(x \pm y, n)$.

Example 3.3. We first give a rather simple NFS factoring example. Let $n = 14885 - 5 \cdot 13 \cdot 229 - 122^2 + 1$. So we put $f(x) = x^2 + 1$ and $m = 122$, such that

$$f(x) \equiv f(m) \equiv 0 \ (mod\ n).$$

If we choose $|a|, |b| \leq 50$, then we can easily find (by sieving) that (Readers should be able to find many such pairs of (a_i, b_i) in the interval, that are smooth up to e.g. 29). So, we have

(a, b)	Norm$(a + bi)$	$a + bm$
$\vdots$	$\vdots$	$\vdots$
$(-49, 49)$	$4802 = 2 \cdot 7^4$	$5929 = 7^2 \cdot 11^2$
$\vdots$	$\vdots$	$\vdots$
$(-41, 1)$	$1682 = 2 \cdot 29^2$	$81 = 3^4$
$\vdots$	$\vdots$	$\vdots$

$$(49 + 49i)(-41 + i) = (49 - 21i)^2,$$

$$f(49 - 21i) = 49 - 21m$$

$$= 49 - 21 \cdot 122$$

$$= -2513 \to x,$$

$$5929 \cdot 81 = (2^2 \cdot 7 \cdot 11)^2$$

$$= 693^2$$

$$\to y = 693.$$

Thus,

$$\gcd(x \pm y, n) = \gcd(-2513 \pm 693, 14885)$$

$$= (65, 229).$$

In the same way, if we wish to fact $n = 84101 = 290^2 + 1$, then we let $m = 290$, and $f(x) = x^2 + 1$ so that

$$f(x) \equiv f(m) \equiv 0 \pmod{n}.$$

We tabulate the sieving process as follows: Clearly, $-38 + i$ and $-22 + 19i$ can produce a product square, since

$$(-38 + i)(-22 + 19i) = (31 - 12i)^2,$$

$$f(31 - 12i) = 31 - 12m$$

$$= -3449 \to x,$$

$$252 \cdot 5488 = (2^3 \cdot 3 \cdot 7^2)^2$$

$$= 1176^2,$$

$$\to y = 1176,$$

$$\gcd(x \pm y, n) = \gcd(-3449 \pm 1176, 84101)$$

$$= (2273, 37).$$

In fact, $84101 = 2273 \times 37$. Note that $-118 + 11i$ and $218 + 59i$ can also produce a product square, since

$$(-118 + 11i)(218 + 59i) = (14 - 163i)^2,$$

(a, b)	Norm$(a + bi)$	$a + bm$
$\vdots$	$\vdots$	$\vdots$
$-50, 1$	$2501 = 41 \cdot 61$	$240 = 2^4 \cdot 3 \cdot 5$
$\vdots$	$\vdots$	$\vdots$
$-50, 3$	$2509 = 13 \cdot 193$	$820 = 2^2 \cdot 5 \cdot 41$
	$\vdots$	$\vdots$
$-49, 43$	$4250 = 2 \cdot 5^3 \cdot 17$	$12421 = 12421$
$\vdots$	$\vdots$	$\vdots$
$-38, 1$	$1445 = 5 \cdot 17^2$	$252 = 2^2 \cdot 3^2 \cdot 7$
$\vdots$	$\vdots$	$\vdots$
$-22, 19$	$845 = 5 \cdot 13^2$	$5488 = 2^4 \cdot 7^3$
$\vdots$	$\vdots$	$\vdots$
$-118, 11$	$14045 = 5 \cdot 53^2$	$3072 = 2^{10} \cdot 3$
$\vdots$	$\vdots$	$\vdots$
$218, 59$	$51005 = 5 \cdot 101^2$	$17328 = 2^4 \cdot 3 \cdot 19^2$
$\vdots$	$\vdots$	$\vdots$

$$f(14 - 163i) = 14 - 163m$$

$$= -47256 \rightarrow x,$$

$$3071 \cdot 173288 = (2^7 \cdot 3 \cdot 19)^2$$

$$= 7296^2,$$

$$\rightarrow y = 7296,$$

$$\gcd(x \pm y, n) = \gcd(-47256 \pm 7296, 84101)$$

$$= (37, 2273).$$

Example 3.4. Next we present a little bit more complicated example. Use NFS to factor $n = 1098413$. First notice that $n = 1098413 = 12 \cdot 45^3 + 17^3$, which is in a special form and can be factored by using SNFS.

[1] (Polynomials selection) Select the two irreducible polynomials $f(x)$ and $g(x)$ and the integer m as follows:

$$m = \frac{17}{45},$$

$$f(x) = x^3 + 12 \implies f(m) = \left(\frac{17}{45}\right)^3 + 12 \equiv 0 \; (\text{mod } n),$$

$$g(x) = 45x - 17 \implies g(m) = 45\left(\frac{17}{45}\right) - 17 \equiv 0 \; (\text{mod } n).$$

[2] (Sieving) Suppose after sieving, we get $U = \{a_i, b_i\}$ as follows:

$$U = \{(6, -1), (3, 2), (-7, 3), (1, 3), (-2, 5), (-3, 8), (9, 10)\}.$$

That is, the chosen polynomial that produces a product square can be constructed as follows (as an exercise. readers may wish to choose some other polynomial which can also produce a product square):

$$\prod_U (a_i + b_i x) = (6 - x)(3 + 2x)(-7 + 3x)(1 + 3x)(-2 + 5x)(-3 + 8x)(9 + 10x).$$

Let $\alpha = \sqrt[3]{-12}$ and $\beta = \frac{17}{45}$. Then

$$\prod_U (a - b\alpha) = 7400772 + 1138236\alpha - 10549\alpha^2$$

$$= (2694 + 213\alpha - 28\alpha^2)^2$$

$$= \left(\frac{5610203}{2025}\right)$$

$$= 270729^2,$$

$$\prod_U (a - b\beta) = \frac{2^8 \cdot 11^2 \cdot 13^2 \cdot 23^2}{3^{12} \cdot 5^4}$$

$$= \left(\frac{52624}{18225}\right)^2$$

$$= 875539^2.$$

So, we get the required square of congruence:

$$270729^2 \equiv 875539^2 \; (\text{mod } 1098413).$$

Thus,

$$\gcd(270729 \pm 875539, 1098413) = (563, 1951).$$

That is,

$$1098413 = 563 \cdot 1951.$$

Example 3.5. We give some large factoring examples using NFS.

1. SNFS examples: One of the largest numbers factored by SNFS is

$$n = (12^{167} + 1)/13 = p_{75} \cdot p_{105}.$$

It was announced by P. Montgomery, S. Cavallar and H. te Riele at CWI in Amsterdam on 3 September 1997. They used the polynomials $f(x) = x^5 - 144$ and $g(x) = 12^{33}x + 1$ with common root $m \equiv 12^{134} \pmod{n}$. The factor base bound was 4.8 million for f and 12 million for g. Both large prime bounds were 150 million, with two large primes allowed on each side. They sieved over $|a| \leq 8.4$ million and $0 < b \leq 2.5$ million. The sieving lasted 10.3 calendar days; 85 SGI machines at CWI contributed a combined 13027719 relations in 560 machine-days. It took 1.6 more calendar days to process the data. This processing included 16 CPU-hours on a Cray C90 at SARA in Amsterdam to process a 1969262×1986500 matrix with 57942503 nonzero entries. The other large number factorized by using SNFS is the 9th Fermat number:

$$F_9 = 2^{2^9} + 1 = 2^{512} + 1 = 2424833 \cdot p_{49} \cdot p_{99},$$

a number with 155 digits; it was completely factored in April 1990. The most wanted factoring number of special form at present is the 12th Fermat number

$$F_{12} = 2^{2^{12}} + 1,$$

we only know its partial prime factorization:

$$F_{12} = 114689 \cdot 26017793 \cdot 63766529 \cdot 190274191361 \cdot 1256132134125569 \cdot c_{1187}$$

and we want to find the prime factors of the remaining 1187-digit composite.
2. GNFS examples:

RSA-130 (130 digits, 430 bits)

$$= 18070820886874048059516561644059055662781025167694013491$$
$$70127021450056662540244048387341127590812303371781887966$$
$$563182013214880557$$

$$= 3968599945959745429016112616288378606757644911 2810064832$$
$$555157243$$

$$\times$$

$$4553449864673597218840368689727440886435630126320 5069600$$
$$999044599.$$

RSA-140 (140 digits, 463 bits)

$$= 21290246318258757547497882016271517497806703963277 21627$$
$$82333832153819499840564959113665738530219183167831 07387$$
$$99531723088956923087344193 6471$$

$$= 33987174230284385545301236276138758356339864959695 97423$$
$$490929302771479$$

$$\times$$

$$62642001874012850961516549482644422193020371786235 09019$$
$$111660653946049.$$

RSA-155 (155 digits, 512 bits)

$$= 10941738641570527421809707322040357612003732945449 20599$$
$$09138421314763499842889347847179972578912673324976 25752$$
$$89978183379707653724402714674353159335 4333897$$

$$= 10263959282974110577205419657399167590071656780803 80668$$
$$03341933521790711307779$$

$$\times$$

$$= 21290246318258757547497882016271517497806703963277 21627$$
$$10660348838016845482092722036001287867920795857598 92915$$
$$2227060823719306280 8643.$$

RSA-576 (174 digits, 576 bits)

$$= 18819881292060796383869723946165043980716356337941 738$$
$$27007633564229888597152346654853190606065047430453 173$$

880113033967161996923212057340318795505699622130516

8759307650257059

$= 3980750864240649373971255005503864911990643623425267$

0840638518957594638895726176858331

7

$\times$

$4727721461074353025362230719730482246329146953020971$

164598521711305207112563635903975

27.

RSA-640 (193 digits, 640 bits)

$= 3107418240490004372135075003588856793003734602284272$

$75457201619488232064405180815045563468296717232867824$

37916272838033415471073

10

$= 1634733645809253848443133883865090859841783670033092$

$312181110852389333100104508151212118167511$

579

$\times$

$= 1900871281664822113126851573935413975471896789968515$

$49366663853908802710380210449895719126146557$

1.

RSA-663 (200 digits, 663 bits)

$= 2799783391122132787082946763872260162107044678695542$

$85375600099293261284001076093456710529553608560618223$

$51910951365788637105954482006576775098580557613579098$

734950144178863178946295187237869221823

983

$= 3532461934402770121272604978198464368671197400197625$

0236493034687761212536794232000585479565280883

49

$\times$

$79258699544783330333470858414800596877379758573642199$

$607343303414557678728181521353814093047401854$

67.

RSA-704 (212 digits, 704 bits)

= 74037563479561712828046796097429573142593188889231289084936232638972765034028266276891996419625117843995894330502127585370118968098286733173273108930900552505116877063299072396380786710086096962537934650563796359

= 909121352959781887844065830260043748589260831032835872042851216896041152864093336782495078836795675680614 1

×

8143859259110045265727809126284429335877899002167627883200914172429324360133004116702003240828777970252499.

RSA-768 (232 digits, 768 bits)

= 12301866845301177551304949583849627207728535695953347921973224521517264005072636575187452021997864693899564749427740638459251925573263034537315482685079170261221429134616704292143116022212404792747377940806653514195974598569021434 13

= 33478071698956898786044169848212690817704794983713768568912431388982883793878002287614711652531743087737814467999489

×

3674604366679959042824463379962795263227915816434308764267603228381573966651127923337341714339681027009279873630891 7.

Remark 3.3. Prior to the NFS, all modern factoring methods had an expected running time of at best

$$\mathcal{O}\left(\exp\left((c+o(1))\sqrt{\log n \log\log n}\right)\right).$$

For example, Dixon's random square method has the expected running time

$$\mathcal{O}\left(\exp\left((\sqrt{2} + o(1))\sqrt{\log n \log\log n}\right)\right),$$

whereas the Multiple Polynomial Quadratic Sieve (MPQS) takes time

$$\mathcal{O}\left(\exp\left((1 + o(1))\sqrt{\log\log n / \log n}\right)\right).$$

Because of the Canfield-Erdös-Pomerance theorem, some people even believed that this could not be improved, except maybe for the term $(c + o(1))$, but the invention of the NFS has changed this belief.

Conjecture 3.1 (Complexity of NFS). Under some reasonable heuristic assumptions, the NFS method can factor an integer n in time

$$\mathcal{O}\left(\exp\left((c + o(1))\sqrt[3]{\log n}\sqrt[3]{(\log\log n)^2}\right)\right),$$

where $c = (64/9)^{1/3} \approx 1.922999427$ if GNFS is used to factor an arbitrary integer n, whereas $c = (32/9)^{1/3} \approx 1.526285657$ if SNFS is used to factor a special integer n.

3.1.3 ρ-Factoring Method

Although NFS is the fastest method of factoring at present, other methods are also useful, one of the particular method is the ρ-factoring method [70]; surprisingly it is the method that is applicable for all the three infeasible problems, IFP, DLP and ECDLP discussed in this book.

ρ uses an iteration of the form

$$\left.\begin{array}{l} x_0 = \text{random}(0,\ n - 1), \\ x_i \equiv f(x_{i-1}) \pmod{n}, \quad i = 1, 2, 3, \ldots \end{array}\right\}$$

where x_0 is a random starting value, n is the number to be factored, and $f \in \mathbb{Z}[x]$ is a polynomial with integer coefficients; usually, we just simply choose $f(x) = x^2 \pm a$ with $a \neq -2, 0$. If p is prime, then the sequence $\{x_i \bmod p\}_{i>0}$ must eventually repeat. Let $f(x) = x^2 + 1, x_0 = 0, p = 563$. Then we get the sequence $\{x_i \bmod p\}_{i>0}$ as follows:

$$x_0 = 0,$$
$$x_1 = x_0^2 + 1 = 1,$$
$$x_2 = x_1^2 + 1 = 2,$$
$$x_3 = x_2^2 + 1 = 5,$$
$$x_4 = x_3^2 + 1 = 26,$$

$$x_5 = x_4^2 + 1 = 114,$$

$$x_6 = x_5^2 + 1 = 48,$$

$$x_7 = x_6^2 + 1 = 53,$$

$$x_8 = x_7^2 + 1 = 558,$$

$$x_9 = x_8^2 + 1 = 26.$$

That is,

$$0, 1, 2, 5, \overline{26, 114, 48, 53, 558}.$$

This sequence symbols a diagram, looks like the Greek letter ρ (Figure 3.1). As an exercise, readers may wish to find the ρ cycle modulo 1951 using $f(x) = x^2 + 1$ and $x_0 = 0$. Of course, to factor n, we do not know its prime factors before hand, but we can simply modulo n (justified by the Chinese Remainder Theorem). For example, to factor $n = 1098413 = 563 \cdot 1951$, we perform (all modulo 1098413):

$$x_0 = \mathbf{0}, \qquad\qquad y_i = x_{2i} \qquad\qquad \gcd(x_i - y_i, n)$$

$$x_1 = x_0^2 + 1 = \mathbf{1},$$

$$x_2 = x_1^2 + 1 = \mathbf{2}, \qquad y_1 = x_2 = 2 \qquad \gcd(1 - 2, n) = 1$$

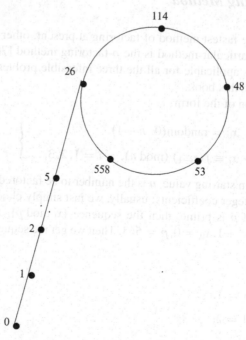

Figure 3.1 ρ cycle modulo 563 using $f(x) = x^2 + 1$ and $x_0 = 0$

$$x_3 = x_2^2 + 1 = \mathbf{5},$$

$$x_4 = x_3^2 + 1 = \mathbf{26}, \qquad y_2 = x_4 = 26 \qquad \gcd(2 - 26, n) = 1$$

$$x_5 = x_4^2 + 1 = 677$$
$$\equiv \mathbf{114},$$

$$x_6 = x_5^2 + 1 = 458330$$
$$\equiv \mathbf{48}, \qquad y_3 = x_6 = 458330 \quad \gcd(5 - 458330, n) = 1$$

$$x_7 = x_6^2 + 1 = 394716$$
$$\equiv \mathbf{53},$$

$$x_8 = x_7^2 + 1 = 722324$$
$$\equiv \mathbf{558}, \qquad y_4 = x_8 = 722324 \quad \gcd(26 - 722324, n) = 1$$

$$x_9 = x_8^2 + 1 = 293912$$
$$\equiv \mathbf{26},$$

$$x_{10} = x_9^2 + 1 = 671773$$
$$\equiv \mathbf{114} \qquad y_5 = x_{10} = 671773 \quad \gcd(677 - 671773, n) = \underline{563}.$$

The following algorithm is an improved version of Brent [11] over Pollard's original ρ-method.

Algorithm 3.2 (Brent-Pollard's ρ-Method). Let n be a composite integer greater than 1. This algorithm tries to find a nontrivial factor d of n, which is small compared with $\sqrt{n}$. Suppose the polynomial to use is $f(x) = x^2 + 1$.

[1] (Initialization) Choose a seed, say $x_0 = 2$, a generating function, say $f(x) = x^2 + 1 \pmod{n}$. Choose also a value for t not much bigger than $\sqrt{d}$, perhaps $t < 100\sqrt{d}$.

[2] (Iteration and computation) Compute x_i and y_i in the following way:

$$x_1 = f(x_0),$$

$$x_2 = f(f(x_0)) = f(x_1),$$

$$x_3 = f(f(f(x_0))) = f(f(x_1)) = f(x_2),$$

$$\vdots$$

$$x_i = f(x_{i-1}),$$

$$y_1 = x_2 = f(x_1) = f(f(x_0)) = f(f(y_0)),$$

$$y_2 = x_4 = f(x_3) = f(f(x_2)) = f(f(y_1)),$$

$$y_3 = x_6 = f(x_5) = f(f(x_4)) = f(f(y_2)),$$

$$\vdots$$

$$y_i = x_{2i} = f(f(y_{i-1})),$$

and simultaneously compare x_i and y_i by computing $d = \gcd(x_i - y_i, n)$.

[3] (Factor found?) If $1 < d < n$, then d is a nontrivial factor of n, print d, and go to Step [5].

[4] (Another search?) If $x_i \equiv y_i \pmod{n}$ for some i or $i \geq \sqrt{t}$, then go to Step [1] to choose a new seed and a new generator and repeat.

[5] (Exit) Terminate the algorithm.

The ρ algorithm has the conjectured complexity:

Conjecture 3.2 (Complexity of the ρ-Method). Let p be a prime dividing n and $p = \mathcal{O}(\sqrt{p})$, then the ρ-algorithm has expected running time

$$\mathcal{O}(\sqrt{p}) = \mathcal{O}(\sqrt{p}\,(\log n)^2) = \mathcal{O}(n^{1/4}(\log n)^2)$$

to find the prime factor p of n.

Remark 3.4. The ρ-method is an improvement over trial division, because in trial division, $\mathcal{O}(p) = \mathcal{O}(n^{1/4})$ divisions is needed to find a small factor p of n. But of course, one disadvantage of the ρ-algorithm is that its running time is only a conjectured expected value, not a rigorous bound.

Problems for Section 3.1

1. Explain why general purpose factoring algorithms are slower than special purpose factoring algorithms, or why the special numbers are easy to factor than general numbers.

2. Show that

   (1) addition of two $\log n$ bit integers can be performed in $\mathcal{O}(\log n)$ bit operations;

   (2) multiplication of two $\log n$ bit integers can be performed in $\mathcal{O}((\log n)^{1+\epsilon})$ bit operations.

3. Show that

   (1) assume the Extended Riemann Hypothesis (ERH), there is deterministic algorithm that factors n in $\mathcal{O}(n^{1/5+\epsilon})$ steps;

   (2) FFT (Fast Fourier Transform) can be utilized to factor an integer n in $\mathcal{O}(n^{1/4+\epsilon})$ steps;

   (3) give two deterministic algorithms that factor integer n in $\mathcal{O}(n^{1/3+\epsilon})$ steps.

4. Show that if $\mathcal{P} = \mathcal{NP}$, then IFP $\in \mathcal{P}$.

5. Prove or disprove that IFP $\in \mathcal{NP}$-Complete.
6. Extend the NFS (Number Field Sieve) to FFS (Function Field Sieve). Give a complete description of the FFS for factoring large integers.
7. Let $x_i = f(x_{i-1})$, $i = 1, 2, 3, \ldots$. Let also $t, u > 0$ be the smallest numbers in the sequence $x_{t+i} = x_{t+u+i}$, $i = 0, 1, 2, \ldots$, where t and u are called the lengths of the ρ tail and cycle, respectively. Give an efficient algorithm to determine t and u exactly, and analyze the running time of your algorithm.
8. Find the prime factorization of the following RSA numbers, each of these numbers has two prime factors.

(1) RSA-896 (270 digits, 896 bits)
41202343698665954385553136533257594817981169984432798284545562643387644556524842619809887042316184187926142024718886949256093177637503342113098239748515094490910691026986103186270411488086697056490290365365886743373172081310410519086425479328260139125762403394637326939l,

(2) RSA-1024 (309 digits, 1024 bits)
1350664108659952233496032162788059699388814756056670275244851438515265106048595338339402871505719094417982072821644715513736804197039641917430464965892742562393410208643832021103729587257623585096431105640735015081875106765946292055636855294752135008528794163773285339061097505443349998111500569772368909275 63,

(3) RSA-1536 (463 digits, 1536 bits)
18476997032117414743068356202001644030185493386634101714717857749106516967111612498593376843054357445856160615445717940522297177325246609606469460712496237204420222697567566873784275623895087646784409332851574965788434150884755282981867264513398633649319080846719904318743812833635027954702826532978029349161558118810498449083195450098483937752272570525785919449938700736957556884369338127796130892303925696952532616208236764903160365513714479139323471695669880 69,

(4) RSA-2048 (617 digits, 2048 bits)
25195908475657893494027183240048398571429282126204032027777137836043662020707595556264018525880784406918290641249515082189298559149176184502808489120072844992687392807287776735971418347270261896375014971824691165077613379859095700097330459748808428401797429100642458691817195118746121515172654632282216869987549182422433637259085141865462043576798423387184774447920739934236584823824281198163815010674810451660377306056201619676256133844143603833904414952634432190114657544454178424020924616515723350778707749817125772467962926386356373289912154831438167899885040445364023527381951378636564391212010397122822120720357.

9. Try to complete the following prime factorization of the smallest unfactored (not completely factored) Fermat numbers:

$$F_{12} = 2^{2^{12}} + 1$$

$$= 114689 \cdot 26017793 \cdot 63766529 \cdot 190274191361 \cdot$$

$$1256132134125569 \cdot c_{1187},$$

$$F_{13} = 2^{2^{13}} + 1$$

$$= 2710954639361 \cdot 2663848877152141313 \cdot 36031098445229199 \cdot$$

$$3195460208205516432206 72513 \cdot c_{2391},$$

$$F_{14} = 2^{2^{14}} + 1$$

$$= c_{4933},$$

$$F_{15} = 2^{2^{15}} + 1$$

$$= 1214251009 \cdot 2327042503868417 \cdot$$

$$168768817029516972383024127016961 \cdot c_{9808},$$

$$F_{16} = 2^{2^{16}} + 1$$

$$= 825753601 \cdot 188981757975021318420037633 \cdot c_{19694},$$

$$F_{17} = 2^{2^{17}} + 1$$

$$= 31065037602817 \cdot c_{39444},$$

$$F_{18} = 2^{2^{18}} + 1$$

$$= 13631489 \cdot 81274690703860512587777 \cdot c_{78884},$$

$$F_{19} = 2^{2^{19}} + 1$$

$$= 70525124609 \cdot 646730219521 \cdot c_{157804},$$

$$F_{20} = 2^{2^{20}} + 1$$

$$= c_{315653},$$

$$F_{21} = 2^{2^{21}} + 1$$

$$= 4485296422913 \cdot c_{631294},$$

$$F_{22} = 2^{2^{22}} + 1$$

$$= c_{1262612},$$

$$F_{23} = 2^{2^{23}} + 1$$

$$= 167772161 \cdot c_{2525215},$$

$$F_{24} = 2^{2^{24}} + 1$$

$$= c_{5050446}.$$

Basically, you are asked to factor the unfactored composite numbers, denoted by c_x, of the Fermat numbers. For example, in F_{12}, c_{1187} is the unfactored 1187 digit composite.

10. Both ECM (Elliptic Curve Method) factoring algorithm and NFS (Number Field Sieve) factoring algorithm are very well suited for parallel implementation. Is it possible to utilize the quantum parallelism to implement ECM and NFS algorithms? If so, give a complete description the quantum ECM and NFS algorithms.

11. Pollard [69] and Strassen [88] showed that FFT can be utilized to factor an integer n in $\mathcal{O}(n^{1/4+\epsilon})$ steps, deterministically. Is it possible to replace the classical FFT with a quantum FFT in the Pollard-Strassen method, in order to obtain a deterministic quantum polynomial-time factoring algorithm (i.e., to obtain a $\mathcal{QP}$ factoring algorithm rather than the $\mathcal{BQP}$ algorithm as proposed by Shor)? If so, give a full description of the $\mathcal{QP}$ factoring algorithm.

12. At the very heart of the Pollard ρ method for IFP lives the phenomenon of periodicity. Develop a quantum period-finding algorithm, if possible, for the ρ factoring algorithm.

3.2 Integer Factorization Based Cryptography

All the existing factoring algorithms up to date, such the NFS and the ρ-method, are all inefficient, and cannot be run in polynomial-time. This unreasonable effectiveness of factoring makes it useful for constructing unbreakable cryptography. In fact, the most famous and widely used RSA cryptographic system is the first factoring based cryptographic system, for which its three inventors, Rivest, Shamir and Adleman received the 2002 Turing award. Note that RSA is also the world's first public-key cryptographic system. The security of RSA and other factoring based cryptographic systems relies heavily on the intractability of the integer factorization problem. Anyone who can solve the integer factorization problem in polynomial-time, can break the RSA cryptographic system in polynomial-time. In this section, we introduce the basic idea of the unbreakable RSA cryptographic system.

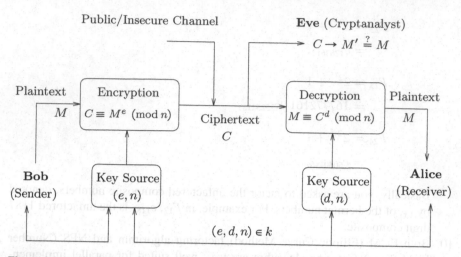

Figure 3.2 RSA public-key cryptography

Definition 3.3. The *RSA public-key cryptosystem* may be formally defined as follows (depicted in Figure 3.2):

$$\text{RSA} = (\mathcal{M}, \mathcal{C}, \mathcal{K}, M, C, e, d, n, E, D)$$

where

1. $\mathcal{M}$ is the set of plaintexts, called the plaintext space.
2. $\mathcal{C}$ is the set of ciphertexts, called the ciphertexts space.
3. $\mathcal{K}$ is the set of keys, called the key space.
4. $M \in \mathcal{M}$ is a piece of particular plaintext.
5. $C \in \mathcal{C}$ is a piece of particular ciphertexts.
6. $n = pq$ is the modulus with p, q prime numbers, usually each with at least 100 digits.
7. $\{(e, n), (d, n)\} \in \mathcal{K}$ with $e \neq d$ are the encryption and encryption keys, respectively, satisfying

$$ed \equiv 1 \ (\mathrm{mod} \ \phi(n)),$$

where $\phi(n) = (p-1)(q-1)$ is the Euler ϕ-function and defined by $\phi(n) = \#(\mathbb{Z}_n^*)$, the number of elements in the multiplicative group $\mathbb{Z}_n^*$.
8. E is the encryption function

$$E_{e,n} : M \mapsto C.$$

That is, $M \in \mathcal{M}$ maps to $C \in C$, using the public-key (e, n), such that

$$C \equiv M^e \pmod{n}.$$

9. D is the decryption function

$$D_{d,n} : C \mapsto M.$$

That is, $C \in C$ maps to $M \in \mathcal{M}$, using the private-key (d, n), such that

$$M \equiv C^d \equiv (M^e)^d \pmod{n}.$$

The idea of RSA can be best depicted in Figure 3.3.

Theorem 3.2 (The Correctness of RSA). *Let M, C, n, e, d be plaintext, cipher-texts, encryption exponent, decryption exponent, and modulus, respectively. Then*

$$(M^e)^d \equiv M \pmod{n}.$$

Proof. Notice first that

$$C^d \equiv (M^e)^d \pmod{n} \qquad \text{(since } C \equiv M^e \pmod{n})$$

$$\equiv M^{1+k\phi(n)} \pmod{n} \qquad \text{(since } ed \equiv 1 \pmod{\phi(n)})$$

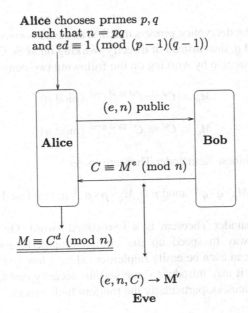

Alice chooses primes p, q
such that $n = pq$
and $ed \equiv 1 \pmod{(p-1)(q-1)}$

(e, n) public

Alice

Bob

$C \equiv M^e \pmod{n}$

$M \equiv C^d \pmod{n}$

$(e, n, C) \to \mathbf{M'}$

Eve

Figure 3.3 RSA encryption and decryption

$$\equiv M \cdot M^{k\phi(n)} \pmod{n}$$

$$\equiv M \cdot (M^{\phi(n)})^k \pmod{n}$$

$$\equiv M \cdot (1)^k \pmod{n} \qquad \text{(by Euler's Theorem } a^{\phi(n)} \equiv 1 \pmod{n}\text{)}$$

$$\equiv M$$

The result thus follows.   □

Both encryption $C \equiv M^e \pmod{n}$ and decryption $M \equiv C^d \pmod{n}$ of RSA can be implemented in polynomial-time by the fast exponentiation method. For example the RSA encryption can be implemented as follows:

Algorithm 3.3. Given (e, M, n), this algorithm finds $C \equiv M^e \pmod{n}$, or given (d, C, n), finds $M \equiv C^d \pmod{n}$ in time polynomial in $\log e$ or $\log d$, respectively.

Encryption:

Given (e, M, n) to find C
Set $C \leftarrow 1$
While $e \geq 1$ do
    if $e \bmod 2 = 1$
        then $C \leftarrow C \cdot M \bmod n$
        $M \leftarrow M^2 \bmod n$
        $e \leftarrow \lfloor e/2 \rfloor$
Print C

Description:

Given (d, C, n) to find M
Set $M \leftarrow 1$
While $d \geq 1$ do
    if $d \bmod 2 = 1$
        then $M \leftarrow M \cdot C \bmod n$
        $C \leftarrow C^2 \bmod n$
        $d \leftarrow \lfloor d/2 \rfloor$
Print M

Remark 3.5. For the decryption process in RSA, as the authorized user knows d and hence knows p and q, thus instead of directly working on $M \equiv C^d \pmod{n}$, he can speed up the computation by working on the following two congruences:

$$M_p \equiv C^d \equiv C^{d \bmod p-1} \pmod{p}$$

$$M_q \equiv C^d \equiv C^{d \bmod q-1} \pmod{q}$$

and then use the Chinese Remainder Theorem to get

$$M \equiv M_p \cdot q \cdot q^{-1} \bmod p + M_q \cdot p \cdot p^{-1} \bmod q \pmod{n}.$$

The Chinese Remainder Theorem is a two-edged sword. On the one hand, it provides a good way to speed up the computation/performance of the RSA decryption, which can even be easily implemented by a low-cost crypto-chip [38]. On the other hand, it may introduce some serious security problems vulnerable to some side-channel attacks, particularly the random fault attacks.

Example 3.6. Let the letter-digit encoding be as follows:

$$\text{space} = 00, A = 01, B = 02, \ldots, Z = 26.$$

(We will use this digital representation of letters throughout the book.) Let also

$e = 9007,$

$M = 20080500130107090300231518041900011805001917210501 1309$

19080015191909061801 0705,

$n = 11438162575788886766923577997614661201021829672124 2362$

56256184293570693524573389783059712356395870505898 9075

1475992900268 79543541.

Then the encryption can be done by using Algorithm 3.3:

$C \equiv M^e$

$\equiv 96869613754622061477140922254355882905759991124574 3198$

74695120930816298225145708356931476622883989628013 3919

9055182994515781 5154 \pmod{n}.$

For the decryption, since the two prime factors p and q of n are known to the authorized person who does the decryption:

$p = 34905295108476509491478496199038981334177646384933 878$

43990820577,

$q = 32769132993266709549961988190834461413177642967992 942$

539798288533,

then

$d \equiv 1/e$

$\equiv 10669861436857802444286877132892015478070990663393 7862$

$\equiv 80122622449663106312591177447087334016859746230655 3968$

$\equiv 544513277109053606095 \pmod{(p-1)(q-1)}.$

Thus, the original plaintext M can be recovered either directly by using Algorithm 3.3, or indirectly by a combined use of Algorithm 3.3 and the Chinese Remainder Theorem:

$$M \equiv C^d$$

$$= 2008050013010709030023151804190001180500191721050 11309$$

$$190800151919090618010705 \pmod{n},$$

which is "THE MAGIC WORDS ARE SQUEAMISH OSSIFRAGE".

Remark 3.6. Prior to RSA, Pohlig and Hellman in 1978 [67] proposed a secret-key cryptography based on arithmetic modulo p, rather than $n = pq$. The Pohlig-Hellman system works as follows: Let M and C be the plaintext and ciphertext, respectively. Choose a prime p, usually with more than 200 digits, and a secret encryption key e such that $e \in \mathbb{Z}^+$ and $e \le p-2$. Compute $d \equiv 1/e \pmod{(p-1)}$. p and of course d must be kept as a secret.

[1] **Encryption:**

$$C \equiv M^e \pmod{p}.$$

This process is easy for the authorized user:

$$\{M, e, p\} \xrightarrow[\text{easy}]{\text{find}} \{C \equiv M^e \pmod{p}\}.$$

[2] **Decryption:**

$$M \equiv C^d \pmod{p}.$$

For the authorized user who knows (e, p), this process is easy, since d can be easily computed from e.

[3] **Cryptanalysis:** The security of this system is based on the infeasibility of the Discrete Logarithm Problem. For example, for a cryptanalyst who does not know e or d would have to compute:

$$e \equiv \log_M C \pmod{p}.$$

Remark 3.7. One of the most important features of RSA encryption is that it can also be used for digital signatures. Let M be a document to be signed, and $n = pq$ with p, q primes, (e, d) the public and private exponents as in RSA encryption scheme. Then the processes of RSA signature signing and signature verification are just the same as that of the decryption and encryption; that is use d for signature signing and e signature verification as follows (see also Figure 3.4):

[1] **Signature signing**:

$$S \equiv M^d \pmod{n}.$$

The signing process can only be done by the authorized person who has the private exponent d.

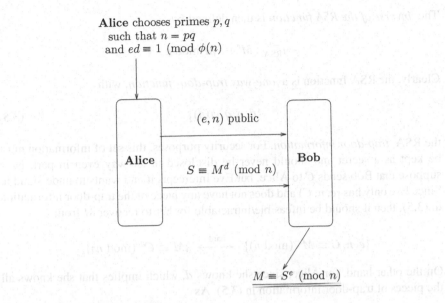

Alice chooses primes p, q
such that $n = pq$
and $ed \equiv 1 \pmod{\phi(n)}$

(e, n) public

Alice

Bob

$S \equiv M^d \pmod{n}$

$M \equiv S^e \pmod{n}$

Figure 3.4 RSA digital signature

[2] Signature verification:

$$M \equiv S^e \pmod{n}.$$

This verification process can be done by anyone since (e, n) is public.

Of course, RSA encryption and RSA signature can be used together to obtain a signed encrypted document to be sent over an insecure network.

As can be seen, the whole idea of the RSA encryption and decryption is as follows:

$$\left. \begin{aligned} C &\equiv M^e \pmod{n}, \\ M &\equiv C^d \pmod{n}, \end{aligned} \right\}$$

where

$$\left. \begin{aligned} ed &\equiv 1 \pmod{\phi(n)}, \\ n &= pq \text{ with } p, q \in \text{Primes}. \end{aligned} \right\}$$

Thus, the *RSA function* can be defined by

$$f_{\text{RSA}} : M \mapsto M^e \bmod n.$$

The *inverse of the RSA function* is then defined by

$$f_{\text{RSA}}^{-1} : M^e \mapsto M \bmod n.$$

Clearly, the RSA function is a *one-way trap-door function*, with

$$\{d, p, q, \phi(n)\} \tag{3.5}$$

the RSA *trap-door information*. For security purposes, this set of information must be kept as a secret and should never be disclosed in anyway even in part. Now suppose that Bob sends C to Alice, but Eve intercepts it and wants to understand it. Since Eve only has (e, n, C) and does not have any piece of the trap-door information in (3.5), then it should be infeasible/intractable for her to recover M from C:

$$\{e, n, C \equiv M^e \ (\bmod \ n)\} \xrightarrow{\text{hard}} \{M \equiv C^d \ (\bmod \ n)\}.$$

On the other hand, for Alice, since she knows d, which implies that she knows all the pieces of trap-door information in (3.5). As

$$\{d\} \overset{\mathcal{P}}{\Longleftrightarrow} \{p\} \overset{\mathcal{P}}{\Longleftrightarrow} \{q\} \overset{\mathcal{P}}{\Longleftrightarrow} \{\phi(n)\},$$

so, it is easy for Alice to recover M from C:

$$\{n, C \equiv M^e \ (\bmod \ n)\} \xrightarrow[\text{easy}]{\{d,p,q,\phi(n)\}} \{M \equiv C^d \ (\bmod \ n)\}.$$

Why is it hard for Eve to recover M from C? This is because Eve is facing a hard computational problem, namely, the *RSA problem* [76]:

The RSA problem: Given the RSA public-key (e, n) and the RSA ciphertext C, find the corresponding RSA plaintext M. That is,

$$\{e, n, C\} \longrightarrow \{M\}.$$

It is conjectured although it has never been proved or disproved that:

The RSA conjecture: Given the RSA public-key (e, n) and the RSA ciphertext C, it is hard to find the corresponding RSA plaintext M. That is,

$$\{e, n, C\} \xrightarrow{\text{hard}} \{M\}.$$

But how hard is it for Alice to recover M from C? This is another version of the RSA conjecture, often called the *RSA assumption*, which again has never been proved or disproved:

The RSA assumption: Given the RSA public-key (e, n) and the RSA ciphertext C, then finding M is as hard as factoring the RSA modulus n. That is,

$$\text{IFP}(n) \iff \text{RSA}(M)$$

provided that n is sufficiently large and randomly generated, and M and C are random integers between 0 and $n - 1$. More precisely, it is conjectured (or assumed) that

$$\text{IFP}(n) \overset{\mathcal{P}}{\iff} \text{RSA}(M).$$

That is, if n can be factorized in polynomial-time, then M can be recovered from C in polynomial-time. In other words, cryptoanalyzing RSA must be as difficult as solving the IFP problem. But the problem is, as we discussed previously, that no-one knows whether or not IFP can be solved in polynomial-time, so RSA is only assumed to be secure, not proved to be secure:

$$\text{IFP}(n) \text{ is hard } \longrightarrow \text{RSA}(M) \text{ is secure.}$$

The real situation is that

$$\text{IFP}(n) \overset{\checkmark}{\implies} \text{RSA}(M),$$

$$\text{IFP}(n) \overset{?}{\impliedby} \text{RSA}(M).$$

Now we can return to answer the question that how hard is it for Alice to recover M from C. By the RSA assumption, cryptanalyzing C is as hard as factoring n. The fastest known integer factorization algorithm, the Number Field Sieve, runs in time

$$\mathcal{O}(\exp(c(\log n)^{1/3}(\log \log n)^{2/3}))$$

where $c = (64/9)^{1/3}$ if a general version of NFS, GNFS, is used for factoring an arbitrary integer n whereas $c = (32/9)^{1/3}$ if a special version of NFS, SNFS, is used for factoring a special form of integer n. As in RSA, the modulus $n = pq$ is often chosen be a large general composite integer $n = pq$ with p and q the same bit size, which makes SNFS is not useful. This means that RSA cannot be broken in polynomial-time, but in subexponential-time, which makes RSA secure, again, by assumption. Thus, readers should note that the RSA problem is *assumed* to be *hard*, and the RSA cryptosystem is *conjectured* to be *secure*.

In the RSA cryptosystem, it is assumed that the cryptanalyst, Eve

1. knows the public-key $\{e, n\}$ with $n = pq$ and also the ciphertext C,
2. does not know any one piece of the trap-door information $\{p, q, \phi(n), d\}$,
3. wants to know $\{M\}$.

That is,

$$\{e, n, C \equiv M^e \pmod{n}\} \xrightarrow{\text{Eve wants to find}} \{M\}.$$

Obviously, there are several ways to recover M from C (i.e., to break the RSA system):

1. Factor n by using say, e.g., QS/MPQS or NFS to find its prime factors $\{p, q\}$ so as to compute

$$M \equiv C^{1/e \ (\text{mod} \ (p-1)(q-1))} \ (\text{mod} \ n).$$

2. Find $\phi(n)$ so as to compute

$$M \equiv C^{1/e \ (\text{mod} \ \phi(n))} \ (\text{mod} \ n).$$

3. Find order(a, n), by using Shor's quantum algorithm in the next section, the order of a random integer $a \in [2, n-2]$ modulo n, then try to find

$$\{p, q\} = \gcd(a^{r/2} \pm 1, n) \text{ and } M \equiv C^{1/e \ (\text{mod} \ (p-1)(q-1))} \ (\text{mod} \ n).$$

4. Find order(C, n), the order of C modulo n, so as to compute

$$M \equiv C^{1/e \ (\text{mod} \ \text{order}(C,n))} \ (\text{mod} \ n).$$

5. Compute $\log_C M \ (\text{mod} \ n)$, the discrete logarithm M to the base C modulo n in order to find

$$M \equiv C^{\log_C M \ (\text{mod} \ n)} \ (\text{mod} \ n).$$

As can be seen from the previous sections, RSA uses M^e for encryption, with $e \geq 3$ (3 is the smallest possible public exponent in RSA); in this way, we might call RSA encryption M^e encryption. In 1979, Michael Rabin [73] proposed a scheme based on M^2 encryption, rather than the M^e for $e \geq 3$ encryption used in RSA. A brief description of the Rabin cryptosystem is as follows (see also Figure 3.5).

[1] **Key generation:** Let $n = pq$ with p, q odd primes satisfying

$$p \equiv q \equiv 3 \ (\text{mod} \ 4).$$

[2] **Encryption:**

$$C \equiv M^2 \ (\text{mod} \ n).$$

[3] **Decryption:** Use the Chinese Remainder Theorem to solve the system of congruences:

$$\begin{cases} M_p \equiv \sqrt{C} \ (\text{mod} \ p) \\ M_q \equiv \sqrt{C} \ (\text{mod} \ q) \end{cases}$$

to get the four solutions: $\{\pm M_p, \pm M_q\}$. The true plaintext M will be one of these four values.

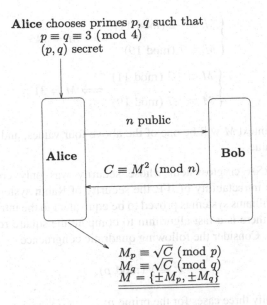

Figure 3.5 Rabin cryptosystem

[4] **Cryptanalysis:** A cryptanalyst who can factor n can compute the four square roots of C modulo n, and hence can recover M from C. Thus, breaking the Rabin system is equivalent to factoring n.

Example 3.7. Let $M = 31$.

[1] **Key generation:** Let $n = 11 \cdot 19$ be the public-key, but keep the prime factors $p = 11$ and $q = 19$ of n as a secret.

[2] **Encryption:**

$$C \equiv 31^2 \equiv 125 \pmod{209}.$$

[3] **Decryption:** Compute

$$\begin{cases} M_p \equiv \sqrt{125} \equiv \pm 2 \pmod{p} \\ M_q \equiv \sqrt{125} \equiv \pm 7 \pmod{q}. \end{cases}$$

Now use the Chinese Remainder Theorem to solve

$$\begin{cases} M \equiv 2 \pmod{11} \\ M \equiv 7 \pmod{19} \end{cases} \implies M = 178$$

$$\begin{cases} M \equiv -2 \pmod{11} \\ M \equiv 7 \pmod{19} \end{cases} \implies M = 64$$

$$\begin{cases} M \equiv -2 \pmod{11} \\ M \equiv 7 \pmod{19} \end{cases} \implies M = 145$$

$$\begin{cases} M \equiv -2 \pmod{11} \\ M \equiv -7 \pmod{19} \end{cases} \implies M = 31.$$

The true plaintext M will be one of the above four values, and in fact, $M = 31$ is the true value.

Unlike the RSA cryptosystem whose security was only conjectured to be equivalent to the intractability of IFP, the security of Rabin system and its variant such as Rabin-Williams system is proved to be equivalent to the intractability of IFP. First notice that there is a fast algorithm to compute the square roots modulo n if $n = pq$ is known. Consider the following quadratic congruence

$$x^2 \equiv y \pmod{p},$$

there are essentially three cases for the prime p:

1. $p \equiv 3 \pmod 4$,
2. $p \equiv 5 \pmod 8$,
3. $p \equiv 1 \pmod 8$.

All three cases may be solved by the following process:

$$\begin{cases} \text{if } p \equiv 3 \pmod 4, \ x \equiv \pm y^{\frac{p+1}{4}} \pmod p, \\ \\ \text{if } p \equiv 5 \pmod 8, \ \begin{cases} \text{if } y^{\frac{p+1}{4}} = 1, \ x \equiv \pm y^{\frac{p+3}{8}} \pmod p \\ \\ \text{if } y^{\frac{p+1}{4}} \neq 1, \ x \equiv \pm 2y(4y)^{\frac{p-5}{8}} \pmod p. \end{cases} \end{cases}$$

Problems for Section 3.2

1. The RSA function $M \mapsto C \bmod n$ is a trap-door one-way, as it is computationally intractable to invert the function if the prime factorization $n = pq$ is unknown. Give your own trap-door one-way functions that can be used to construct public-key cryptosystems. Justify your answer.
2. Show that

$$M \equiv M^{ed} \pmod n,$$

where $ed \equiv 1 \pmod{\phi(n)}$.

3. Let the ciphertexts $C_1 \equiv M_1^e \pmod{n}$ and $C_2 \equiv M_2^e \pmod{n}$, be as follows, where and n is the following RSA-129 number:

$e = 9137,$

$C_1 = 46604906435060096392391122387112023736039163470082768$
$24341038329668507346202721798200029792506708833728356$
$78045323838911140719579,$

$C_2 = 65064096938511069741528313342475396648978551735813836$
$77796350373814720928779386178787818974157439185718360$
$8196124160093438830158,$

$n = 11438162575788886766923577997614661201021829672124236$
$25625618429357069352457338978305971235639587050589890$
$75147599290026879543541.$

Find M_1 and M_2.

4. Let

$e_1 = 9007,$

$e_2 = 65537,$

$n = 11438162575788886766923577997614661201021829672124236$
$25625618429357069352457338978305971235639587050589890$
$75147599290026879543541,$

$C_1 \equiv M^{e_1} \pmod{n}$
$\equiv 10420225094119623841363838260797412577444908472492959$
$12574337458892652977717171824130246429380783519790899$
$4534340746416137797212,$

$C_2 \equiv M^{e_2} \bmod n$
$\equiv 76452750729188700180719970517544574710944757317909896$
$04134098748828557319028078348030908497802156339649075$
$9750600519496071304348.$

Find the plaintext M.

5. (Rivest) Let

$$k = 2^{2^t} \pmod{n},$$

where

$n = 6314466083072888893799357126131292332363298818330841375588990772701957128924885547308446$
$0557532065136183466288489480886635003684803965881713619876605218972678101622805574753938$
$3830826175971321892666861177695452639157012069093997368008972127446466642331918780683055$
$2067951253070082020241246233982410737753705127344494169501180975241890667963858754856319$
$8055072737099043971197336146667015439053601525433739825245793135753176536463319890646514$
$0213398526580034199190398219284471021246488745938885358207031808428902320971090703239693$
$4919962778995323320184064522476463966355937367009369212758092086293198727008292431243681,$

$t = 79685186856218.$

Find k. (Note that to find k, one needs to find $2^t \pmod{\phi(n)}$ first, however, to find $\phi(n)$ one needs to factor n first.)

6. (Knuth) Let

$$\{C_1, C_2\} \equiv \{M_1^3, M_2^3\} \bmod n,$$

where

$C_1 = 6875028364370892898789953506044079907168981402585834430355355882374792710800902930496305666512681123340562743326121428231872037311815196394426165689989243682712275123771458797372299204125753023665954875641382171,$

$C_2 = 7130139886169274645420466503586462247282166640137557785672232197970115932208495578642497037753313173775326965348797392018688875678295190326816326888127500602518223884462866157583604931628056686669968333451929466 3,$

$n = 77903022885101595423624756547055783624857676209739839410844022221357287251170999858504838764813194434051093 2$

$$26513681516857411993477558685427409422564450008791272 3$$

$$25857493370618539583402784340582088810854850 78737.$$

Find $\{M_1, M_2\}$. (Note that there are two known ways to find $\{M_1, M_2\}$:

$$M_i \equiv \sqrt[3]{C_i} \pmod{n},$$

$$M_i \equiv C_i^d \pmod{n},$$

where $i = 1, 2$. But in either way, one needs to find n first.)

7. The original version of the RSA cryptosystem:

$$C \equiv M^e \pmod{n}, \quad M \equiv C^d \pmod{n},$$

with

$$ed \equiv 1 \pmod{\phi(n)}$$

is a type of deterministic cryptosystem, in which the same ciphertext is obtained for the same plaintext even at a different time. That is,

$$M_1 \xrightarrow{\text{Encryption at Time 1}} C_1 \ ,$$

$$M_1 \xrightarrow{\text{Encryption at Time 2}} C_1 \ ,$$

$$\vdots$$

$$M_1 \xrightarrow{\text{Encryption at Time } t} C_1 \ .$$

A randomized cryptosystem is one in which different ciphertext is obtained at a different time even for the same plaintext

$$M_1 \xrightarrow{\text{Encryption at Time 1}} C_1 \ ,$$

$$M_1 \xrightarrow{\text{Encryption at Time 2}} C_2 \ ,$$

$$\vdots$$

$$M_1 \xrightarrow{\text{Encryption at Time } t} C_t \ ,$$

with $C_1 \neq C_2 \neq \cdots \neq C_t$. Describe a method to make RSA a randomized cryptosystem.

8. Show that if IFP can be solved in polynomial-time, then RSA can be broken in polynomial-time.

9. Let

$$n = 21290246318258757547497882016271517497806703963277216278233$$
$$383215384705704132501028901089769825481925825513509252260960$$
$$2369983944024335907529,$$

$$C \equiv M^2 \pmod{n}$$

$$= 5128520506024348118812210987654066112214090680743732729 0641$$
$$60633920242479741450841196687149365272035106423411648279363$$
$$932042884271651389234.$$

Find the plaintext M.

3.3 Shor's Algorithm for Integer Factorization

As just discussed in the previous two sections, there is no efficient algorithms for integer factorization, so RSA and all other integer factorization based cryptographic systems are secure and unbreakable in polynomial-time. However, there is a quantum polynomial-time algorithm, proposed by Shor in 1994. This algorithm, if run on a practical quantum computer, can solve the integer factorization problem, break RSA and all other factoring based cryptographic systems in polynomial-time, efficiently and completely.

3.3.1 Quantum Order Finding Algorithm

The key idea of Shor's quantum algorithm for factoring n is to find the order of a random element x in the multiplicative group $\mathbb{Z}_n^*$. So we first present some basic concepts of the *order* of an element in a multiplicative group.

Definition 3.4. Let $G = \mathbb{Z}_n^*$ be a finite multiplicative group, and $x \in G$ a randomly chosen integer (element). Then order of x in G, or order of an element x modulo n, some times denoted by order(x, n), is the smallest positive integer r such that

$$x^r \equiv 1 \pmod{n}.$$

Example 3.8. Let $5 \in \mathbb{Z}_{104}^*$. Then order$(5, 104) = 4$, since 4 is the smallest positive integer satisfying

$$5^4 \equiv 1 \pmod{104}.$$

Theorem 3.3. *Let G be a finite group and suppose that $x \in G$ has finite order r. If $x^k = 1$, then $r \mid k$.*

Example 3.9. Let $5 \in \mathbb{Z}^*_{104}$. As $5^{24} \equiv 1$ (mod 104), so, $4 \mid 24$.

Definition 3.5. Let G be a finite group, then the number of elements in G, denoted by $|G|$, is called the *order* of G.

Example 3.10. Let $G = \mathbb{Z}^*_{104}$. Then there are 48 elements in G that are relatively prime to 104 (two numbers a and b are relatively prime if $\gcd(a, b) = 1$), namely;

$$1, 3, 5, 7, 9, 11, 15, 17, 19, 21, 23, 25, 27, 29, 31, 33, 35, 37, 41, 43$$
$$45, 47, 49, 51, 53, 55, 57, 59, 61, 63, 67, 69, 71, 73, 75, 77, 79, 81$$
$$83, 85, 87, 89, 93, 95, 97, 99, 101, 103.$$

Thus, $|G| = 48$. That is, the order of the group G is 48.

Theorem 3.4 (Lagrange). *Let G be a finite group. Then the order of an element $x \in G$ divides the order of the group G.*

Example 3.11. Let $G = \mathbb{Z}^*_{104}$. Then the order of G is 48, whereas the order of the element $5 \in G$ is 4. Clearly $4 \mid 48$.

Corollary 3.1. *If a finite group G has order r, then $x^r = 1$ for all $x \in G$.*

Example 3.12. Let $G = \mathbb{Z}^*_{104}$ and $|G| = 48$. Then

$$1^{48} \equiv 1 \ (\text{mod } 104)$$

$$3^{48} \equiv 1 \ (\text{mod } 104)$$

$$5^{48} \equiv 1 \ (\text{mod } 104)$$

$$7^{48} \equiv 1 \ (\text{mod } 104)$$

$$\vdots$$

$$101^{48} \equiv 1 \ (\text{mod } 104)$$

$$103^{48} \equiv 1 \ (\text{mod } 104).$$

Finding the order of an element x in G is, in theory, not a problem: just keep multiplying until we get to "1", the identity element of the multiplicative group G. For example, let $n = 179359$, $x = 3 \in G$, and $G = \mathbb{Z}^*_{179359}$, such that $\gcd(3, 179359) = 1$. To find $r = \text{order}(3, 179359)$, we just keep multiplying until we get to "1":

3^1	mod	179359	=	3
3^2	mod	179359	=	9
3^3	mod	179359	=	27

$$\vdots$$

$$3^{1000} \quad \mathrm{mod} \quad 179359 \quad = \quad 31981$$
$$3^{1001} \quad \mathrm{mod} \quad 179359 \quad = \quad 95943$$
$$3^{1002} \quad \mathrm{mod} \quad 179359 \quad = \quad 108470$$

$$\vdots$$

$$3^{14716} \quad \mathrm{mod} \quad 179359 \quad = \quad 99644$$
$$3^{14717} \quad \mathrm{mod} \quad 179359 \quad = \quad 119573$$
$$3^{14718} \quad \mathrm{mod} \quad 179359 \quad = \quad 1.$$

Thus, the order r of 3 in the multiplicative group $\mathcal{G} = (\mathbb{Z}/179359\mathbb{Z})^*$ is 14718, that is, $\mathrm{ord}_{179359}(3) = 14718$.

Example 3.13. Let

$$n = 5515596313,$$
$$e = 1757316971,$$
$$C = 763222127,$$
$$r = \mathrm{order}(C, n) = 114905160.$$

Then

$$M \equiv C^{1/e \bmod r} \ (\mathrm{mod} \ n)$$

$$\equiv 763222127^{1/1757316971 \bmod 114905160} \ (\mathrm{mod} \ 5515596313)$$

$$\equiv 1612050119.$$

Clearly, this result is correct, since

$$M^e \equiv 1612050119^{1757316971}$$

$$\equiv 763222127$$

$$\equiv C \ (\mathrm{mod} \ 5515596313).$$

It must also be noted, however, that in practice, the above computation for finding the order of $x \in \mathbb{Z}_n^*$ may not work, since for an element x in a large group $\mathcal{G}$ with n having more than 200 digits, the computation of r may require more than 10^{150} multiplications. Even if these multiplications could be carried out at the rate of 1000 billion per second on a supercomputer, it would take approximately $3 \cdot 10^{80}$ years to arrive at the answer. Thus, the order finding problem is intractable on conventional digital computers. The problem is, however, tractable on quantum computers, provided that a practical quantum computer is available.

It is worthwhile pointing out that although the order is hard to find, the exponentiation is easy to compute. Suppose we want to compute $x^e \bmod n$ with $x, e, n \in \mathbb{N}$. Suppose moreover that the binary form of e is as follows:

$$e = \beta_k 2^k + \beta_{k-1} 2^{k-1} + \cdots + \beta_1 2^1 + \beta_0 2^0,$$

where each β_i $(i = 0, 1, 2, \cdots k)$ is either 0 or 1. Then we have

$$x^e = x^{\beta_k 2^k + \beta_{k-1} 2^{k-1} + \cdots + \beta_1 2^1 + \beta_0 2^0}$$

$$= \prod_{i=0}^{k} x^{\beta_i 2^i}$$

$$= \prod_{i=0}^{k} \left(x^{2^i} \right)^{\beta_i}.$$

Furthermore, by the exponentiation law

$$x^{2^{i+1}} = (x^{2^i})^2,$$

and so the final value of the exponentiation can be obtained by *repeated squaring and multiplication* operations. For example, to compute a^{100}, we first write $100_{10} = 1100100_2 := e_6 e_5 e_4 e_3 e_2 e_1 e_0$, and then compute

$$a^{100} = (((((a)^2 \cdot a)^2)^2)^2 \cdot a)^2)^2$$

$$\Rightarrow a, a^3, a^6, a^{12}, a^{24}, a^{25}, a^{50}, a^{100}.$$

Note that for each e_i, if $e_i = 1$, we perform a *squaring* and a *multiplication* operation (except "$e_6 = 1$", for which we just write down a, as indicated in the first bracket), otherwise, we perform only a *squaring* operation. That is,

e_6	1	a	a	initialization
e_5	1	$(a)^2 \cdot a$	a^3	squaring and multiplication
e_4	0	$((a)^2 \cdot a)^2$	a^6	squaring
e_3	0	$(((a)^2 \cdot a)^2)^2$	a^{12}	squaring
e_2	1	$((((a)^2 \cdot a)^2)^2)^2 \cdot a$	a^{25}	squaring and multiplication
e_1	0	$(((((a)^2 \cdot a)^2)^2)^2 \cdot a)^2$	a^{50}	squaring
e_0	0	$((((((a)^2 \cdot a)^2)^2)^2 \cdot a)^2)^2$	a^{100}	squaring

$$\parallel$$
$$a^{100}$$

The following is the algorithm, which runs in $\mathcal{O}(\log e)$ arithmetic operations and $\mathcal{O}\left((\log e)(\log n)^2\right)$ bit operations.

Algorithm 3.4 (Fast Modular Exponentiation $x^e \bmod n$). This algorithm will compute the modular exponentiation

$$c \equiv x^e \pmod{n},$$

where $x, e, n \in \mathbb{N}$ with $n > 1$. It requires at most $2 \log e$ and $2 \log e$ divisions (divisions are only needed for modular operations; they can be removed if only $c = x^e$ are required to be computed).

[1] [Precomputation] Let

$$e_{\beta-1} e_{\beta-2} \cdots e_1 e_0$$

be the binary representation of e (i.e., e has β bits). For example, for $562 = 1000110010$, we have $\beta = 10$ and

$$
\begin{array}{cccccccccc}
1 & 0 & 0 & 0 & 1 & 1 & 0 & 0 & 1 & 0 \\
\uparrow & \uparrow & \uparrow & \uparrow & \uparrow & \uparrow & \uparrow & \uparrow & \uparrow & \uparrow \\
e_9 & e_8 & e_7 & e_6 & e_5 & e_4 & e_3 & e_2 & e_1 & e_0
\end{array}
$$

[2] [Initialization] Set $c \leftarrow 1$.

[3] [Modular exponentiation] Compute $c = x^e \bmod n$ in the following way:

> for i from $\beta - 1$ down to 0 do
> $\quad c \leftarrow c^2 \bmod n$ (squaring)
> $\quad$ if $e_i = 1$ then
> $\quad\quad c \leftarrow c \cdot x \bmod n$ (multiplication)

[4] [Exit] Print c and terminate the algorithm.

Now we are in a position to present the quantum algorithm for computing the order of an element x in the multiplicative group $\mathbb{Z}_n^*$, due to Shor [81]. The main idea of Shor's algorithm is as follows. First of all, we create two quantum registers for our quantum computer: Register-1 and Register-2. Of course, we can create just one single quantum memory register partitioned into two parts. Secondly, we create in Register-1, a superposition of the integers $a = 0, 1, 2, 3, \ldots$ which will be the arguments of $f(a) = x^a \pmod{n}$, and load Register-2 with all zeros. Thirdly, we compute in Register-2, $f(a) = x^a \pmod{n}$ for each input a. (Since the values of a are kept in Register-1, this can be done reversibly.) Fourthly, we perform the discrete Fourier transform on Register-1. Finally we observe both registers of the machine and find the order r that satisfies $x^r \equiv 1 \pmod{n}$. Here is the algorithm.

Algorithm 3.5 (Quantum Algorithm for Order Finding). Given a random integers x and n, the algorithm will Assume the machine has two quantum registers: Register-1 and Register-2, which hold integers in binary form.

[1] (Initialization) Find a number q, a power of 2, say 2^t, with $n^2 < q < 2n^2$.

[2] (Preparation for quantum registers) Put in the first t-qubit register, Register-1, the uniform superposition of states representing numbers $a \pmod q$, and load Register-2 with all zeros. This leaves the machine in the state $| \Psi_1 \rangle$:

$$| \Psi_1 \rangle = \frac{1}{\sqrt{q}} \sum_{a=0}^{q-1} | a \rangle | 0 \rangle .$$

(Note that the joint state of both registers are represented by $| Register\text{-}1 \rangle$ and $| Register\text{-}2 \rangle$). What this step does is put each qubit in Register-1 into the superposition

$$\frac{1}{\sqrt{2}} (| 0 \rangle + | 1 \rangle) .$$

[3] (Base selection) Choose a random $x \in [2, n-2]$ such that $\gcd(x, n) = 1$.

[4] (Power creation) Fill in the second t-qubit register, Register-2, with powers $x^a \pmod n$. This leaves the machine in state $| \Psi_2 \rangle$:

$$| \Psi_2 \rangle = \frac{1}{\sqrt{q}} \sum_{a=0}^{q-1} | a \rangle | x^a \pmod n \rangle .$$

This step can be done reversibly since all the a's were kept in Register-1.

[5] (Perform a quantum FFT) Apply FFT on Register-1. The FFT maps each state $| a \rangle$ to

$$\frac{1}{\sqrt{q}} \sum_{c=0}^{q-1} \exp(2\pi i a c / q) | c \rangle .$$

That is, we apply the unitary matrix with the (a, c) entry equal to $\frac{1}{\sqrt{q}} \exp(2\pi i a c / q)$. This leaves the machine in the state $| \Psi_3 \rangle$:

$$| \Psi_3 \rangle = \frac{1}{q} \sum_{a=0}^{q-1} \sum_{c=0}^{q-1} \exp(2\pi i a c / q) | c \rangle | x^a \pmod n \rangle .$$

[6] (Periodicity detection in x^a) Observe both $| c \rangle$ in Register-1 and $| x^a \pmod n \rangle$ in Register-2 of the machine, measure both arguments of this superposition, obtaining the values of $| c \rangle$ in the first argument and some $| x^k \pmod n \rangle$ as the answer for the second one $(0 < k < r)$.

[7] (Extract r) Extract the required value of r. Given the pure state $| \Psi_3 \rangle$, the probabilities of different results for this measurement will be given by the probability distribution:

$$\text{Prob}(c, x^k \ (\text{mod } n)) = \left| \frac{1}{q} \sum_{\substack{a=0 \\ x^a \equiv x^k \ (\text{mod } n)}}^{q-1} \exp(2\pi i a c/q) \right|^2$$

$$= \left| \frac{1}{q} \sum_{B=0}^{\lfloor (q-k-1)/r \rfloor} \exp(2\pi i (br + k)c/q) \right|^2$$

$$= \left| \frac{1}{q} \sum_{B=0}^{\lfloor (q-k-1)/r \rfloor} \exp(2\pi i b \{rc\}/q) \right|^2$$

where $\{rc\}$ is $rc \bmod n$. As showed in [81],

$$\frac{-r}{2} \le \{rc\} \le \frac{-r}{2} \implies \frac{-r}{2} \le rc - dq \le \frac{-r}{2}, \text{ for some } d$$

$$\implies \text{Prob}(c, x^k \ (\text{mod } n)) > \frac{1}{3r^2}.$$

then we have

$$\left| \frac{c}{q} - \frac{d}{r} \right| \le \frac{1}{2q}.$$

Since $\frac{c}{q}$ were known, r can be obtained by the continued fraction expansion of $\frac{c}{q}$.

[8] (Exit) Output r and stop the algorithm.

Theorem 3.5 (Complexity of Quantum Order Finding Algorithm). *Algorithm 3.5 for finding the order r of an element x in the multiplicative group $\mathbb{Z}_n^*$, i.e.,* order(x, n), *runs in polynomial-time, $\mathcal{O}((\log n)^{2+\epsilon})$.*

3.3.2 Quantum Integer Factoring Algorithm

The above order finding algorithm can be further extended to an integer factorization algorithm by adding one more step, as follows.

Algorithm 3.6 (Quantum Integer Factoring). Given a composite number n, usually $n = pq$ with p, q prime, and a random element $x \in \mathbb{Z}_n^*$ with $\gcd(x, n) = 1$, this algorithm will find the two prime factors p, q of n if $n = pq$ with the probability $> 1/2$.

[1]–[7] (Pre-computation) The steps of [1] to [7] are just the same as that in Algorithm 3.5.

[8] (Resolution) If r is odd, go to Step [3] to start a new random element $x \in \mathbb{Z}_n^*$. If r is even, then try to compute

$$\gcd(x^{r/2} \pm 1, n) = \{p, q\}.$$

The probability for this computation to success will be greater than $1/2$ if n has two prime factors.

Theorem 3.6 (Complexity of Integer Factoring). *Algorithm 3.6 for factoring* n *runs in polynomial-time,* $\mathcal{O}((\log n)^{2+\epsilon})$.

On 19 December 2001, IBM made the first experimental demonstration of Shor's quantum factoring algorithm [90], that correctly identified 3 and 5 as the factors of 15. Although the answer may appear to be trivial, it may have a good potential and practical implication. In the next example, we give a step by step illustration of how to factor 15 quantum-mechanically.

Example 3.14. Let $n = 15$. This example shows Shor's quantum algorithm for factoring the integer 15.

[1] Find a number q such that $15^2 < q = 2^8 = 256 < 2 \cdot 15^2$.
[2] Initialize the two quantum registers with zeroes

$$|\Psi_0\rangle = |0\rangle|0\rangle.$$

[3] Perform a Hadamard transform on Reg1, we get

$$H : |\Psi_0\rangle \to |\Psi_1\rangle = \frac{1}{\sqrt{256}} \sum_{a=0}^{255} |a\rangle|0\rangle.$$

[4] Choose a random $x = 7 \in [2, 13]$ such that $\gcd(7, 15) = 1$.
[5] Perform the modular exponentiations on Reg2, we get

$$U_f : |\Psi_1\rangle \to |\Psi_2\rangle = \frac{1}{\sqrt{q}} \sum_{a=0}^{q-1} |a\rangle|f(a)\rangle$$

$$= \frac{1}{\sqrt{256}} \sum_{a=0}^{255} |a\rangle|7^a \pmod{15}\rangle$$

$$= \frac{1}{\sqrt{256}}[|0\rangle|1\rangle + |1\rangle|7\rangle + |2\rangle|4\rangle + |3\rangle|13\rangle +$$

$$|4\rangle|1\rangle + |5\rangle|7\rangle + |6\rangle|4\rangle + |7\rangle|13\rangle +$$

$$|8\rangle|1\rangle + |9\rangle|7\rangle + |10\rangle|4\rangle + |11\rangle|13\rangle +$$

$$\cdots +$$

$$|252\rangle|1\rangle + |253\rangle|7\rangle + |254\rangle|4\rangle + |255\rangle|13\rangle].$$

[6] Measure Reg2. Suppose $|4\rangle$ is observed, this means that the states in Reg1 are collapsed into a superposition over all a such that $7^a \equiv 4 \mod 15$. That leaves Reg1 in states

$$|\Psi_3\rangle = \frac{1}{\sqrt{64}} (|2\rangle + |6\rangle + |10\rangle + |14\rangle + \cdots + |254\rangle).$$

[7] Perform QFT on Reg1.

$$QFT(|\Psi_3\rangle)$$

$$= QFT \left(\frac{1}{\sqrt{64}} (|2\rangle + |6\rangle + |10\rangle + |14\rangle + \cdots + |254\rangle) \right)$$

$$= \frac{1}{\sqrt{64}} QFT(|2\rangle + |6\rangle + |10\rangle + |14\rangle + \cdots + |254\rangle)$$

$$= \frac{1}{\sqrt{64}} \frac{1}{\sqrt{256}} \left(\sum_{c=0}^{255} e^{\frac{2\pi i 2c}{256}} |c\rangle + \sum_{c=0}^{255} e^{\frac{2\pi i 6c}{256}} |c\rangle + \sum_{c=0}^{255} e^{\frac{2\pi i 10c}{256}} |c\rangle + \cdots \right.$$
$$\left. + \sum_{c=0}^{255} e^{\frac{2\pi i 254c}{256}} |c\rangle \right)$$

$$= \frac{1}{8\sqrt{256}} \left(\sum_{c=0}^{255} e^{\frac{2\pi 2c}{256}} + \sum_{c=0}^{255} e^{\frac{2\pi 6c}{256}} + \sum_{c=0}^{255} e^{\frac{2\pi 10c}{256}} + \cdots + \sum_{c=0}^{255} e^{\frac{2\pi 254c}{256}} \right)$$

$$= \frac{1}{2}|0\rangle - \frac{1}{2}|64\rangle + \frac{1}{2}|128\rangle - \frac{1}{2}|192\rangle.$$

[8] Measure Reg1. The final measurement gives $0, 64, 128, 192$, each with probability almost exactly $1/4$. Suppose $c = 192$ is observed from the measurement. Then we compute the continued fraction expansion

$$\frac{c}{q} = \frac{192}{256} = \frac{1}{1 + \frac{1}{3}}, \text{ with convergents } \left[0, 1, \frac{3}{4} \right]$$

Thus, $r = 4 = \text{order}_{15}(7)$. Therefore,

$$\gcd(x^{r/2} \pm 1, n) = \gcd(7^2 \pm 1, 15) = (5, 3).$$

This gives the prime factorization of $15 = 3 \cdot 5$.

3.3.3 Quantum Algorithm for Breaking RSA

The above quantum order finding algorithm (i.e., Algorithm 3.5) and quantum factoring algorithm (i.e., Algorithm 3.6) can be further extended to an algorithm for breaking RSA.

Algorithm 3.7 (Quantum Algorithm for Breaking RSA). Let $n = pq$ be the RSA modulus, $C \equiv M^e$ (mod n) the ciphertext, (e, n) the public-key satisfying $ed \equiv 1$ (mod $(p-1)(q-1)$). Then by first execute Algorithm 3.6, this algorithm will break RSA efficiently.

[1]–[8] (Pre-computation) The steps from [1] to [8] are just the same as that in Algorithm 3.6.

[9] (Computing d) Once n is factored and p and q are found, then compute

$$d \equiv 1/e \ (\text{mod } (p-1)(q-1)).$$

[10] (Code break) As soon as d is found, the RSA plaintext can be computed immediately as follows:

$$M \equiv C^d \ (\text{mod } n).$$

Theorem 3.7 (Complexity of RSA Breaking). *Algorithm 3.7 for breaking RSA runs in polynomial-time,* $\mathcal{O}((\log n)^{2+\epsilon})$.

However, if we just wish to recover the RSA plaintext M from C, we could do this straightforward by finding the order of C in $\mathbb{Z}_n^*$ without explicitly factoring.

Theorem 3.8. *Let C be the RSA ciphertext, and* $\text{order}(C, n)$ *the order of $C \in \mathbb{Z}_n^*$. Then*

$$d \equiv 1/e \ (\text{mod } \text{order}(C, n)).$$

Corollary 3.2. *Let C be the RSA ciphertext, and* $\text{order}(C, n)$ *the order of $C \in \mathbb{Z}_n^*$. Then*

$$M \equiv C^{1/e \ (\text{mod } \text{order}(C,n))} \ (\text{mod } n)$$

Thus, to recover the RSA plaintext M from ciphertext C, it suffices to just find the order of C in $\mathbb{Z}_n^*$. Here is the algorithm.

Algorithm 3.8 (Quantum Order Finding Attack for RSA). Given the RSA ciphertext C and the modulus n, this algorithm shall first find the order r of C in $\mathbb{Z}_n^*$, such that $C^r \equiv 1$ (mod n), then recover the plaintext M from the ciphertext C. Assume the quantum computer has two quantum registers: Register-1 and Register-2, which hold integers in binary form.

[1] (Initialization) Find a number q, a power of 2, say 2^t, with $n^2 < q < 2n^2$.

[2] (Preparation for quantum registers) Put in the first t-qubit register, Register-1, the uniform superposition of states representing numbers $a \pmod{q}$, and load Register-2 with all zeros. This leaves the machine in the state $|\Psi_1\rangle$:

$$|\Psi_1\rangle = \frac{1}{\sqrt{q}} \sum_{a=0}^{q-1} |a\rangle\, |0\rangle .$$

(Note that the joint state of both registers are represented by $|$*Register*-1$\rangle$ and $|$*Register*-2$\rangle$). What this step does is put each qubit in Register-1 into the superposition

$$\frac{1}{\sqrt{2}} \left(|0\rangle + |1\rangle\right).$$

[3] (Power creation) Fill in the second t-qubit register, Register-2, with powers $C^a \pmod{n}$. This leaves the machine in state $|\Psi_2\rangle$:

$$|\Psi_2\rangle = \frac{1}{\sqrt{q}} \sum_{a=0}^{q-1} |a\rangle\, |C^a \pmod{n}\rangle .$$

This step can be done reversibly since all the a's were kept in Register-1.

[4] (Perform a quantum FFT) Apply FFT on Register-1. The FFT maps each state $|a\rangle$ to

$$\frac{1}{\sqrt{q}} \sum_{c=0}^{q-1} \exp(2\pi iac/q)\, |c\rangle .$$

That is, we apply the unitary matrix with the (a, c) entry equal to $\frac{1}{\sqrt{q}} \exp(2\pi iac/q)$. This leaves the machine in the state $|\Psi_3\rangle$:

$$|\Psi_3\rangle = \frac{1}{q} \sum_{a=0}^{q-1} \sum_{c=0}^{q-1} \exp(2\pi iac/q)\, |c\rangle\, |C^a \pmod{n}\rangle .$$

[5] (Periodicity detection in x^a) Observe both $|c\rangle$ in Register-1 and $|C^a \pmod{n}\rangle$ in Register-2 of the machine, measure both arguments of this superposition, obtaining the values of $|c\rangle$ in the first argument and some $|x^k \pmod{n}\rangle$ as the answer for the second one ($0 < k < r$).

[6] (Extract r) Extract the required value of r. Given the pure state $|\Psi_3\rangle$, the probabilities of different results for this measurement will be given by the probability distribution:

$$\text{Prob}(c, C^k \ (\text{mod } n)) = \left| \frac{1}{q} \sum_{\substack{a=0 \\ C^a \equiv C^k \ (\text{mod } n)}}^{q-1} \exp(2\pi i a c / q) \right|^2$$

$$= \left| \frac{1}{q} \sum_{B=0}^{\lfloor (q-k-1)/r \rfloor} \exp(2\pi i (br+k)c/q) \right|^2$$

$$= \left| \frac{1}{q} \sum_{B=0}^{\lfloor (q-k-1)/r \rfloor} \exp(2\pi i b \{rc\}/q) \right|^2$$

where $\{rc\}$ is $rc \mod n$. As shown in [81],

$$\frac{-r}{2} \leq \{rc\} \leq \frac{-r}{2} \implies \frac{-r}{2} \leq rc - dq \leq \frac{-r}{2}, \text{ for some } d$$

$$\implies \text{Prob}(c, C^k \ (\text{mod } n)) > \frac{1}{3r^2}.$$

then we have

$$\left| \frac{c}{q} - \frac{d}{r} \right| \leq \frac{1}{2q}.$$

Since $\frac{c}{q}$ were known, r can be obtained by the continued fraction expansion of $\frac{c}{q}$.

[7] (Code break) Once the order r, $r = \text{order}(C, n)$, is found, then compute:

$$M \equiv C^{1/e \mod r} \ (\text{mod } n),$$

recovering M from C.

Theorem 3.9 (Complexity of Quantum Order Finding Attack for RSA). *Algorithm 3.8 for finding* order(C, n) *and recovering M from C runs in polynomial-time,* $\mathcal{O}((\log n)^{2+\epsilon})$.

Remark 3.8. The above quantum order finding attack is for finding order(C, n), then use this order information to recover M from C without explicitly factoring n.

Problems for Section 3.3

1. Show that if in Shor's factoring algorithm, we have

$$\left| \frac{c}{2^m} - \frac{d}{r} \right| < \frac{1}{2n^2}$$

and

$$\left| \frac{c}{2^m} - \frac{d_1}{r_1} \right| < \frac{1}{2n^2},$$

then

$$\frac{d}{r} = \frac{d_1}{r_1}.$$

2. Show that in case $r \nmid 2^n$, Shor's factoring algorithm [82] needs to be repeated only $\mathcal{O}(\log \log r)$ steps in order to achieve the high probability of success.
3. Let $0 < s \le m$. Fix an integer x_0 with $0 \le x_0 < 2^s$. Show that

$$\sum_{\substack{0 \le c < 2^m \\ c \equiv c_0 \ (\mathrm{mod}\ 2^s)}} e^{2\pi i c x / 2^m} = \begin{cases} 0 & \text{if } x \not\equiv 0 \ (\mathrm{mod}\ 2^{m-s}), \\ 2^{m-s} e^{2\pi i x c_0 / 2^m} & \text{if } x \equiv 0 \ (\mathrm{mod}\ 2^{m-s}). \end{cases}$$

4. There are currently many pseudo-simulations of Shor's quantum factoring algorithm; for example, the paper by Schneiderman et al. [80] gives one of the simulations in Maple, whereas Browne [13] presents an efficient classical simulation of the quantum Fourier transform based on [80]. Construct your own Java (C/C++, Mathematica or Maple) program to simulate Shor's quantum factoring algorithm and discrete logarithm algorithm.
5. Shor's algorithm for solving the integer factorization problem runs in polynomial-time. Can you find another quantum polynomial-time factoring algorithm, but different from Shor's algorithm?
6. Shor's algorithm belongs to $\mathcal{BQP}$. Can you design a quantum factoring algorithm that belongs to $\mathcal{P}$?

3.4   Variations of Quantum Factoring Algorithms

It would be nice to implement the full version of Shor's algorithm directly on a quantum computer, but this has been shown to be difficult and impossible, as there is no practical quantum computer that is capable of running the algorithm. Thus various improved and compiled versions of Shor's algorithm using different technics have been proposed and studied. In what follows, we list some of the notable algorithms and methods.

1. A compiled version of Shor's factoring algorithm with a demonstration of factoring 15 using *photonic qubits* is proposed in [53].
2. A compiled version of Shor's factoring algorithm with a demonstration of factoring 15 using *quantum entanglement* is proposed in [47].

3. A factoring method using a Josephson phase quantum bit processor was proposed [54].
4. An experimental demonstration of a factoring method with temporal talbot effect for factoring the number 19403 was proposed in [8].
5. Gauss sum was used in classical factoring method, but Gilowski et al. [33] presented a quantum version of the Gauss sum method with cold atoms; a demonstration of this method for factoring the number 263193 was also given.
6. An experimental demonstration of an adiabatic quantum factoring algorithm in nuclear magnetic resonance with an example of factoring the number 21 was given [66].
7. An experimental demonstration of the factorization of 143 on a dipolar-coupling nuclear magnetic resonance system was proposed in [98].
8. By using the similar method in [98], Dattani and Bryans [23] gave a demonstration of the factorization of 156153 on a quantum computer with only 4 qubits.
9. Geller and Zhou [32] constructed simplified quantum circuits for Shor's factoring algorithm and gave an example for factoring the numbers 51 and 85 with 8 qubits.
10. An experimental realization of Shor's algorithm for factoring 21 using qubit recycling was proposed [56].
11. A realization of Shor's algorithm of factoring 15 on a photonic chip was proposed in [68].
12. Since the bottleneck of Shor's algorithm is the modular exponentiation, Martkov and Saeedi [55] presented a fast version via circuit synthesis.
13. An interesting but different factoring method based on waves was proposed in [105], where a demonstration on factoring the numbers 157575 and 52882363 were briefly discussed.
14. A fast and highly parallelized version of Shor's algorithm was proposed in [104], with a sizable quantum computer, it is possible to factor numbers with millions of digits, as it claimed.
15. Rather than finding the order r of the element a in $\mathbb{Z}_n^*$ such that $a^r \equiv 1 \pmod{n}$, Smolin et al. [87] proposed a quantum computing idea to find the number a such that $a^2 \equiv 1 \pmod{n}$, since once a is found, one can compute $\gcd(a \pm 1, n) = \{p, q\}$ with probability greater than $1/2$, if $n = pq$.
16. Parker and Plenio [65] proposed an efficient quantum factoring method with a pure qubit and $\log n$ mixed qubits for factoring integer n.
17. Reducing qubits in Shor's algorithm is helpful in constructing practical quantum computer, Seifert [77] proposed a quantum factoring algorithm using fewer qubits via simultaneously Diophantine approximation.

This list will enlarge as the time goes, and the factored numbers by various new and improved quantum factoring algorithms will also become bigger and bigger, hopefully, these algorithms will become practical at the end. Now, we give an example and demonstration of a variant described in [98].

Most of the modern classical factoring algorithms such as the continued fraction method (CFRAC), the quadratic sieve (QS) and the number field sieve (NFS) are based on the fact that if one can find the pair of integer solution (x, y) in the square congruence $x^2 \equiv y^2 \pmod{n}$, then one can compute $\gcd(x \pm y, n) = (p, q)$ with high probability if $n = pq$. As we know, all the classical algorithms based on this approach run in subexponential-time. We would naturally ask: can we speed up the process for finding (x, y) exponentially (more precisely, superpolynomially) or polynomially? The answer is that it is possible to speed up polynomially, but it can be hard exponentially. In what follows, we present a polynomially speedup quantum algorithm for finding the solution (x, y) [103]; it actually consists of two new algorithms: Algorithm 3.9 for finding x and Algorithm 3.10 for finding y. Here are the two algorithms.

Algorithm 3.9. This algorithm tries to find a pair of positive integers (x, y) such that $x^2 \equiv y^2 \pmod{n}$ in an attempt to factor n by computing $\gcd(x \pm y, n) = (p, q)$, provided that $n = pq$. By the fundamental law of quantum mechanics, although (x, y) can be computed at once, when x is measured, y will be destroyed, so this algorithm will only find the required x.

[1] Find a number q, a power of 2, say, e.g., 2^t, such that $t = \lfloor \log n \rfloor$.
[2] Initialize the two quantum registers, Reg1 and Reg2 with zeroes

$$|\Psi_0\rangle = |0\rangle|0\rangle.$$

[3] Perform a Hadamard transform on Reg1, we get

$$H: |\Psi_0\rangle \to |\Psi_1\rangle = \frac{1}{\sqrt{q}} \sum_{x=0}^{q-1} |x\rangle|0\rangle.$$

[4] Perform the modular exponentiations on Reg2, we get

$$U_f: |\Psi_1\rangle \to |\Psi_2\rangle = \frac{1}{\sqrt{q}} \sum_{x=0}^{q-1} |x\rangle|f(x)\rangle$$

$$= \frac{1}{\sqrt{q}} \sum_{x=0}^{q-1} |x\rangle|x^2 \pmod{n}\rangle.$$

[5] Perform a conditional phase shift on Reg2, with the same state receiving a phase shift of -1, that is, the states $|x\rangle, |y\rangle$, satisfying $x^2 \equiv y^2 \pmod{n}$ receive a phase shift of -1, thus

$$|\Psi_2\rangle \to |\Psi_3\rangle = \frac{1}{\sqrt{q}} \sum_{x=0}^{q-1} (-1)^{\delta_{x^2 \bmod n, \ y^2 \bmod n}} |x\rangle|x^2 \pmod{n}\rangle.$$

[6] Perform the unitary operation U on Reg2, where $U : |x\rangle|b\rangle \rightarrow |x\rangle|b \oplus x^2 \pmod{n}\rangle$, we obtain

$$|\Psi_3\rangle \rightarrow |\Psi_4\rangle = \frac{1}{\sqrt{q}} \sum_{x=0}^{q-1} (-1)^{\delta_{x^2 \bmod n, \ y^2 \bmod n}} |x\rangle|0\rangle.$$

[7] Perform a Hadamard transform on Reg1.

[8] Perform a conditional phase shift on Reg1 with every computational basis state, except $|0\rangle^{\otimes t}$ receiving a phase shift of -1.

[9] Perform a Hadamard transform on Reg1.

[10] Measure Reg1. Suppose we observe the state $|x\rangle$; in fact, by the fundamental law of quantum mechanics, the states $|x\rangle$ and $|y\rangle$, satisfying the congruence $x^2 \equiv y^2 \pmod{n}$, are observed with the same and higher probability, but when x is observed, y will be destroyed, in this case, we continue to go to run Algorithm 2.

Remark 3.9. When x in $x^2 \equiv y^2 \pmod{n}$ is measured, the value y will be destroyed immediately by the fundamental law of quantum mechanics, so we cannot measure y at the same time. Ideally, we can run Algorithm 3.9 again to determine y, but this may require exponentially many times to run Algorithm 1 in order to determine y. To speed up the computation, we let $a = x^2$, so that our square congruence $x^2 \equiv y^2 \pmod{n}$ becomes to the quadratic congruence $y^2 \equiv a \pmod{n}$. In this case, we use the following quantum algorithm to solve the Quadratic Congruence Problem, that is, to solve y in $y^2 \equiv a \pmod{n}$.

Algorithm 3.10. This algorithm tries to find a solution y to the quadratic congruence $y^2 \equiv a \pmod{n}$, where $a = x^2$ is obtained previously from Algorithm 3.9.

[1] Find a number q, a power of 2, say, e.g., 2^t, such that $t = \lceil \log \frac{n}{2} \rceil$.

[2] Initialize the two quantum registers, Reg1 and Reg2 with zeroes

$$|\Psi_0\rangle = |0\rangle|0\rangle.$$

[3] Perform a Hadamard transform on Reg1, we get

$$H : |\Psi_0\rangle \rightarrow |\Psi_1\rangle = \frac{1}{\sqrt{q}} \sum_{y=0}^{q-1} |y\rangle|0\rangle.$$

[4] Perform the modular exponentiations on Reg2, we get

$$U_f : |\Psi_1\rangle \rightarrow |\Psi_2\rangle = \frac{1}{\sqrt{q}} \sum_{y=0}^{q-1} |y\rangle|f(y)\rangle$$

$$= \frac{1}{\sqrt{q}} \sum_{y=0}^{q-1} |y\rangle|y^2 \pmod{n}\rangle.$$

[5] Perform a conditional phase shift on Reg2, with the state $|a\rangle$ receiving a phase shift of -1, thus

$$|\Psi_2\rangle \to |\Psi_3\rangle = \frac{1}{\sqrt{q}} \sum_{y=0}^{q-1} (-1)^{\delta_{a,\ y^2 \bmod n}} |y\rangle |y^2 \ (\bmod \ n)\rangle.$$

[6] Perform the unitary operation U on Reg2, where $U: |y\rangle|b\rangle \to |y\rangle|b \oplus y^2 \ (\bmod \ n)\rangle$, we obtain

$$|\Psi_3\rangle \to |\Psi_4\rangle = \frac{1}{\sqrt{q}} \sum_{y=0}^{q-1} (-1)^{\delta_{a,\ y^2 \bmod n}} |y\rangle |0\rangle.$$

[7] Perform a Hadamard transform on Reg1.
[8] Perform a conditional phase shift on Reg1 with every computational basis state, except $|0\rangle^{\otimes t}$ receiving a phase shift of -1.
[9] Perform a Hadamard transform on Reg1.
[10] Measure Reg1. Suppose we observe the state $|y\rangle$, if y satisfies the congruence $y^2 \equiv a \ (\bmod \ n)$, then y is a solution to the congruence $y^2 \equiv a \ (\bmod \ n)$, otherwise, we need to run the algorithm several times. In fact, we observe the y satisfying the congruence $y^2 \equiv a \ (\bmod \ n)$ with a higher probability.

In what follows, some numerical examples for factoring $n = 15$ and $n = 21$ are given to simulate and illustrate the execution of the two algorithms.

Example 3.15. Let $n = 15$. We first run Algorithm 3.9.

[1] Find a number q, a power of 2, say, e.g., 2^t, such that $t = \lfloor \log 15 \rfloor = 3$.
[2] Initialize the two quantum registers, Reg1 and Reg2 with zeroes

$$|\Psi_0\rangle = |0\rangle|0\rangle.$$

[3] Perform a Hadamard transform on Reg1, we get

$$H: |\Psi_0\rangle \to |\Psi_1\rangle = \frac{1}{\sqrt{8}} \sum_{x=0}^{7} |x\rangle|0\rangle.$$

[4] Perform the modular exponentiations on Reg2, we get

$$U_f: |\Psi_1\rangle \to |\Psi_2\rangle = \frac{1}{\sqrt{8}} \sum_{x=0}^{7} |x\rangle|f(x)\rangle$$

$$= \frac{1}{\sqrt{8}} \sum_{x=0}^{7} |x\rangle|x^2 \ (\bmod \ 15)\rangle.$$

[5] Perform a conditional phase shift on Reg2, with the same state receiving a phase shift of -1, that is, the states $|2\rangle, |7\rangle$, satisfying $2^2 \equiv 7^2$ (mod 15) receive a phase shift of -1, thus

$$|\Psi_2\rangle \rightarrow |\Psi_3\rangle = \frac{1}{\sqrt{8}} \sum_{x=0}^{7} (-1)^{\delta_{x^2 \bmod 15, \, y^2 \bmod 15}} |x\rangle |x^2 \text{ (mod 15)}\rangle$$

$$= \frac{1}{\sqrt{8}} (|0\rangle|0\rangle + |1\rangle|1\rangle - |2\rangle|4\rangle + |3\rangle|9\rangle + |4\rangle|1\rangle + |5\rangle|10\rangle +$$

$$|6\rangle|6\rangle - |7\rangle|4\rangle).$$

[6] Perform the unitary operation U on Reg2, where $U : |x\rangle|b\rangle \rightarrow |x\rangle|b \oplus x^2$ (mod 15)$\rangle$, we obtain

$$|\Psi_3\rangle \rightarrow |\Psi_4\rangle = \frac{1}{\sqrt{8}} \sum_{x=0}^{7} (-1)^{\delta_{x^2 \bmod 15, \, y^2 \bmod 15}} |x\rangle |0\rangle$$

$$= \frac{1}{\sqrt{8}} (|0\rangle + |1\rangle - |2\rangle + |3\rangle + |4\rangle + |5\rangle + |6\rangle - |7\rangle)|0\rangle.$$

[7] Perform a Hadamard transform on Reg1.

$$H : |\Psi_4\rangle \rightarrow |\Psi_5\rangle$$

$$= H \left(\frac{1}{\sqrt{8}} (|000\rangle + |001\rangle - |010\rangle + |011\rangle + |100\rangle + |101\rangle + |110\rangle - |111\rangle) \right)$$

$$= \frac{1}{\sqrt{8}} H(|000\rangle + |001\rangle - |010\rangle + |011\rangle + |100\rangle + |101\rangle + |110\rangle - |111\rangle)$$

$$= \frac{1}{\sqrt{8}} \frac{1}{\sqrt{8}} [(|0\rangle + |1\rangle) \otimes (|0\rangle + |1\rangle) \otimes (|0\rangle + |1\rangle) + (|0\rangle + |1\rangle) \otimes$$

$$(|0\rangle + |1\rangle) \otimes (|0\rangle - |1\rangle)(|0\rangle + |1\rangle) \otimes (|0\rangle - |1\rangle) \otimes (|0\rangle + |1\rangle) +$$

$$(|0\rangle + |1\rangle) \otimes (|0\rangle - |1\rangle) \otimes (|0\rangle - |1\rangle) + (|0\rangle - |1\rangle) \otimes (|0\rangle + |1\rangle) \otimes$$

$$(|0\rangle + |1\rangle) + (|0\rangle - |1\rangle) \otimes (|0\rangle + |1\rangle) \otimes (|0\rangle - |1\rangle) + (|0\rangle - |1\rangle) \otimes$$

$$(|0\rangle - |1\rangle) \otimes (|0\rangle + |1\rangle) - (|0\rangle - |1\rangle) \otimes (|0\rangle - |1\rangle) \otimes (|0\rangle - |1\rangle)]$$

$$= \frac{1}{2} (|000\rangle + |010\rangle - |101\rangle + |111\rangle).$$

[8] Perform a conditional phase shift on Reg1 with every computational basis state, except $|0\rangle^{\otimes 3}$ receiving a phase shift of -1.

$$|\Psi_6\rangle = \frac{1}{2} (|000\rangle - |010\rangle + |101\rangle - |111\rangle).$$

[9] Perform a Hadamard transform on Reg1.

$$H: |\Psi_6\rangle \rightarrow |\Psi_7\rangle$$

$$= H\left(\frac{1}{2}(|000\rangle - |010\rangle + |101\rangle - |111\rangle)\right)$$

$$= \frac{1}{4\sqrt{2}}[(|0\rangle + |1\rangle) \otimes (|0\rangle + |1\rangle) \otimes (|0\rangle + |1\rangle) - (|0\rangle + |1\rangle) \otimes$$

$$(|0\rangle - |1\rangle) \otimes (|0\rangle + |1\rangle) + (|0\rangle - |1\rangle) \otimes (|0\rangle + |1\rangle) \otimes (|0\rangle - |1\rangle) -$$

$$(|0\rangle - |1\rangle) \otimes (|0\rangle - |1\rangle) \otimes (|0\rangle - |1\rangle)]$$

$$= \frac{1}{4\sqrt{2}}(4|010\rangle + 4|111\rangle)$$

$$= \frac{1}{\sqrt{2}}(|010\rangle + |111\rangle).$$

[10] Measure Reg1. Suppose we observe the state $x = |010\rangle$. In fact, the states $|010\rangle$ and $|111\rangle$ are observed with the same and higher probability, but according to the fundamental law of quantum mechanics, we can only observe one of them, say, e.g., the first. Thus, we obtain $x = |010\rangle = 2$, then we continue to go to run Algorithm 3.10.

Example 3.16. Now we continue to run Algorithm 3.10 for $n = 15$. At the end of the execution of Algorithm 1, we have observed the state $x = |010\rangle$, that is, we get $x = 2$. Now let $a = x^2$. Algorithm 3.10 tries to find a solution y to the quadratic congruence $y^2 \equiv a \pmod{15}$, where $a = x^2 = 4$.

[1] Find a number q, a power of 2, say, e.g., 2^t, such that $t = \lceil \log \frac{15}{2} \rceil = 3$.
[2] Initialize the two quantum registers, Reg1 and Reg2 with zeroes

$$|\Psi_0\rangle = |0\rangle|0\rangle.$$

[3] Perform a Hadamard transform on Reg1, we get

$$H: |\Psi_0\rangle \rightarrow |\Psi_1\rangle = \frac{1}{\sqrt{8}} \sum_{y=0}^{7} |y\rangle|0\rangle.$$

[4] Perform the modular exponentiations on Reg2, we get

$$U_f : |\Psi_1\rangle \to |\Psi_2\rangle = \frac{1}{\sqrt{8}} \sum_{y=0}^{7} |y\rangle |f(y)\rangle$$

$$= \frac{1}{\sqrt{8}} \sum_{y=0}^{7} |y\rangle |y^2 \ (\text{mod } 15)\rangle.$$

[5] Perform a conditional phase shift on Reg2, with $|4\rangle$ receiving a phase shift of -1, thus

$$|\Psi_2\rangle \to |\Psi_3\rangle = \frac{1}{\sqrt{8}} \sum_{y=0}^{7} (-1)^{\delta_{4, \ y^2 \bmod 15}} |y\rangle |y^2 \ (\text{mod } 15)\rangle$$

$$= \frac{1}{\sqrt{8}} (|0\rangle|0\rangle + |1\rangle|1\rangle - |2\rangle|4\rangle + |3\rangle|9\rangle + |4\rangle|1\rangle + |5\rangle|10\rangle +$$

$$|6\rangle|6\rangle - |7\rangle|4\rangle).$$

[6] Perform the unitary operation U on Reg2, where $U : |y\rangle|b\rangle \to |y\rangle|b \oplus y^2(\text{mod } 15)\rangle$, we obtain

$$|\Psi_3\rangle \to |\Psi_4\rangle = \frac{1}{\sqrt{8}} \sum_{y=0}^{7} (-1)^{\delta_{4, \ y^2 \bmod 15}} |y\rangle |0\rangle$$

$$= \frac{1}{\sqrt{8}} (|0\rangle + |1\rangle - |2\rangle + |3\rangle + |4\rangle + |5\rangle + |6\rangle - |7\rangle)|0\rangle.$$

[7] Perform a Hadamard transform on Reg1.
$$H : |\Psi_4\rangle \to |\Psi_5\rangle$$

$$= H\left[\frac{1}{\sqrt{8}} (|000\rangle + |001\rangle - |010\rangle + |011\rangle + |100\rangle + |101\rangle + |110\rangle - |111\rangle)\right]$$

$$= \frac{1}{\sqrt{8}} H(|000\rangle + |001\rangle - |010\rangle + |011\rangle + |100\rangle + |101\rangle + |110\rangle - |111\rangle)$$

$$= \frac{1}{\sqrt{8}} \frac{1}{\sqrt{8}} [(|0\rangle + |1\rangle) \otimes (|0\rangle + |1\rangle) \otimes (|0\rangle + |1\rangle) + (|0\rangle + |1\rangle) \otimes (|0\rangle + |1\rangle)$$

$$\otimes (|0\rangle - |1\rangle)(|0\rangle + |1\rangle) \otimes (|0\rangle - |1\rangle) \otimes (|0\rangle + |1\rangle) + (|0\rangle + |1\rangle)$$

$$\otimes (|0\rangle - |1\rangle) \otimes (|0\rangle - |1\rangle) + (|0\rangle - |1\rangle) \otimes (|0\rangle + |1\rangle)(|0\rangle + |1\rangle)$$

$$\otimes (|0\rangle - |1\rangle) + (|0\rangle - |1\rangle) \otimes (|0\rangle - |1\rangle)$$

$$\otimes (|0\rangle + |1\rangle) - (|0\rangle - |1\rangle) \otimes (|0\rangle - |1\rangle) \otimes (|0\rangle - |1\rangle)]$$

$$= \frac{1}{2} (|000\rangle + |010\rangle - |101\rangle + |111\rangle).$$

[8] Perform a conditional phase shift on Reg1 with every computational basis state, except $|0\rangle^{\otimes 3}$ receiving a phase shift of -1.

$$|\Psi_6\rangle = \frac{1}{2}(|000\rangle - |010\rangle + |101\rangle - |111\rangle).$$

[9] Perform a Hadamard transform on Reg1.
$H : |\Psi_6\rangle \to |\Psi_7\rangle$

$$= H\left(\frac{1}{2}(|000\rangle - |010\rangle + |101\rangle - |111\rangle)\right)$$

$$= \frac{1}{4\sqrt{2}}[((|0\rangle + |1\rangle) \otimes (|0\rangle + |1\rangle) \otimes (|0\rangle + |1\rangle) - (|0\rangle + |1\rangle) \otimes (|0\rangle - |1\rangle)$$

$$\otimes (|0\rangle + |1\rangle) + (|0\rangle - |1\rangle) \otimes (|0\rangle + |1\rangle) \otimes (|0\rangle - |1\rangle) - (|0\rangle - |1\rangle) \otimes$$

$$(|0\rangle - |1\rangle) \otimes (|0\rangle - |1\rangle)]$$

$$= \frac{1}{4\sqrt{2}}(4|010\rangle + 4|111\rangle)$$

$$= \frac{1}{\sqrt{2}}(|010\rangle + |111\rangle).$$

[10] Measure Reg1. Suppose we observe the state $|010\rangle$, that is $y = |010\rangle = 2 = x$, in this worse case, the value of y is not suitable for us, thus we need to run Algorithm 2 several times to observe another state $y = |111\rangle = 7$; in fact, the state $|010\rangle$ and $|111\rangle$ are observed with the same probability, that is $P(|010\rangle) = P(|111\rangle) = \frac{1}{2}$. Of course, we may first observe the state $y = |111\rangle = 7$, in this case we get the desired value for y and do not need to run the algorithm again. So, at the end of the execution of Algorithm 2, we get $x = |010\rangle = 2$, $y = |111\rangle = 7$, satisfying $x^2 \equiv y^2 \pmod{15}$.

[11] Since the desired (x, y) is obtained, we can efficiently compute $\gcd(2\pm7, 15) = (3, 5)$ on a classical computer, leading to the required prime factorization $15 = 3 \times 5$.

Problems for Section 3.4

1. Smolin et al. [87] discussed the idea of a simplified version of the Shor's quantum factoring algorithm by computing the suitable a such that $a^2 \equiv 1 \pmod{n}$, rather than computing the order r of a such that $a^r \equiv 1 \pmod{n}$, so as to factor n. Give a description of the simplified version of the quantum algorithm, as well as the complexity measure of the algorithm.

2. Give a computing demonstration of factoring the integer 21 by using the compiled version of Shor's algorithm developed in [53].
3. Give a factoring simulation of the number 291311 by using the quantum factorization method described in [23]. What is the complexity of this method?
4. Give an experimental demonstration the compiled version of Shor's factoring algorithm developed in [98] to a large number than 143.
5. Develop a quantum version of the classical number field sieve factoring algorithm.
6. Develop a quantum version of the classical Pollard's ρ integer factoring algorithm.

3.5 Chapter Notes and Further Reading

The theory of prime numbers is one of the oldest subject in number theory and indeed in the whole of mathematics, whereas the Integer Factorization problem is one of the oldest number-theoretic problems in the field. The root of the problem may be traced back to Euclid's *Elements* [27], although it was first clearly stated in Gauss' *Disquisitiones* [31]. With the advent of modern public-key cryptography, it has an important application in the construction of unbreakable public-key cryptographic schemes and protocols, such as RSA (see [30, 75]), Rabin [73] and zero-knowledge proofs [37]. IFP is currently a very hot and applicable research topic, and there are many good references in the field, for a general reading, the following references are highly recommended: [1, 3, 4, 12, 14, 18, 20, 22, 25, 44, 51, 72, 74, 102].

IFP-based cryptography forms an important class of public-key cryptography. In particular, RSA cryptography is the most famous and widely used cryptographic schemes in today's Internet world. More information on IFP-based cryptography can be found in [9, 10, 21, 34–36, 40, 41, 43, 45, 58, 60, 61, 89, 96, 101].

Shor's discovery of the quantum factoring algorithm [81, 82, 82–85] in 1994 generated a great deal of research and interest in the field. Quantum computers provided a completely new paradigm for the theory of computation, and it was the first time to show that IFP can be solved efficiently in polynomial-time on a quantum computer. Now there are many good references on quantum computation, particularly on quantum factoring. Readers who wish to know more about quantum computers and quantum computation are suggested to consult the following references: [2, 5–7, 17, 24, 26, 39, 47, 52, 59, 64, 86, 90–95, 97, 99, 100, 104]. Feynman is perhaps the father of quantum computation whose original idea about quantum computers may be found in [28, 29].

In addition to quantum computation for factoring, there are also some other non-classical computations for factoring such as molecular DNA-based factoring and attacking. For example, Chang et al. proposed some fast parallel molecular DNA algorithms for factoring large integers [15] and for breaking RSA cryptography [16].

References

1. L.M. Adleman, Algorithmic number theory – the complexity contribution, in *Proceedings of the 35th Annual IEEE Symposium on Foundations of Computer Science* (IEEE, New York, 1994), pp. 88–113
2. L.M. Adleman, J. DeMarrais, M.D.A. Huang, Quantum computability. SIAM J. Comput. **26**(5), 1524–1540 (1997)
3. D. Atkins, M. Graff, A.K. Lenstra, P.C. Leyland, The magic words are squeamish ossifrage, in *Advances in Cryptology – ASIACRYPT 1994*. Lecture Notes in Computer Science, vol. 917 (Springer, Berlin, 1995), pp. 261–277
4. M. Agrawal, N. Kayal, N. Saxena, Primes is in P. Ann. Math. **160**(2), 781–793 (2004)
5. C.H. Bennett, E. Bernstein et al., Strengths and weakness of quantum computing. SIAM J. Comput. **26**(5), 1510–1523 (1997)
6. C.H. Bennett, D.P. DiVincenzo, Quantum information and computation. Nature **404**(6775), 247–255 (2000)
7. E. Bernstein, U. Vazirani, Quantum complexity theory. SIAM J. Comput. **26**(5), 1411–1473 (1997)
8. D. Bigourd, B. Chatel, W.P. Schleich et al., Factorization of numbers with the temporal talbot effect: optical implementation by a sequence of shaped ultrashort pulse. Phys. Rev. Lett. **100**(3), 030202 1–4 (2008)
9. M. Blum, S. Goldwasser, An efficient probabilistic public-key encryption scheme that hides all partial information, in *Advances in Cryptography – CRYPTO 1984*. Lecture Notes in Computer Science, vol. 196 (Springer, Heidelberg, 1985), pp. 289–302
10. D. Boneh, Twenty years of attacks on the RSA cryptosystem. Not. AMS **46**(2), 203–213 (1999)
11. R.P. Brent, An improved monte Carlo factorization algorithm. BIT **20**(2), 176–184 (1980)
12. D.M. Bressound, *Factorization and Primality Testing* (Springer, Berlin, 1989)
13. D.E. Browne, Efficient classical simulation of the quantum fourier transform. New J. Phys. **9**(146), 1–7 (2007)
14. J.P. Buhler, P. Stevenhagen (eds.), *Algorithmic Number Theory* (Cambridge University Press, Cambridge, 2008)
15. W.L. Chang, M. Guo, M.S.H. Ho, Fast parallel molecular algorithms for DNA-based computation: factoring integers. IEEE Trans. Nanobiosci. **4**(2), 149–163 (2005)
16. W.L. Chang, K.W. Lin et al., Molecular solutions of the RSA public-key cryptosystem on a DNA-based computer. J. Supercomput. 31 May 2011 (On-Line Version)
17. I.L Chuang, R. Laflamme, P. Shor, W.H. Zurek, Quantum computers, factoring, and decoherence. Science **270**(5242), 1633–1635 (1995)
18. H. Cohen, *A Course in Computational Algebraic Number Theory*. Graduate Texts in Mathematics, vol. 138 (Springer, Berlin, 1993)
19. D. Coppersmith, Small solutions to polynomial equations, and low exponent RSA vulnerability. J. Cryptol. **10**(4), 233–260 (1997)
20. T.H. Cormen, C.E. Ceiserson, R.L. Rivest, *Introduction to Algorithms*, 3rd edn. (MIT, Cambridge, 2009)
21. J.S. Coron, A. May, Deterministic polynomial-time equivalence of computing the RSA secret key and factoring. J. Cryptol. **20**(1), 39–50 (2007)
22. R. Crandall, C. Pomerance, *Prime Numbers – A Computational Perspective*, 2nd edn. (Springer, New York, 2005)
23. N.S. Dattani, N. Bryans, *Quantum Factorization of 56153 with only 4 Qubits* (2014), 6 p. arXiv:1411.6758v3 [quantum-ph]
24. D. Deutsch, Quantum theory, the Church–Turing principle and the universal quantum computer. Proc. R. Soc. Lond. Ser. A **400**(1818), 96–117 (1985)
25. J.D. Dixon, Factorization and primality tests. Am. Math. Mon. **91**(6), 333–352 (1984)

26. A. Ekert, R. Jozsa, Quantum computation and Shor's factoring algorithm. SIAM J. Comput. **26**(5), 1510–1523 (1997)
27. Euclid, *The Thirteen Books of Euclid's Elements*, 2nd edn. (Dover, New York, 1956) [Translated by T.L. Heath]. Great Books of the Western World, vol. 11 (William Benton Publishers, New York, 1952)
28. R.P. Feynman, Simulating physics with computers. Int. J. Theor. Phys. **21**(6), 467–488 (1982)
29. R.P. Feynman, *Feynman Lectures on Computation*, ed. by A.J.G. Hey, R.W. Allen (Addison-Wesley, Reading, 1996)
30. M. Gardner, Mathematical games – a new kind of cipher that would take millions of years to break. Sci. Am. **237**(2), 120–124 (1977)
31. C.F. Gauss, *Disquisitiones Arithmeticae*, ed. by G. Fleischer (Leipzig in commissis apud Gerh. Fleischerlun, 1801) [English translation by A.A. Clarke] (Yale University Press, Yale, 1966) [Revised English translation by W.C. Waterhouse (Springer, Berlin, 1975)]
32. M.R. Geller, Z. Zhou, Factoring 51 and 85 with 8 qubits. Sci. Rep. **3**(3023), 1–5 (2007)
33. M. Gilowski, T. Wendrich, T. Müller et al., Gauss sum factoring with cold atoms. Phys. Rev. Lett. **100**(3), 030201 1–4 (2008)
34. O. Goldreich, *Foundations of Cryptography: Basic Tools* (Cambridge University Press, Cambridge, 2001)
35. O. Goldreich, *Foundations of Cryptography: Basic Applications* (Cambridge University Press, Cambridge, 2004)
36. S. Goldwasser, S. Micali, Probabilistic encryption. J. Comput. Syst. Sci. **28**(2), 270–299 (1984)
37. S. Goldwasser, S. Micali, C. Rackoff, The knowledge complexity of interactive proof systems. SIAM J. Comput. **18**(1), 186–208 (1989)
38. J. Grobchadl, The Chinese remainder theorem and its application in a high-speed RSA crypto chip, in *Proceedings of the 16th Annual Computer Security Applications Conference* (IEEE, New York, 2000), pp. 384–393
39. Grustka, J. *Quantum Computing* (McGraw-Hill, New York, 1999)
40. M.J. Hinek, *Cryptanalysis of RSA and Its Variants* (Chapman & Hall/CRC, London/West Palm Beach, 2009)
41. J. Hoffstein, J. Pipher, J.H. Silverman, *An Introduction to Mathematical Cryptography* (Springer, New York, 2008)
42. K. Ireland, M. Rosen, *A Classical Introduction to Modern Number Theory*, 2nd edn. Graduate Texts in Mathematics, vol. 84 (Springer, Heidelberg, 1990)
43. S. Katzenbeisser, *Recent Advances in RSA Cryptography* (Kluwer Academic, Dordrecht, 2001)
44. T. Kleinjung, K. Aoki, J. Franke et al., Factorization of a 768-Bit RSA modulus, in *Advances in Cryptology – CRYPTO 2010*. Lecture Notes in Computer Science, vol. 6223 (Springer, Berlin, 2010), pp. 333–350
45. A.G. Konheim, *Computer Security and Cryptography* (Wiley, Chichester, 2007)
46. D.E. Knuth, *The Art of Computer Programming III – Sorting and Searching*, 2nd edn. (Addison-Wesley, Reading, 1998)
47. B.P. Lanyon, T.J. Weinhold, N.K. Langford et al., Experimental demonstration of a compiled version of Shor's algorithm with quantum entanglement. Phys. Rev. lett. **99**(25), 250505 1–4 (2007)
48. R.S. Lehman, Factoring large integers. Math. Comput. **28**(126), 637–646 (1974)
49. H.W. Lenstra Jr., Factoring integers with elliptic curves. Ann. Math. **126**(3), 649–673 (1987)
50. A.K. Lenstra, H.W. Lenstra Jr. (eds.), *The Development of the Number Field Sieve*. Lecture Notes in Mathematics, vol. 1554 (Springer, Berlin, 1993)
51. A.K. Lenstra, Integer factoring. Des. Codes Crypt. **19**(2/3), 101–128 (2000)
52. S.J. Lomonaco Jr., Shor's quantum factoring algorithm. AMS Proc. Symp. Appl. Math. **58**, 1–19 (2002)
53. C. Lu, D. Browne, T. Yang et al., Demonstration of a compiled version of Shor's quantum algorithm using photonic qubits. Phys. Rev. Lett. **99**(25), 250504 1–4 (2007)

54. E. Lucero, R. Barends, Y. Chen et al., Computing prime factors with a Josephson phase qubit quantum processor. Nat. Phys. **8**(10), 719–723 (2012)
55. I. Martkov, M. Saeedi, Fast quantum number factoring via circuit synthesis. Phys. Rev. A **87**(1), 012310 1–5 (2012)
56. E. Martín-López, A. Laing, T. Lawson et al., Experimental realization of Shor's quantum factoring algorithm using qubit recycling. Nat. Photon. **6**(11), 773–776 (2012)
57. J.F. McKee, Turning Euler's factoring methods into a factoring algorithm. Bull. Lond. Math. Soc. **28**(4), 351–355 (1996)
58. J.F. McKee, R. Pinch, Old and new deterministic factoring algorithms, in *Algorithmic Number Theory*. Lecture Notes in Computer Science, vol.1122 (Springer, Berlin, 1996), pp. 217–224
59. N.D. Mermin, *Quantum Computer Science* (Cambridge University Press, Cambridge, 2007)
60. R.A. Mollin, *RSA and Public-Key Cryptography* (Chapman & Hall/CRC, Boca Raton, 2003)
61. P.L. Montgomery, Speeding Pollard's and Elliptic curve methods of factorization. Math. Comput. **48**(177), 243–264 (1987)
62. P.L. Montgomery, A survey of modern integer factorization algorithms. CWI Q. **7**(4), 337–394 (1994)
63. M.A. Morrison, J. Brillhart, A method of factoring and the factorization of F_7. Math. Comput. **29**(129), 183–205 (1975)
64. M.A. Nielson, I.L. Chuang, *Quantum Computation and Quantum Information*, 10th anniversary edition. (Cambridge University Press, Cambridge, 2010)
65. S. Parker, M.B. Plenio, Efficient factorization a single pure qubit and $\log N$ mixed qubit. Phys. Rev. Lett. **85**(14), 3049–3052 (2004)
66. X. Peng, Z. Liao, N. Xu et al., Quantum adiabatic algorithm for factorization and its experimental implementation. Phys. Rev. Lett. **101**(22), 220405 1–4 (2008)
67. S.C. Pohlig, M.E. Hellman, An improved algorithm for computing logarithms over GF(p) and its cryptographic significance. IEEE Trans. Inf. Theory **24**(1), 106–110 (1978)
68. A. Politi, J.C.F. Matthews, J.L. O'Brient, Shor's quantum algorithm on a photonic chip. Science **325**(5945), 122 (2009)
69. J.M. Pollard, Theorems on factorization and primality testing. Proc. Camb. Philos. Soc. **76**(3), 521–528 (1974)
70. J.M. Pollard, A Monte Carlo method for factorization. BIT **15**(3), 331–332 (1975),
71. C. Pomerance, The quadratic sieve factoring algorithm, in *Proceedings of Eurocrypt 1984*. Lecture Notes in Computer Science, vol. 209 (Springer, Berlin, 1985), pp. 169–182
72. C. Pomerance, A tale of two sieves. Not. AMS **43**(12), 1473–1485 (1996)
73. M. Rabin, Digitalized signatures and public-key functions as intractable as factorization. Technical Report MIT/LCS/TR-212, MIT Laboratory for Computer Science, 1979
74. H. Riesel, *Prime Numbers and Computer Methods for Factorization* (Birkhäuser, Boston, 1990)
75. R.L. Rivest, A. Shamir, L. Adleman, A method for obtaining digital signatures and public key cryptosystems. Commun. Assoc. Comput. Mach. **21**(2), 120–126 (1978)
76. R.L. Rivest, B. Kaliski, RSA problem, in *Encyclopedia of Cryptography and Security*, ed. by H.C.A. van Tilborg (Springer, Berlin, 2005)
77. J.P. Seifert, Using fewer qubits in Shor's factorization algorithm via simultaneous diophantine approximation, in *Topics in Cryptology – CT-RSA 2001*. Lecture Notes in Computer Science, vol. 2020 (Springer, Berlin, 2001), pp. 319–327
78. D. Shanks, Class number, a theory of factorization, and genera, in *Proceedings of Symposium of Pure Mathematics*, vol. XX (The State University of New York, Stony Brook, 1969) (American Mathematical Society, Providence, 1971), pp. 415–440
79. D. Shanks, Analysis and improvement of the continued fraction method of factorization, Abstract 720-10-43. Am. Math. Soc. Not. **22**, A-68 (1975)
80. J.F. Schneiderman, M.E. Stanley, P.K. Aravind, A Pseudo-simulation of Shor's Quantum Factoring Algorithm (2002), 20 p. arXiv:quant-ph/0206101v1

81. P. Shor, Algorithms for quantum computation: discrete logarithms and factoring, in *Proceedings of 35th Annual Symposium on Foundations of Computer Science* (IEEE Computer Society, New York, 1994), pp. 124–134

82. P. Shor, Polynomial-time algorithms for prime factorization and discrete logarithms on a quantum computer. SIAM J. Comput. **26**(5), 1484–1509 (1997)

83. P. Shor, Quantum computing. Doc. Math. **Extra Vol. ICM I**, 467–486 (1998)

84. P. Shor, Introduction to quantum algorithms. AMS Proc. Symp. Appl. Math. **58**, 143–159 (2002)

85. P. Shor, Why haven't more quantum algorithms been found? J. ACM **50**(1), 87–90 (2003)

86. D.R. Simon, On the power of quantum computation. SIAM J. Comput. **26**(5), 1471–1483 (1997)

87. J.A. Smolin, G. Smith, A. Vargo, Oversimplifying quantum factoring. Nature **499**(7457), 163–165 (2013)

88. V. Strassen, Einige Resultate über Berechnungskomplexität. Jahresber. Deutsch. Math. Vereinigung **78**, 1–84 (1976/1997)

89. W. Trappe, L. Washington, *Introduction to Cryptography with Coding Theory*, 2nd edn. (Prentice-Hall, Englewood Cliffs, 2006)

90. L.M.K. Vandersypen, M. Steffen, G. Breyta et al., Experimental realization of Shor's quantum factoring algorithm using nuclear magnetic resonance. Nature **414**(6866), 883–887 (2001)

91. R. Van Meter, K.M. Itoh, Fast quantum modular exponentiation. Phys. Rev. A **71**(5), 052320 1–12 (2005)

92. R. Van Meter, W.J. Munro, K. Nemoto, Architecture of a quantum multicomputer implementing Shor's algorithm, in *Theory of Quantum Computation, Communication and Cryptography*, ed. by Y. Kawano, M. Mosca. Lecture Notes in Computer Science, vol. 5106 (Springer, New York, 2008), pp. 105–114

93. U.V. Vazirani, On the power of quantum computation. Phil. Trans. R. Soc. Lond. **A356**(1743), 1759–1768 (1998)

94. U.V. Vazirani, A survey of quantum complexity theory. AMS Proc. Symp. Appl. Math. **58**, 28 p. (2002)

95. J. Watrous, Quantum computational complexity, in *Encyclopedia of Complexity and System Science* (Springer, New York, 2009), pp. 7174–7201

96. H. Wiener, Cryptanalysis of short RSA secret exponents. IEEE Trans. Inf. Theory **36**(3), 553–558 (1990)

97. C.P. Williams, *Explorations in Quantum Computation*, 2nd edn. (Springer, New York, 2011)

98. N. Xu, J. Zhu, D. Lu, X. Zhou et al., Quantum factorization of 143 on a dipolar-coupling nuclear magnetic resonance system. Phys. Rev. Lett. **108**(13), 130501 1–5 (2012)

99. N.S. Yanofsky, M.A. Mannucci, *Quantum Computing for Computer Scientists* (Cambridge University Press, Cambridge, 2008)

100. A.C. Yao, Quantum circuit complexity, in *Proceedings of Foundations of Computer Science* (IEEE, New York, 1993), pp. 352–361

101. S.Y. Yan, *Cryptanalyic Attacks on RSA* (Springer, New York, 2008)

102. S.Y. Yan, *Primality Testing and Integer Factorization in Public-Key Cryptography*, 2nd edn. Advances in Information Security, vol. 11 (Springer, New York, 2009)

103. S.Y. Yan, Y.H. Wang, *New Quantum Algorithm for Finding the Solution x, y in $x^2 \equiv y^2 \pmod{n}$* (Computer School, Wuhan University, Wuhan, 2015)

104. C. Zalka, *Fast Versions of Shor's Quantum Factoring Algorithm* (1998), 37 p. arXiv:quant-ph/9806084v1

105. M.S. Zubairy, Factoring numbers with waves. Science **318**(5824), 5541–5555 (2007)

Chapter 4
Quantum Computing for Discrete Logarithms

The best way to get a good idea is to get a lot of ideas.

LINUS PAULING (1901–1994)
The 1954 Nobel Laureate in Chemistry

The Discrete Logarithm Problem (DLP) may be the first intractable computational number-theoretic problem to be considered for constructing cryptographic schemes by Diffie, Hellman and Merle at Stanford in 1976 and also by Ellis, Cocks and Williamson at the British GCHQ in 1970–1976. Today, DLP are widely used for constructing cryptographic systems and digital signatures, and the security of these systems depends heavily on the intractability of DLP. In this chapter, we discuss the quantum computing methods for solving the Discrete Logarithm Problem (DLP) and its extension Elliptic Curve Discrete Logarithm Problem (ECDLP).

4.1 Classical Algorithms for Discrete Logarithms

4.1.1 Basic Concepts

There are three main types of DLP problems, with respect to the level of the difficulty for solving them:

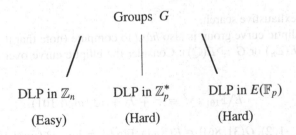

Groups G

DLP in $\mathbb{Z}_n$ DLP in $\mathbb{Z}_p^*$ DLP in $E(\mathbb{F}_p)$

(Easy)   (Hard)   (Hard)

© Springer International Publishing Switzerland 2015
S.Y. Yan, *Quantum Computational Number Theory*,
DOI 10.1007/978-3-319-25823-2_4

1. DLP in additive group $G = \mathbb{Z}_n$ is *easy* to compute: Let us consider the additive (cyclic) group $G = \mathbb{Z}_{100}$ of order 100: Find

$$n \equiv \log_3 17 \pmod{100},$$

such that

$$3n \equiv 17 \pmod{100}.$$

This type of DLP can be computed in polynomial-time by using Euclid's algorithm for multiplicative inverse as follows:

$$n = \frac{1}{3} \cdot 17$$
$$= 67 \cdot 17$$
$$= 39.$$

2. DLP in multiplicative group $G = \mathbb{Z}_n^*$ is *hard* to compute (note that when $n = p$ or $n = p^k$ is prime or prime power, then G is a field): Let us consider the multiplicative (cyclic) group $G = \mathbb{Z}_{101}^*$ of order 100. Find

$$n \equiv \log_3 17 \pmod{101},$$

such that

$$3^n \equiv 17 \pmod{101}.$$

This type of DLP is generally hard and there is no polynomial-time algorithm to solve it. Of course, for this artificially small example, one can find

$$\log_3 17 \equiv 70 \pmod{101}$$

easily by exhaustive search.

3. DLP in elliptic curve group is also *hard* to compute (note that it is also possible for $G = E(\mathbb{Z}_n)$ or $G = E(\mathbb{Q})$): Consider the elliptic curve over a finite field as follows:

$$E \backslash \mathbb{F}_{101} : y^2 \equiv x^3 + 7x + 12 \pmod{101},$$

where $\{P(-1, 2), Q(31, 86)\} \in E(\mathbb{F}_{101})$. Find $k \equiv \log_P Q \pmod{101}$ such that

$$Q \equiv kP \pmod{101}.$$

This type of DLP is also generally hard and there is no polynomial-time algorithm to solve it. Again, for this artificially small example, one can find

$$\log_P Q \equiv 78 \ (\text{mod } 101)$$

easily by exhaustive search.

In the next sections of this chapter, we consider the classical and quantum algorithms for DLP over a multiplicative group $\mathbb{Z}_n^*$, or a finite field $\mathbb{F}_{p^k}$ with $k \geq 1$; the ECDLP over $E(\mathbb{F}_p)$ will be discussed in the next chapter.

4.1.2 Shanks' Baby-Step Giant-Step Algorithm

Let G be a finite cyclic group of order n, a a generator of G and $b \in G$. The *obvious* algorithm for computing successive powers of a until b is found takes $\mathcal{O}(n)$ group operations. For example, to compute $x = \log_2 15 \ (\text{mod } 19)$, we compute 2^x mod 19 for $x = 0, 1, 2, \ldots, 19 - 1$ until 2^x mod $19 = 15$ for some x is found, that is:

x	0	1	2	3	4	5	6	7	8	9	10	11
a^x	1	2	4	8	16	13	7	14	9	18	17	15

So $\log_2 15 \ (\text{mod } 19) = 11$. It is clear that when n is large, the algorithm is inefficient. In this section, we introduce a type of square root algorithm, called the baby-step giant-step algorithm, for taking discrete logarithms, which is better than the above mentioned *obvious* algorithm. The algorithm, due to Daniel Shanks (1917–1996), works on arbitrary groups [59].

Let $m = \lfloor \sqrt{n} \rfloor$. The baby-step giant-step algorithm is based on the observation that if $x = \log_a b$, then we can uniquely write $x = i + jm$, where $0 \leq i, j < m$. For example, if $11 = \log_2 15$ mod 19, then $a = 2$, $b = 15$, $m = 5$, so we can write $11 = i + 5j$ for $0 \leq i, j < m$. Clearly here $i = 1$ and $j = 2$ so we have $11 = 1 + 5 \cdot 2$. Similarly, for $14 = \log_2 6$ mod 19 we can write $14 = 4 + 5 \cdot 2$, for $17 = \log_2 10$ mod 19 we can write $17 = 2 + 5 \cdot 3$, etc. The following is a description of the algorithm:

Algorithm 4.1 (Shanks' Baby-Step Giant-Step Algorithm). This algorithm computes the discrete logarithm x of y to the base a, modulo n, such that $y = a^x \ (\text{mod } n)$:

[1] (Initialization) Computes $s = \lfloor \sqrt{n} \rfloor$.
[2] (Computing the baby step) Compute the first sequence (list), denoted by S, of pairs (ya^r, r), $r = 0, 1, 2, 3, \ldots, s - 1$:

$$S = \{(y, 0), (ya, 1), (ya^2, 2), (ya^3, 3), \ldots, (ya^{s-1}, s - 1) \ \text{mod } n\}$$

and sort S by ya^r, the first element of the pairs in S.

[3] (Computing the giant step) Compute the second sequence (list), denoted by T, of pairs (a^{ts}, ts), $t = 1, 2, 3, \ldots, s$:

$$T = \{(a^s, 1), (a^{2s}, 2), (a^{3s}, 3), \ldots, (a^{s^2}, s) \bmod n\}$$

and sort T by a^{ts}, the first element of the pairs in T.

[4] (Searching, comparing and computing) Search both lists S and T for a match $ya^r = a^{ts}$ with ya^r in S and a^{ts} in T, then compute $x = ts - r$. This x is the required value of $\log_a y \pmod n$.

This algorithm requires a table with $\mathcal{O}(m)$ entries ($m = \lfloor \sqrt{n} \rfloor$, where n is the modulus). Using a sorting algorithm, we can sort both the lists S and T in $\mathcal{O}(m \log m)$ operations. Thus this gives an algorithm for computing discrete logarithms that uses $\mathcal{O}(\sqrt{n} \log n)$ time and space for $\mathcal{O}(\sqrt{n})$ group elements. Note that Shanks' idea was originally for computing the order of a group element g in the group G, but here we use his idea to compute discrete logarithms. Note also that although this algorithm works on arbitrary groups, if the order of a group is larger than 10^{40}, it will be infeasible.

Example 4.1. Suppose we wish to compute the discrete logarithm $x = \log_2 6 \bmod 19$ such that $6 = 2^x \bmod 19$. According to Algorithm 4.1, we perform the following computations:

[1] $y = 6$, $a = 2$ and $n = 19$, $s = \lfloor \sqrt{19} \rfloor = 4$.
[2] Computing the baby step:

$$S = \{(y, 0), (ya, 1), (ya^2, 2), (ya^3, 3) \bmod 19\}$$
$$= \{(6, 0), (6 \cdot 2, 1), (6 \cdot 2^2, 2), (6 \cdot 2^3, 3) \bmod 19\}$$
$$= \{(6, 0), (12, 1), (5, 2), (10, 3)\}$$
$$= \{(5, 2), (6, 0), (10, 3), (12, 1)\}.$$

[3] Computing the giant step:

$$T = \{(a^s, s), (a^{2s}, 2s), (a^{3s}, 3s), (a^{4s}, 4s) \bmod 19\}$$
$$= \{(2^4, 4), (2^8, 8), (2^{12}, 12), (2^{16}, 16) \bmod 19\}$$
$$= \{(16, 4), (9, 8), (11, 12), (5, 16)\}$$
$$= \{(5, 16), (9, 8), (11, 12), (16, 4)\}.$$

[4] Matching and computing: The number 5 is the common value of the first element in pairs of both lists S and T with $r = 2$ and $st = 16$, so $x = st - r = 16 - 2 = 14$. That is, $\log_2 6 \pmod{19} = 14$, or equivalently, $2^{14} \pmod{19} = 6$.

Example 4.2. Suppose now we wish to find the discrete logarithm $x = \log_{59} 67 \bmod 113$, such that $67 = 59^x \bmod 113$. Again by Algorithm 4.1, we have:

[1] $y = 67$, $a = 59$ and $n = 113$, $s = \lfloor \sqrt{113} \rfloor = 10$.
[2] Computing the baby step:

$$S = \{(y, 0), (ya, 1), (ya^2, 2), (ya^3, 3), \ldots, (ya^9, 9) \bmod 113\}$$

$$= \{(67, 0), (67 \cdot 59, 1), (67 \cdot 59^2, 2), (67 \cdot 59^3, 3), (67 \cdot 59^4, 4),$$

$$(67 \cdot 59^5, 5), (67 \cdot 59^6, 6), (67 \cdot 59^7, 7), (67 \cdot 59^8, 8),$$

$$(67 \cdot 59^9, 9) \bmod 113\}$$

$$= \{(67, 0), (111, 1), (108, 2), (44, 3), (110, 4), (49, 5), (66, 6),$$

$$(52, 7), (17, 8), (99, 9)\}$$

$$= \{(17, 8), (44, 3), (49, 5), (52, 7), (66, 6), (67, 0), (99, 9),$$

$$(108, 2), (110, 4), (111, 1)\}.$$

[3] Computing the giant-step:

$$T = \{(a^s, s), (a^{2s}, ss), (a^{3s}, 3s), \ldots (a^{10s}, 10s) \bmod 113\}$$

$$= \{(59^{10}, 10), (59^{2 \cdot 10}, 2 \cdot 10), (59^{3 \cdot 10}, 3 \cdot 10), (59^{4 \cdot 10}, 4 \cdot 10),$$

$$(59^{5 \cdot 10}, 5 \cdot 10), (59^{6 \cdot 10}, 6 \cdot 10), (59^{7 \cdot 10}, 7 \cdot 10), (59^{8 \cdot 10}, 8 \cdot 10),$$

$$(59^{9 \cdot 10}, 9 \cdot 10) \bmod 113\}$$

$$= \{(72, 10), (99, 20), (9, 30), (83, 40), (100, 50), (81, 60),$$

$$(69, 70), (109, 80), (51, 90), (56, 100)\}$$

$$= \{(9, 30), (51, 90), (56, 100), (69, 70), (72, 10), (81, 60), (83, 40),$$

$$(99, 20), (100, 50), (109, 80)\}.$$

[4] Matching and computing: The number 99 is the common value of the first element in pairs of both lists S and T with $r = 9$ and $st = 20$, so $x = st - r = 20 - 9 = 11$. That is, $\log_{59} 67 \pmod{113} = 11$, or equivalently, $59^{11} \pmod{113} = 67$.

Shanks' baby-step giant-step algorithm is a type of *square root method* for computing discrete logarithms. In 1978 Pollard also gave two other types of square root methods, namely the ρ-method and the λ-method for taking discrete logarithms. Pollard's methods are probabilistic but remove the necessity of precomputing the lists S and T, as with Shanks' baby-step giant-step method. Again, Pollard's algorithm requires $\mathcal{O}(n)$ group operations and hence is infeasible if the order of the group G is larger than 10^{40}.

4.1.3 Silver–Pohlig–Hellman Algorithm

In 1978, Pohlig and Hellman proposed an important special algorithm, now widely
known as the Silver–Pohlig–Hellman algorithm for computing discrete logarithms
over $GF(q)$ with $\mathcal{O}(\sqrt{p})$ operations and a comparable amount of storage, where p is
the largest prime factor of $q - 1$. Pohlig and Hellman showed that if

$$q - 1 = \prod_{i=1}^{k} p_i^{\alpha_i},$$

where p_i are distinct primes and α_i natural numbers, and if $r_1, \ldots, r_k$ are any real
numbers with $0 \le r_i \le 1$, then logarithms over $GF(q)$ can be computed in

$$\mathcal{O}\left(\sum_{i=1}^{k} \left(\log q + p_i^{1-r_i} \left(1 + \log p_i^{r_i} \right) \right) \right)$$

field operations, using

$$\mathcal{O}\left(\log q \sum_{i=1}^{k} \left(1 + p_i^{r_i} \right) \right)$$

bits of memory, provided that a precomputation requiring

$$\mathcal{O}\left(\sum_{i=1}^{k} p_i^{r_i} \log p_i^{r_i} + \log q \right)$$

field operations is performed first. This algorithm is very efficient if q is "smooth",
i.e., all the prime factors of $q - 1$ are small. We shall give a brief description of the
algorithm as follows:

Algorithm 4.2 (Silver–Pohlig–Hellman Algorithm). This algorithm computes
the discrete logarithm $x = \log_a b \bmod q$:

[1] Factor $q - 1$ into its prime factorization form:

$$q - 1 = \prod_{i=1}^{k} p_1^{\alpha_1} p_2^{\alpha_2} \cdots p_k^{\alpha_k}.$$

[2] Precompute the table $r_{p_i j}$ for a given field:

$$r_{p_i j} = a^{j(q-1)/p_i} \bmod q, \quad 0 \le j < p_i.$$

This only needs to be done once for any given field.

[3] Compute the discrete logarithm of b to the base a modulo q, i.e., compute $x = \log_a b \bmod q$:

  [3-1]   Use an idea similar to that in the baby-step giant-step algorithm to find the individual discrete logarithms $x \bmod p_i^{\alpha_i}$: To compute $x \bmod p_i^{\alpha_i}$, we consider the representation of this number to the base p_i:

$$x \bmod p_i^{\alpha_i} = x_0 + x_1 p_i + \cdots + x_{\alpha_i - 1} p_i^{\alpha_i - 1},$$

  where $0 \le x_n < p_i - 1$.

  (a) To find x_0, we compute $b^{(q-1)/p_i}$ which equals $r_{p_i, j}$ for some j, and set $x_0 = j$ for which

$$b^{(q-1)/p_i} \bmod q = r_{p_i, j}.$$

  This is possible because

$$b^{(q-1)/p_i} \equiv a^{x(q-1)/p} \equiv a^{x_0(q-1)/p} \bmod q = r_{p_i, x_0}.$$

  (b) To find x_1, compute $b_1 = ba^{-x_0}$. If

$$b_1^{(q-1)/p_i^2} \bmod q = r_{p_i, j},$$

  then set $x_1 = j$. This is possible because

$$b_1^{(q-1)/p_i^2} \equiv a^{(x-x_0)(q-1)/p_i^2} \equiv a^{(x_1 + x_2 p_i + \cdots)(q-1)/p_i}$$
$$\equiv a^{x_1(q-1)/p} \bmod q = r_{p_i, x_1}.$$

  (c) To obtain x_2, consider the number $b_2 = ba^{-x_0 - x_1 p_i}$ and compute

$$b_2^{(q-1)/p_i^3} \bmod q.$$

  The procedure is carried on inductively to find all $x_0, x_1, \ldots, x_{\alpha_i - 1}$.

  [3-2]   Use the Chinese Remainder Theorem to find the unique value of x from the congruences $x \bmod p_i^{\alpha_i}$.

We now give an example of how the above algorithm works:

Example 4.3. Suppose we wish to compute the discrete logarithm $x = \log_2 62 \bmod 181$. Now we have $a = 2$, $b = 62$ and $q = 181$ (2 is a generator of $\mathbb{F}_{181}^*$). We follow the computation steps described in the above algorithm:

[1] Factor $q - 1$ into its prime factorization form:

$$180 = 2^2 \cdot 3^2 \cdot 5.$$

[2] Use the following formula to precompute the table $r_{p_i,j}$ for the given field $\mathbb{F}_{181}^*$:

$$r_{p_i,j} = a^{j(q-1)/p_i} \bmod q, \quad 0 \le j < p_i.$$

This only needs to be done once for this field.

[2-1] Compute

$$r_{p_1,j} = a^{j(q-1)/p_1} \bmod q = 2^{90j} \bmod 181 \text{ for } 0 \le j < p_1 = 2:$$

$$r_{2,0} = 2^{90 \cdot 0} \bmod 181 = 1,$$

$$r_{2,1} = 2^{90 \cdot 1} \bmod 181 = 180.$$

[2-2] Compute

$$r_{p_2,j} = a^{j(q-1)/p_2} \bmod q = 2^{60j} \bmod 181 \text{ for } 0 \le j < p_2 = 3:$$

$$r_{3,0} = 2^{60 \cdot 0} \bmod 181 = 1,$$

$$r_{3,1} = 2^{60 \cdot 1} \bmod 181 = 48,$$

$$r_{3,2} = 2^{60 \cdot 2} \bmod 181 = 132.$$

[2-3] Compute

$$r_{p_3,j} = a^{j(q-1)/p_3} \bmod q = 2^{36j} \bmod 181 \text{ for } 0 \le j < p_3 = 5:$$

$$r_{5,0} = 2^{36 \cdot 0} \bmod 181 = 1,$$

$$r_{5,1} = 2^{36 \cdot 1} \bmod 181 = 59,$$

$$r_{5,2} = 2^{36 \cdot 2} \bmod 181 = 42,$$

$$r_{5,3} = 2^{36 \cdot 3} \bmod 181 = 125,$$

$$r_{5,4} = 2^{36 \cdot 4} \bmod 181 = 135.$$

Construct the $r_{p_i,j}$ table as follows:

	j				
p_i	0	1	2	3	4
2	1	180			
3	1	48	132		
5	1	59	42	125	135

This table is manageable if all p_i are small.

[3] Compute the discrete logarithm of 62 to the base 2 modulo 181, that is, compute $x = \log_2 62 \bmod 181$. Here $a = 2$ and $b = 62$:

[3-1]   Find the individual discrete logarithms $x \bmod p_i^{\alpha_i}$ using

$$x \bmod p_i^{\alpha_i} = x_0 + x_1 p_i + \cdots + x_{\alpha_i - 1} p_i^{\alpha_i - 1}, \quad 0 \leq x_n < p_i - 1.$$

(a-1)   Find the discrete logarithms $x \bmod p_1^{\alpha_1}$, i.e., $x \bmod 2^2$:

$$x \bmod 181 \iff x \bmod 2^2 = x_0 + 2x_1.$$

(i) To find x_0, we compute

$$b^{(q-1)/p_1} \bmod q = 62^{180/2} \bmod 181 = 1 = r_{p_1, j} = r_{2,0}$$

hence $x_0 = 0$.

(ii) To find x_1, compute first $b_1 = ba^{-x_0} = b = 62$, then compute

$$b_1^{(q-1)/p_1^2} \bmod q = 62^{180/4} \bmod 181 = 1 = r_{p_1, j} = r_{2,0}$$

hence $x_1 = 0$. So

$$x \bmod 2^2 = x_0 + 2x_1 \implies x \bmod 4 = 0.$$

(a-2)   Find the discrete logarithms $x \bmod p_2^{\alpha_2}$, that is, $x \bmod 3^2$:

$$x \bmod 181 \iff x \bmod 3^2 = x_0 + 2x_1.$$

(i) To find x_0, we compute

$$b^{(q-1)/p_2} \bmod q = 62^{180/3} \bmod 181 = 48 = r_{p_2, j} = r_{3,1}$$

hence $x_0 = 1$.

(ii) To find x_1, compute first $b_1 = ba^{-x_0} = 62 \cdot 2^{-1} = 31$, then compute

$$b_1^{(q-1)/p_2^2} \bmod q = 31^{180/3^2} \bmod 181 = 1 = r_{p_2, j} = r_{3,0}$$

hence $x_1 = 0$. So

$$x \bmod 3^2 = x_0 + 2x_1 \implies x \bmod 9 = 1.$$

(a-3)   Find the discrete logarithms $x \bmod p_3^{\alpha_3}$, that is, $x \bmod 5^1$:

$$x \bmod 181 \iff x \bmod 5^1 = x_0.$$

To find x_0, we compute

$$b^{(q-1)/p_3} \bmod q = 62^{180/5} \bmod 181 = 1 = r_{p_3,j} = r_{5,0}$$

hence $x_0 = 0$. So we conclude that

$$x \bmod 5 = x_0 \implies x \bmod 5 = 0.$$

[3-2]   Find the x in

$$x \bmod 181,$$

such that

$$\begin{cases} x \bmod 4 = 0, \\ x \bmod 9 = 1, \\ x \bmod 5 = 0. \end{cases}$$

To do this, we just use the Chinese Remainder Theorem to solve the following system of congruences:

$$\begin{cases} x \equiv 0 \ (\bmod\ 4), \\ x \equiv 1 \ (\bmod\ 9), \\ x \equiv 0 \ (\bmod\ 5). \end{cases}$$

The unique value of x for this system of congruences is $x = 100$. (This can be easily done by using, for example, the Maple function chrem([0, 1, 0], [4,9, 5]).) So the value of x in the congruence $x \bmod 181$ is 100. Hence $x = \log_2 62 = 100$.

4.1.4 ρ Method for DLP

We have seen that the Pollard ρ-method [48] can be used to solve the IFP problem. We shall see that there is a corresponding algorithm of ρ for solving the DLP problem [49], which has the same expected running time as the Baby-Step and Giant-Step, but which requires a negligible amount of storage. Assume we wish to find x such that

$$\alpha^x \equiv \beta \ (\bmod\ n).$$

Note that we assume the order of the element α in the multiplicative group $\mathbb{Z}_n^*$ is r. In ρ for DLP, the group $G = \mathbb{Z}_n^*$ is partitioned into three sets G_1, G_2 and G_3 of roughly equal size. Define a sequence of group elements $\{x_i\}$: $x_0, x_1, x_2, x_3, \cdots$ as follows:

$$\begin{cases} x_0 = 1, \\ x_{i+1} = f(x_i) = \begin{cases} \beta \cdot x_i, & \text{if } x_i \in G_1, \\ x_i^2, & \text{if } x_i \in G_1, \\ \alpha \cdot x_i, & \text{if } x_i \in G_1, \end{cases} \end{cases} \tag{4.1}$$

for $i \geq 0$. This sequence in turn defines two sequences of integers $\{a_i\}$ and $\{b_i\}$ as follows:

$$\begin{cases} a_0 = 0, \\ a_{i+1} = \begin{cases} a_i, & \text{if } x_i \in G_1, \\ 2a_i, & \text{if } x_i \in G_1, \\ a_i + 1, & \text{if } x_i \in G_1, \end{cases} \end{cases} \tag{4.2}$$

and

$$\begin{cases} b_0 = 0, \\ b_{i+1} = \begin{cases} b_i + 1, & \text{if } x_i \in G_1, \\ 2b_i, & \text{if } x_i \in G_2, \\ b_i, & \text{if } x_i \in G_3. \end{cases} \end{cases} \tag{4.3}$$

Just the same as ρ for IFP, we find two group elements x_i and x_{2i} such that $x_i = x_{2i}$. Hence

$$\alpha^{a_i} \beta^{b_i} = \alpha^{2a_i} \beta^{2b_i}.$$

Therefore

$$\beta^{b_i - 2b_i} = \alpha^{2a_i - a_i}. \tag{4.4}$$

By taking logarithm to the base α of both sides in (4.4), we get

$$x = \log_\alpha \beta \equiv \frac{2a_i - a_i}{b_i - 2b_i} \pmod{r}, \tag{4.5}$$

provided that $b_i \not\equiv 2b_i \pmod{n}$. The corresponding ρ algorithm may be described as follows.

Algorithm 4.3 (ρ for DLP). This algorithm tries to find x such that

$$\alpha^x \equiv \beta \pmod{n}.$$

Set $x_0 = 1, a_0 = 0, b_0 = 0$
For $i = 1, 2, 3, \cdots$ do
    Using (4.1), (4.2) and (4.3) to compute (x_i, a_i, b_i) and (x_{2i}, a_{2i}, b_{2i})
    If $x_i = x_{2i}$, do
        Set $r \leftarrow b_i - b_{2i}$ mod n
        If $r = 0$ terminate the algorithm with failure
        else compute $x \equiv r^{-1}(a_{2i} - a_i) \pmod{n}$
        output x

Example 4.4. Solve x such that

$$89^x \equiv 618 \pmod{809}.$$

Let G_1, G_2, G_3 be as follows:

$$G_1 = \{x \in \mathbb{Z}_{809} : x \equiv 1 \pmod 3\},$$
$$G_2 = \{x \in \mathbb{Z}_{809} : x \equiv 0 \pmod 3\},$$
$$G_3 = \{x \in \mathbb{Z}_{809} : x \equiv 2 \pmod 3\}.$$

For $i = 1, 2, 3, \cdots$ we calculate (x_i, a_i, b_i) and (x_{2i}, a_{2i}, b_{2i}) until $x_i = x_{2i}$ as follows:

i	$(\mathbf{x_i}, a_i, b_i)$	$(\mathbf{x_{2i}}, a_{2i}, b_{2i})$
1	$(681, 0, 1)$	$(76, 0, 2)$
2	$(76, 0, 2)$	$(113, 0, 4)$
3	$(46, 0, 3)$	$(488, 1, 5)$
4	$(113, 0, 4)$	$(605, 4, 10)$
5	$(349, 1, 4)$	$(422, 5, 11)$
6	$(488, 1, 5)$	$(683, 7, 11)$
7	$(555, 2, 5)$	$(451, 8, 12)$
8	$(605, 4, 10)$	$(344, 9, 13)$
9	$(451, 5, 10)$	$(112, 11, 13)$
10	$(\mathbf{422}, 5, 11)$	$(\mathbf{422}, 11, 15)$

At $i = 10$, a match has been found:

$$x_{10} = x_{20} = 422.$$

Since the order of 89 in $\mathbb{Z}_{809}^*$ is 101, we have

$$x \equiv \frac{a_{2i} - a_i}{b_i - b_{2i}},$$

$$\equiv \frac{11 - 5}{11 - 15}$$

$$\equiv 49 \ (\text{mod } 101).$$

Clearly,

$$89^{49} \equiv 618 \ (\text{mod } 809).$$

4.1.5   Index Calculus Algorithm

In 1979, Adleman [1] proposed a general purpose, subexponential-time algorithm for computing discrete logarithms in $\mathbb{Z}_n^*$ with n composite, called the *index calculus method*, with the following expected running time:

$$\mathcal{O}\left(\exp\left(c\sqrt{\log n \log \log n}\right)\right).$$

The index calculus is, in fact, a wide range of methods, including CFRAC, QS and NFS for IFP. In what follows, we discuss a variant of Adleman's index calculus for DLP in $\mathbb{Z}_p^*$ with p prime.

Algorithm 4.4 (Index Calculus for DLP). This algorithm tries to find an integer k such that

$$k \equiv \log_\beta \alpha \ (\text{mod } p) \quad \text{or} \quad \alpha \equiv \beta^k \ (\text{mod } p).$$

[1] Precomputation

    [1-1]   (Choose factor base) Select a factor base Γ, consisting of the first m prime numbers,

$$\Gamma = \{p_1, p_2, \ldots, p_m\},$$

    with $p_m \leq B$, the bound of the factor base.

    [1-2]   (Compute $\beta^e \bmod p$) Randomly choose a set of exponent $e \leq p-2$, compute $\beta^e \bmod p$, and factor it as a product of prime powers.

    [1-3]   (Smoothness) Collect only those relations $\beta^e \bmod p$ that are smooth with respect to B. That is,

$$\beta^e \bmod p = \prod_{i=1}^{m} p_i^{e_i}, e_i \geq 0. \tag{4.6}$$

When such relations exist, get

$$e \equiv \sum_{j=1}^{m} e_j \log_\beta p_j \ (\bmod \ p - 1). \tag{4.7}$$

[1-4] (Repeat) Repeat [1-3] to find at least m such e in order to find m relations as in (4.7) and solve $\log_\beta p_j$ for $j = 1, 2, \ldots, m$.

[2] Compute $k \equiv \log_\beta \alpha \ (\bmod \ p)$

[2-1] For each e in (4.7), determine the value of $\log_\beta p_j$ for $j = 1, 2, \ldots, m$ by solving the m modular linear equations with unknown $\log_\beta p_j$.

[2-2] (Compute $\alpha\beta^r \bmod p$) Randomly choose exponent $r \leq p - 2$ and compute $\alpha\beta^r \bmod p$.

[2-3] (Factor $\alpha\beta^r \bmod p$ over Γ)

$$\alpha\beta^r \bmod p = \prod_{j=1}^{m} p_j^{r_i}, r_j \geq 0. \tag{4.8}$$

If (4.8) is unsuccessful, go back to Step [2-2]. If it is successful, then

$$\log_\beta \alpha \equiv -r + \sum_{j=1}^{m} r_j \log_\beta p_j.$$

Example 4.5 (Index Calculus for DLP). Find

$$x \equiv \log_{22} 4 \ (\bmod \ 3361)$$

such that

$$4 \equiv 22^x \ (\bmod \ 3361).$$

[1] Precomputation

[1-1] (Choose factor base) Select a factor base Γ, consisting of the first 4 prime numbers,

$$\Gamma = \{2, 3, 5, 7\},$$

with $p_4 \leq 7$, the bound of the factor base.

[1-2]   (Compute 22^e mod 3361) Randomly choose a set of exponent $e \leq 3359$, compute 22^e mod 3361, and factor it as a product of prime powers:

$$22^{48} \equiv 2^5 \cdot 3^2 \ (\text{mod } 3361),$$
$$22^{100} \equiv 2^6 \cdot 7 \ (\text{mod } 3361),$$
$$22^{186} \equiv 2^9 \cdot 5 \ (\text{mod } 3361),$$
$$22^{2986} \equiv 2^3 \cdot 3 \cdot 5^2 \ (\text{mod } 3361).$$

[1-3]   (Smoothness) The above four relations are smooth with respect to $B = 7$. Thus

$$48 \equiv 5 \log_{22} 2 + 2 \log_{22} 3 \ (\text{mod } 3360),$$
$$100 \equiv 6 \log_{22} 2 + \log_{22} 7 \ (\text{mod } 3360),$$
$$186 \equiv 9 \log_{22} 2 + \log_{22} 5 \ (\text{mod } 3360),$$
$$2986 \equiv 3 \log_{22} 2 + \log_{22} 3 + 2 \log_{22} 5 \ (\text{mod } 3360).$$

[2] Compute $k \equiv \log_\beta \alpha \ (\text{mod } p)$

[2-1]   Compute

$$\log_{22} 2 \equiv 1100 \ (\text{mod } 3360),$$
$$\log_{22} 3 \equiv 2314 \ (\text{mod } 3360),$$
$$\log_{22} 5 \equiv 366 \ (\text{mod } 3360),$$
$$\log_{22} 7 \equiv 220 \ (\text{mod } 3360).$$

[2-2]   (Compute $4 \cdot 22^r$ mod p) Randomly choose exponent $r = 754 \leq 3659$ and compute $4 \cdot 22^{754}$ mod 3361.

[2-3]   (Factor $4 \cdot 22^{754}$ mod 3361 over Γ)

$$4 \cdot 22^{754} \equiv 2 \cdot 3^2 \cdot 5 \cdot 7 \ (\text{mod } 3361).$$

Thus,

$$\log_{22} 4 \equiv -754 + \log_{22} 2 + 2 \log_{22} 3 + \log_{22} 5 + \log_{22} 7$$

$$\equiv 2200.$$

That is,

$$22^{2200} \equiv 4 \ (\text{mod } 3361).$$

Example 4.6. Find $k \equiv \log_{11} 7 \ (\text{mod } 29)$ such that $\beta^k \equiv 11 \ (\text{mod } 29)$.

[1] (Factor base) Let the factor base $\Gamma = \{2, 3, 5\}$.
[2] (Compute and factor β^e mod p) Randomly choose $e < p$, compute and factor β^e mod $p = 11^e$ mod 29 as follows:

$$
\begin{aligned}
&(1)\ 11^2 \equiv 5 \ (\mathrm{mod}\ 29) &&\text{(success)}, \\
&(2)\ 11^3 \equiv 2 \cdot 13 \ (\mathrm{mod}\ 29) &&\text{(fail)}, \\
&(3)\ 11^5 \equiv 2 \cdot 7 \ (\mathrm{mod}\ 29) &&\text{(fail)}, \\
&(4)\ 11^6 \equiv 3^2 \ (\mathrm{mod}\ 29) &&\text{(success)}, \\
&(5)\ 11^7 \equiv 2^3 \cdot 3 \ (\mathrm{mod}\ 29) &&\text{(success)}, \\
&(6)\ 11^9 \equiv 2 \cdot 7 \ (\mathrm{mod}\ 29) &&\text{(success)}.
\end{aligned}
$$

[3] (Solve the systems of congruences for the quantities $\log_\beta p_i$)

$$
\begin{aligned}
&(1)\ \log_{11} 5 \equiv 2 \ (\mathrm{mod}\ 28), \\
&(4)\ \log_{11} 3 \equiv 3 \ (\mathrm{mod}\ 28), \\
&(6)\ \log_{11} 2 \equiv 9 \ (\mathrm{mod}\ 28), \\
&(5)\ 2 \cdot \log_{11} 2 + \log_{11} 3 \equiv 7 \ (\mathrm{mod}\ 28), \\
&\quad\ \log_{11} 3 \equiv 17 \ (\mathrm{mod}\ 28).
\end{aligned}
$$

[4] (Compute and factor $\alpha\beta^e \bmod p$) Randomly choose $e < p$, compute and factor $\alpha\beta^e \bmod p = 7 \cdot 11^e \bmod 29$ as follows:

$$
\begin{aligned}
&7 \cdot 11 \equiv 19 \ (\mathrm{mod}\ 29) &&\text{(fail)}, \\
&7 \cdot 11^2 \equiv 2 \cdot 3 \ (\mathrm{mod}\ 29) &&\text{(success)}.
\end{aligned}
$$

Thus

$$
\log_{11} 7 \equiv \log_{11} 2 + \log_{11} 3 - 2 \equiv 24 \ (\mathrm{mod}\ 28).
$$

This is true since

$$
11^{24} \equiv 7 \ (\mathrm{mod}\ 29).
$$

For more than 10 years since its invention, Adleman's method and its variants were the fastest algorithms for computing discrete logarithms. But the situation changed when Gordon [25] in 1993 proposed an algorithm for computing discrete logarithms in finite field $\mathbb{F}_p$. Gordon's algorithm is based on the Number Field Sieve (NFS) for integer factorization, with the heuristic expected running time

$$
\mathcal{O}\left(\exp\left(c(\log p)^{1/3}(\log\log p)^{2/3}\right)\right),
$$

the same as that used in factoring. The algorithm can be briefly described as follows:

Algorithm 4.5 (Gordon's NFS). This algorithm computes the discrete logarithm x such that $a^x \equiv b \ (\mathrm{mod}\ p)$ with input a, b, p, where a and b are generators and p is prime:

[1] (Precomputation): Find the discrete logarithms of a factor base of small rational primes, which must only be done once for a given p.

[2] (Compute individual logarithms): Find the logarithm for each $b \in \mathbb{F}_p$ by finding the logarithms of a number of "medium-sized" primes.

[3] (Compute the final logarithm): Combine all the individual logarithms (by using the Chinese Remainder Theorem) to find the logarithm of b.

Interested readers are referred to Gordon's paper [25] for more detailed information.

Example 4.7. We present in the following some DLP records and examples using various variants (modifications) of the Number Field Sieve (NFS).

1. Hamza Jeljeli at al (NUMTTHRY List, 11 Jun 2014) solved the following discrete logarithm modulo a 180 digit (596-bit) prime using NFS. Let

$$y \equiv g^k \ (\text{mod } p),$$

where

$p = $ RSA-180 + 625942

       191147927718986609689229466631454649812986246276667 3548

       641885036388072607034367990587762013651351612781342 5829

       612810920004670291298456875280033022177775277395740 4540

       495707852046983,

$g = 5,$

$y = $ 135066410865995223349603216278805969938881475605667 0275

       244851438515265106048595338339402871505719094417982 0728

       216447155137368041970396419174304649658927425623934 1020

       864383202110372958725762358509643110564073501508187 5106

       765946292055636855294752135008528794163773285339061 0975

       05443349998111500569772368909275 63.

Then discrete logarithm k is

$k = \log_g y \ (\text{mod } p)$

    = 138670566126823584879625861326333326312363943825621 0392

       202155833461537833362725599555219703573013029120463 1078

       290865945075854910809291833135221575134605475521667 3005

       939933186397777.

2. Thorsten Kleinjung (NUMTTHRY List, 5 Feb 2007) solved the following discrete logarithm modulo a 160 digits (530 bits) prime using NFS. Let

$$p = \lfloor 10^{159}\pi \rfloor + 119849$$

$$3141592653589793238462643383279502884197169399375105820$$
$$9749445923078164062862089986280348253421170679821480865$$
$$13282306647093844609550582231725359408128481237299,$$

$$g = 2,$$

$$y = \lfloor 10^{159}e \rfloor$$

$$2718281828459045235360287471352662497757247093699959574$$
$$9669676277240766303535475945713821785251664274274663919$$
$$3200305992181741359662904357290033429526059563 0738.$$

Then discrete logarithm k is

$$k = \log_g y \ (\text{mod } p)$$
$$= 8298971646503489705186468026407578440249614693231264721$$
$$9853184518689598402644834266625285046612688143761738165$$
$$3942624307537679319636711561053526082423513665596.$$

3. Dmitry Matyukhin et al. (NUMTTHRY List, 22 Dec 2006) solved the following discrete logarithm modulo a 135 digits (448 bits) prime using NFS. Let

$$p = \lfloor 2^{446}\pi \rfloor + 63384$$

$$= 5708577991479139431420732981594532907473762955504519051$$
$$1386537591186591858802294523702070250020343761541967996$$
$$1659928369778961422486479,$$

$$g = 7,$$

$$y = 11.$$

Then discrete logarithm k is

$$k = \log_g y \ (\text{mod } p)$$
$$= 2638094154425326843577938327776267044837001100509616312$$
$$4033661054514364572303487227503001638396257384118164938$$
$$8921540310684960074271 2.$$

4. Antoine Joux et al. (NUMTTHRY List, 18 Jun 2005) solved the following discrete logarithm modulo a 130 digits (431 bits) prime using NFS. Let

$$p = \lfloor 10^{129}\pi \rfloor + 38914$$

$$= 314159265358979323846264338327950288419716939937510582097494459230781640628620899862803482534211706798214808651328230664709388352 3$$

$$g = 2,$$

$$y = 271828182845904523536028747135266249775724709369995957496696762772407663035354759457138217852516642742746639193200305992181741359 6.$$

Then discrete logarithm k is

$$k = \log_g y \pmod{p}$$
$$2113848822378679565759046301222860744437727641443507757730839547200952585495202128754210118376422361373301079194266697766848291 09.$$

4.1.6 Discrete Logarithm in Small Characteristic Fields Using FFS

Let $\mathbb{F}_{p^k}$ be a finite field, with p^k a prime power and $k \geq 1$, and Q the cardinality of the field. Let also

$$L_Q(c, a) = L_Q(\mathcal{O}(\exp(c(\log Q)^a(\log\log Q)^{1-a}))).$$

Then for medium and large p, the fastest algorithm for DLP over $\mathbb{F}_{p^k}$ is still the Number Field Sieve with the complexity

$$L_Q\left(\left(\frac{128}{9}\right)^{1/3}, \frac{1}{3}\right),$$

and

$$L_Q\left(\left(\frac{64}{9}\right)^{1/3}, \frac{1}{3}\right).$$

However, for small p, the Function Field Sieve (FFS) (see [4]) for Discrete Logarithm Problem (DLP) over small characteristic fields runs in time proportion to

$$L_Q\left(\left(\frac{32}{9}\right)^{1/3}, \frac{1}{3}\right),$$

little bit faster than NFS.

Based on works in [31, 33], Gologlu et al. [24] proposed in 2013 an improved version of FFS with complexity

$$L_Q\left(\left(\frac{4}{9}\right)^{1/3}, \frac{1}{3}\right),$$

for DLP over small characteristic fields; they also presented two computation examples of DLP problems over $\mathbb{F}_{2^{1971}}$ and $\mathbb{F}_{2^{3164}}$ using their algorithm. Joux [32] also proposed in 2013 an index calculus algorithm with complexity

$$L_Q\left(c, \frac{1}{4} + o(1)\right)$$

for a small characteristic finite field of size $Q = p^k$. More recently, Barbulescu et al. proposed an even faster algorithm for discrete logarithm in finite fields of small characteristic, called quasi-polynomial algorithm with complexity $\mathcal{O}(n^{\log n})$, where n is the bit-size of the input.

Example 4.8. We give some computational examples of some recent progress in discrete logarithm of small characteristic fields using various variants (modifications) of the Function Field Sieve (FFS), and also NFS.

1. The following discrete logarithm

12577963165105635828352323153204142813405530977815918880154198919721124146930407233594105928
19620054540516726070297615221914385977996245594986628850744829762781379786539611876027859635
21103901153526044534603535422931573797074810398000395495638366455630035992529559929902108679
71589545353496625057851714199506077426599152479284551830406501129185767604943174058395008676
98950480424124992381486947135040691585318036322784283286505743723222916012003228122646787787
60812744846463014185368022969784377362738090039234572180767410866981269956062794778194643992
12708824867777648955338284933948899929899623865017456977463629503923943113103473591974384794
21926417535028150113691845480725642558782528984067457912635161678026919865775699076751288844
96679163247930275647343962891386236813287231696706514618918217999365307761347126655737419414
13893918400092260108486064404849439510367029755672281052702454897269358687249058588987873030
20603799802524293269325348977508513764535408533816752555623074363282273238382125649384955044
57572672007040234538095688669323195326252650693733552443986277025096145247868633522829296001
33618627260962596937676406978422629530723830723742640962354006238224015786085592229860420288
07542464936596853381863393340066643552700210891690213197575446887508091818149816922182720710
85945801198188215225189053189071240027777779380846406126349881480760793162005304774313385188
24856720976442747801073589406770953706872827831279003639075078401078283635730539702158853291
12020386618107876604970297230000308455240418160289565859726786046788491755695501878920244414
40063307155903389049268143763947368963141177709409668219060530210360059490951914011317445172
01908271067081208526487624386979946240202580649411051901851873021974963495470736580919286102
71053635873086802217940591502232862169337148524943727127651097394341372490996098855428920483
41587764062851417107029620945039590888940428098881858968507894858644623403448200740038167
9
15607983989209641706387321499724846988000657546850482405689080003957242722281882144664819226
95800965893402125816541710867996612898132154172132147347259096117374083080124194212521065
94
39961063363459160880859647302371434619662588848231727776340648840935726815387332949033100658

0785678288079185481076831613191857815421115194794969864570034744985160109907748052845110383
28517626386479635241779860392192412319930500261758798773211851188419870966987533549792746212
96687116204686444661810616017020932218916723885416696338016337850625213728173158748135473789
82896334961006121223586898316784941832140014605473361593596572512749882671779148934982863203
39419218271773917636439613324554287610224404525212307785056810461628707919731127095852418872
83847881669191194373349483920170984988952264442328316871533916286465088943094602878183734703
78767297858757572603,

in the finite field $\mathbb{F}_{2^{9234}}$ of characteristic 2, was found in January 2014 by Jen Zumbragel et al. (NUMTTHRY List, 31 Jan 2014), using FFS and spending about 400,000 core hours.

2. A discrete logarithm problem

77505588309444688883926502525134195106654673359423275661795094781621005215134978921361692545
31868849080347908279137658196354900390645498674188900527693235714921590847773054685284711762
88203760651495351559483913150688303752942529997080820548879268135773254808881021486584055763
85785627397055569076940082329730662934624337706494540699542317415746847480016650679479553177
98080977805480255602112956415163465333236163036161283551074339372118791785271068106754394547
16046071108893996448315543572254693416847303317942731872527210679215932698342472719828852892
08850945684950386713303311242731912854342662964589632571637782776220760760823673502138428497
21903406144006720815440449238920557641092436103031596737885884237055588427387341153051723735
96435722205711435175019406137919975700734056170958172298368056240527587735168461043124390372
28717205677060849469042549119669012597735073658430974437293430811219606905750793076266849922
93076114839659496542304412068009364228123317413313229981414515284667588346679273388415737139
23437376509652355872697854174452315802595958954351878312106461627929675514505816157907548584
06581643175264075781190106248059254483,

in the finite field $\mathbb{F}_{3^{2395}} = F_{(4^{479})^5}$ with 3796 bits, was solved in Sept 2014 by Cecile Pierrot et al. using under 8600 CPU hours (NUMTTHRY List, 15 Sep 2014).

3. The following discrete logarithm

4654012645531337673666669197479736917408020801989599595299657583
3066592958510118253230789917498104078593703566578479326592024301
0310280270908733113443497535707468938130765937538614277595176682
0507481582315458109232748306942144971304637051675435855273618145
6654264264960971602341334000598135868436603190762154255904911334
9119590964506643565574541978457160668934080970416111086483769489
8079818213966946690517120289920823006197801890468593528581063945
4110901899167671331438925478333634467622665486691712919356152287
049994352667585939913423425594615552854732,

in the finite field $\mathbb{F}_{2^{6168}} = \mathbb{F}_{(2^{257})^{24}}$ of characteristic 2, was found in May 2013 by Antoine Joux (NUMTTHRY List, 21 May 2013).

4. The following discrete logarithm problem in finite field $\mathbb{F}_{2^{1279}}$ of characteristic 2, was solved by Thorsten Kleinjung et al. (NUMTTHRY List, 17 Oct 2014). The solved logarithm is:

321275076038354244271788784435322541827019023388947750652050900
525115180566148243219392434968714055419806450499337950042809584
372691453133999605576037085342759765883954703008707139154520404
779119388599440952424301842309263415143084451713777855919414897
549477153722892113859834687536270307065104110274816485776366785
659989081124775994769960293808614458121740694009191847021263785
7540496.

Problems for Section 4.1

1. Use the exhaustive method to find the following discrete logarithms k over $\mathbb{Z}_{1009}^*$, if exist:

   (1) $k \equiv \log_3 57 \pmod{1009}$.
   (2) $k \equiv \log_{11} 57 \pmod{1009}$.
   (3) $k \equiv \log_3 20 \pmod{1009}$.

2. Use the baby-step giant-step algorithm to compute the following discrete logarithms k:

   (1) $k \equiv \log_5 96 \pmod{317}$.
   (2) $k \equiv \log_{37} 15 \pmod{123}$.
   (3) $k \equiv \log_5 57105961 \pmod{58231351}$.

3. Use Silver-Pohliq-Hellman algorithm to solve the discrete logarithms k:

   (1) $3^k \equiv 2 \pmod{65537}$.
   (2) $5^k \equiv 57105961 \pmod{58231351}$.
   (3) $k \equiv \log_5 57105961 \pmod{58231351}$.

4. Use Pollard's ρ method to find the discrete logarithms k such that

   (1) $2^k \equiv 228 \pmod{383}$.
   (2) $5^k \equiv 3 \pmod{2017}$.

5. Let the factor base $\Gamma = \{2, 3, 5, 7\}$. Use the index calculus method to find the discrete logarithm k:

   $$k \equiv \log_2 37 \pmod{131}.$$

6. Use the index calculus with factor base $\Gamma = (2, 3, 5, 7, 11)$ to solve the DLP problem

   $$k \equiv \log_7 13 \pmod{2039}.$$

7. Let

   $$p = 31415926535897932384626433832795028841971693993751058209$$
   $$= 74944592307816406286208998628034825342117067982148086513$$
   $$= 282306647093844609550582231725359408128481237299,$$

   $$x = 2,$$

   $$y = 27182818284590452353602874713526624977572470936999595749$$
   $$6697627724076630353547594571382178525166427427466391932$$
   $$003059921817413596629043572900334295260595630738.$$

(1) Use Gordon's index calculus method (Algorithm 4.5) to compute the k such that

$$y \equiv x^k \pmod{p}.$$

(2) Verify that if your k is as follows:

829897164650348970518646802640757844024961469323126472198531845186895984026448342666252850466126881437617381653942624307537679319636711561053526082423513665596.

4.2   Discrete Logarithm Based Cryptography

As discussed in the previous section, the Discrete Logarithm Problem (DLP) is intractable on classical computers and all the existing algorithms for DLP are inefficient. So just the same as IFP for RSA, this unreasonable effectiveness of DLP can also be used to construct cryptographic systems. In fact, the world's first public-key system, the DHM (Diffie-Hellman-Merkle) key-exchange scheme, was proposed in 1976 [18], its security relies directly on the intractability of the DLP problem. In this section we give a brief account of the DHM scheme and some other DLP based cryptographic systems.

4.2.1   The Diffie-Hellman-Merkle Key-Exchange Protocol

Diffie and Hellman [18] in 1976 proposed for the first time the concept and idea of public-key cryptography, and the first public-key system based on the infeasible Discrete Logarithm Problem (DLP). Their system is not a public-key cryptographic system, but a public-key distribution system based on Merkle's seminal work in 1978 [42]. Such a public-key distribution scheme does not send secret messages directly, but rather allows the two parties to agree on a common private-key over public networks to be used later in exchanging messages through conventional secret-key cryptography. Thus, the Diffie-Hellman-Merkle scheme has the nice property that a very fast encryption scheme such as DES or AES can be used for actual encryption (just using the agreed key), yet it still enjoys one of the main advantages of public-key cryptography. The Diffie-Hellman-Merkle key-exchange protocol works in the following way (see Figure 4.1):

[1] A prime q and a generator g are made public (assume all users have agreed upon a finite group over a fixed finite field $\mathbb{F}_q$),

[2] Alice chooses a random number $a \in \{1, 2, \ldots, q-1\}$ and sends $g^a \bmod q$ to Bob,

[3] Bob chooses a random number $b \in \{1, 2, \ldots, q-1\}$ and sends $g^b \bmod q$ to Alice,

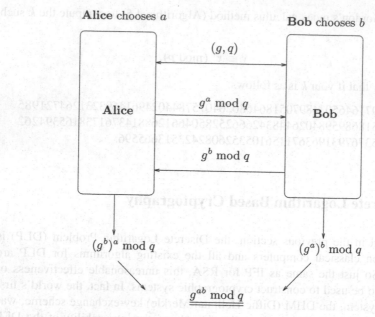

Figure 4.1 DHM key-exchange protocol

[4] Alice and Bob both compute g^{ab} mod q and use this as a private key for future communications.

Clearly, an eavesdropper has g, q, g^a mod q and g^b mod q, so if he can take discrete logarithms, he can calculate g^{ab} mod q and understand the communications. That is, if the eavesdropper can use his knowledge of g, q, g^a mod q and g^b mod q to recover the integer a, then he can easily break the Diffie-Hellman-Merkle system. So, the security of the Diffie-Hellman-Merkle system is based on the following assumption:

Diffie-Hellman-Merkle assumption: It is computationally infeasible to compute g^{ab} mod q from g, q, g^a mod q and g^b mod q. That is,

$$\{g, q, g^a \bmod q, g^b \bmod q\} \xrightarrow{\text{hard to find}} \{g^{ab} \bmod q\}.$$

The Diffie-Hellman-Merkle assumption is, in turn, depends on the following Discrete Logarithm Problem assumption, i.e.,

$$\{g, q, g^a \bmod q\} \xrightarrow{\text{hard to find}} \{a\},$$

or

$$\{g, q, g^b \bmod q\} \xrightarrow{\text{hard to find}} \{b\}.$$

In theory, there could be a way to use knowledge of $g^a \bmod q$ and $g^b \bmod q$ to find $g^{ab} \bmod q$. But at present, we simply cannot imagine a way to go from $g^a \bmod q$ and $g^b \bmod q$ to $g^{ab} \bmod q$ without essentially solving the following Discrete Logarithm Problem:

$$\{g, q, g^a \bmod q\} \xrightarrow{\text{find}} \{a\},$$

or

$$\{g, q, g^b \bmod q\} \xrightarrow{\text{find}} \{b\}.$$

If either a or b can be find efficiently, then DHM can be broken easily, since

$$\{g, q, b, g^a \bmod q\} \xrightarrow{\text{easy to find}} \{(g^a)^b \equiv g^{ab} \ (\bmod \ q)\},$$

or

$$\{g, q, a, g^b \bmod q\} \xrightarrow{\text{easy to find}} \{(g^b)^a \equiv g^{ab} \ (\bmod \ q)\}.$$

Example 4.9. The following DHM challenge problem was proposed in [40].

[1] Let p be following prime number:

$$p = 2047062703855328380597445351669742748036083943401234596957986745915265913726852295106528473397057976220755050698310434866516682279.$$

[2] Alice chooses a random number a modulo p, computes $7^a \ (\bmod \ p)$, and sends the result to Bob, keeping a secret.

[3] Bob receives

$$7^a \equiv 1274021801199739468242692443343228497493820425869316216545577352903229146790959986818609788130465951664554581442805880767660337 81 \ (\bmod \ p).$$

[4] Bob chooses a random number residue b modulo p, computes $7^b \ (\bmod \ p)$, and sends the result to Alice, keeping b secret.

[5] Alice receives

$$7^b \equiv 1801622852874531024447828348367998950159670466953466973130251217340599537720584759581769106253806921016518486623621379340268030 49 \ (\bmod \ p).$$

[6] Now both Alice and Bob can compute the private key $7^{ab} \ (\bmod \ p)$.

McCurley offered a prize of $100 in 1989 to the first person or group to find the private key constructed from the above communication.

Example 4.10. McCurley's 129-digit discrete logarithm challenge was actually solved on 25 January 1998 using the NFS method, by the two German computer scientists, Weber at the Institut für Techno-und Wirtschaftsmathematik in Kaiserslautern and Denny at the Debis IT Security Services in Bonn [74]. Their solution to McCurley's DLP problem is as follows.

$$a \equiv 3812728041119001413807839150792963419399864355101867028556137516504552396692940392210217251405327092887266394263$$
$$70063532797740808 \ (\text{mod } p),$$

$$(7^b)^a \equiv 6185869085965188327359333166520379042679876430695217134591462221849525998156144877820757492182909777408338791850457946749734.$$

As we have already mentioned earlier the Diffie-Hellman-Merkle scheme is not intended to be used for actual secure communications, but for key-exchanges. There are, however, several other cryptosystems based on discrete logarithms, that can be used for secure message transmissions.

4.2.2 ElGamal Cryptography

In 1985, ElGamal [21], a PhD student of Hellman at Stanford then, proposed the first DLP-based public-key cryptosystem, since the plaintext M can be recovered by taking the following discrete logarithms

$$M \equiv \log_{M^e} M \ (\text{mod } q).$$

The ElGamal cryptosystem can be described as follows (see also Figure 4.2).

[1] A prime q and a generator $g \in \mathbb{F}_q^*$ are made public.
[2] Alice chooses at random a private integer

$$a \in \{1, 2, \ldots, q-1\}.$$

This a is the private decryption key. The public encryption key is $\{g, q, g^a \bmod q\}$.
[3] Suppose now Bob wishes to send a message to Alice. He chooses a random number $b \in \{1, 2, \ldots, q-1\}$ and sends Alice the following pair of elements of $\mathbb{F}_q$:

$$(g^b, Mg^{ab})$$

where M is the message.
[4] Since Alice knows the private decryption key a, she can recover M from this pair by computing $g^{ab} \ (\bmod \ q)$ and dividing this result into the second element. That is,

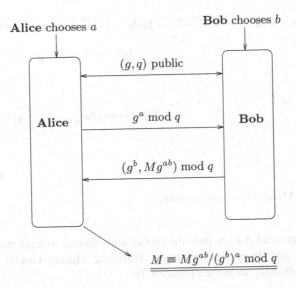

Figure 4.2 ElGamal cryptography

$$M \equiv Mg^{ab}/(g^b)^a \pmod{q}.$$

[5] Cryptanalysis: Find the private a by solving the DLP problem

$$a \equiv \log_g x \pmod{q-1}$$

such that

$$x \equiv g^a \pmod{q}.$$

Remark 4.1. Anyone who can solve the discrete logarithm problem in $\mathbb{F}_q$ breaks the cryptosystem by finding the secret decryption key a from the public encryption key g^a. In theory, there could be a way to use knowledge of g^a and g^b to find g^{ab} and hence break the cipher without solving the discrete logarithm problem. But as we have already seen in the Diffie-Hellman scheme, there is no known way to go from g^a and g^b to g^{ab} without essentially solving the discrete logarithm problem. So, the ElGamal cryptosystem is equivalent to the Diffie-Hellman key-exchange system.

4.2.3   Massey-Omura Cryptography

The Massey-Omura cryptosystem is another popular public-key cryptosystem based on discrete logarithms over the finite field $\mathbb{F}_q$, with $q = p^r$ prime power. It was proposed by James Massey and Jim K. Omura in 1982 [39] as a possible improvement over Shamir's original three-pass cryptographic protocol developed around 1980, in which the sender and the receiver do not exchange any keys,

$$\text{Alice} \leadsto M \xrightarrow{\;M^{e_A}\;(\bmod\;q-1)\;} \text{Bob} \xrightarrow{\;M^{e_A e_B}\;(\bmod\;q-1)\;} \text{Alice}$$

$$M^{e_A e_B d_A}\;(\bmod\;q-1)\qquad\Big\downarrow$$

$$\text{Bob}$$

$$M^{e_A e_B d_A d_B}\;(\bmod\;q-1)\qquad\Big\downarrow$$

$$M$$

$$\text{Bob}$$

Figure 4.3 The Massey-Omura cryptography

however, the protocol does require the sender and receiver to have two private keys for encrypting and decrypting messages. Thus, the Massey-Omura cryptosystem works in the following steps (see Figure 4.3):

[1] All the users have agreed upon a finite group over a fixed finite field $\mathbb{F}_q$ with q a prime power.

[2] Each user secretly selects a random integer e between 0 and $q-1$ such that $\gcd(e, q-1) = 1$, and computes $d = e^{-1} \bmod (q-1)$ by using the extended Euclidean algorithm. At the end of this step, Alice gets (e_A, d_A) and Bib gets (e_B, d_B).

[3] Now suppose that user Alice wishes to send a secure message M to user Bob, then they follow the following procedure:

    [3-1]   Alice first sends M^{e_A} to Bob.

    [3-2]   On receiving Alice's message, Bob sends $M^{e_A e_B}$ back to Alice (note that at this point, Bob cannot read Alice's message M).

    [3-3]   Alice sends $M^{e_A e_B d_A} = M^{e_B}$ to Bob.

    [3-4]   Bob then computes $M^{d_B e_B} = M$, and hence recovers Alice's original message M.

[4] Cryptanalysis: Eve shall be hard to find M from the three-pass protocol between Alice and Bob unless she can solve the discrete logarithm problem involved efficiently.

The Massey-Omura cryptosystem may also be described in detail as follows.

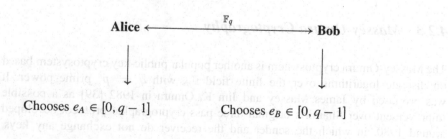

$$\text{Alice} \xleftarrow{\qquad\qquad\mathbb{F}_q\qquad\qquad} \text{Bob}$$

$$\Big\downarrow\qquad\qquad\qquad\qquad\qquad\Big\downarrow$$

Chooses $e_A \in [0, q-1]$ Chooses $e_B \in [0, q-1]$

such that $\gcd(e_a, q-1) = 1$ such that $\gcd(e_a, q-1) = 1$

Computes $d_A = e_A^{-1} \pmod{q-1}$ Computes $d_B = e_B^{-1} \pmod{q-1}$

$$\xrightarrow{\quad M^{e_A} \pmod{q-1} \quad}$$

$$\xleftarrow{\quad M^{e_A e_B} \pmod{q-1} \quad}$$

$$\xrightarrow{\quad M^{e_A e_B d_A} \pmod{q-1} \quad}$$

$$\big\downarrow$$

$$M \equiv M^{e_A e_B d_A d_B} \pmod{q-1}$$

Example 4.11. Let

$$p = 8000000000000001239,$$

$$M = 20210519040125 \text{ (Tuesday)},$$

$$e_A = 6654873997,$$

$$e_B = 7658494001.$$

Then

$$d_A \equiv \frac{1}{e_A} \equiv 70094446778448900393 \pmod{p-1},$$

$$d_B \equiv \frac{1}{e_B} \equiv 14252518250422012923 \pmod{p-1},$$

$$M^{e_A} \equiv 56964332403383118724 \pmod{p},$$

$$M^{e_A e_B} \equiv 37671804887541585024 \pmod{p},$$

$$M^{e_A e_B d_A} \equiv 50551151743565447865 \pmod{p},$$

$$M^{e_A e_B d_A d_B} \equiv 20210519040125 \pmod{p},$$

$$\downarrow$$

$$M$$

4.2.4 DLP-Based Digital Signatures

The ElGamal's cryptosystem [21] can also be used for digital signatures; the security of such a signature scheme depends on the intractability of discrete logarithms over a finite field.

Algorithm 4.6 (ElGamal Signature Scheme). This algorithm tries to generate digital signature $S = (a, b)$ for message m. Suppose that Alice wishes to send a signed message to Bob.

[1] [ElGamal key generation] Alice does the following:

> [1-1]   Choose a prime p and two random integers g and x, such that both g and x are less than p.
>
> [1-2]   Compute $y \equiv g^x \pmod{p}$.
>
> [1-3]   Make (y, g, p) public (both g and p can be shared among a group of users), but keep x as a secret.

[2] [ElGamal signature generation] Alice does the following:

> [2-1]   Choose at random an integers k such that $\gcd(k, p - 1) = 1$.
>
> [2-2]   Compute

$$\left. \begin{aligned} a &\equiv g^k \pmod{p}, \\[6pt] b &\equiv k^{-1}(m - xa) \pmod{(p-1)}. \end{aligned} \right\}$$

> Now Alice has generated the signature (a, b). She must keep the random integer, k, as secret.

[3] [ElGamal signature verification] To verify Alice's signature, Bob confirms that

$$y^a a^b \equiv g^m \pmod{p}.$$

In August 1991, the U.S. government's National Institute of Standards and Technology (NIST) proposed an algorithm for digital signatures. The algorithm is known as DSA, for Digital Signature Algorithm. The DSA has become the U.S. Federal Information Processing Standard 186 (FIPS 186). It is called the Digital Signature Standard (DSS) [12], and is the first digital signature scheme recognized by any government. The role of DSA/DSS is expected to be analogous to that of the Data Encryption Standard (DES). The DSA/DSS is similar to a signature scheme proposed by Schnorr; it is also similar to a signature scheme of ElGamal. The DSA is intended for use in electronic mail, electronic funds transfer, electronic data interchange, software distribution, data storage, and other applications which require data integrity assurance and data authentication. The DSA/DSS consists of two main processes:

1. Signature generation (using the private key),
2. Signature verification (using the public key).

A one-way hash function is used in the signature generation process to obtain a condensed version of data, called a message digest. The message digest is then signed. The digital signature is sent to the intended receiver along with the signed data (often called the message). The receiver of the message and the signature verifies the signature by using the sender's public key. The same hash function must also be used in the verification process. In what follows, we shall give the formal specifications of the DSA/DSS.

Algorithm 4.7 (Digital Signature Algorithm, DSA). This is a variation of ElGamal signature scheme. It generates a signature $S = (r, s)$ for the message m.

[1] [DSA key generation] To generate the DSA key, the sender performs the following:

    [1-1]   Find a 512-bit prime p (which will be public).

    [1-2]   Find a 160-bit prime q dividing evenly into $p - 1$ (which will be public).

    [1-3]   Generate an element $g \in \mathbb{Z}/p\mathbb{Z}$ whose multiplicative order is q, i.e., $g^q \equiv 1 \pmod{p}$.

    [1-4]   Find a one-way function H mapping messages into 160-bit values.

    [1-5]   Choose a secret key x, with $0 < x < q$.

    [1-6]   Choose a public key y, where $y \equiv g^x \pmod{p}$.

Clearly, the secret x is the discrete logarithm of y, modulo p, to the base g.

[2] [DSA signature generation] To sign the message m, the sender produces his signature as (r, s), by selecting a random integer $k \in \mathbb{Z}/q\mathbb{Z}$ and computing

$$\left. \begin{array}{l} r \equiv \left(g^k \pmod{p} \right) \pmod{q}, \\[2mm] s \equiv k^{-1}(H(m) + xr) \pmod{q}. \end{array} \right\}$$

[3] [DSA signature verification] To verify the signature (r, s) for the message m from the sender, the receiver first computes:

$$t \equiv s^{-1} \pmod{q},$$

and then accepts the signature as valid if the following congruence holds:

$$r \equiv \left(g^{H(m)t} y^{rt} \pmod{p} \right) \pmod{q}. \tag{4.9}$$

If the congruence (4.9) does not hold, then the message either may have been incorrectly signed, or may have been signed by an impostor. In this case, the message is considered to be invalid.

There are, however, many responses solicited by the (US) Association of Computing Machinery (ACM), positive and negative, to the NIST's DSA. Some positive aspects of the DSA include:

1. The U.S. government has finally recognized the utility and the usefulness of public-key cryptography. In fact, the DSA is the only signature algorithm that has been publicly proposed by any government.
2. The DSA is based on reasonable familiar number-theoretic concepts, and it is especially useful to the financial services industry.
3. Signatures in DSA are relatively short (only 320 bits), and the key generation process can be performed very efficiently.

4. When signing, the computation of r can be done even before the message m is available, in a "precomputation" step.

Whilst some negative aspects of the DSA include:

1. The DSA does not include key exchanges, and cannot be used for key distribution and encryption.
2. The key size in DSA is too short; it is restricted to a 512-bit modulus or key size, which is too short and should be increased to at least 1024 bits.
3. The DSA is not compatible with existing international standards; for example, the international standards organizations such as ISO, CCITT and SWIFT all have accepted the RSA as a standard.

Nevertheless, the DSA is the only one publicly known government digital signature standard.

Problems for Section 4.2

1. In McCurley's DLP problem, we have

$$7^b \equiv 18016228528774531024447828348367998950159670466953466973113025121734059953772058475958176910625380692101651848662362137934026803049 \pmod{p},$$

$$p = 2047062703855328380597445351669742748036083943401234596957986745915265913726852295106528473397057976220755050698310434866651682279.$$

(1) Find the discrete logarithm b.
(2) Compute $(7^a)^b \bmod p$.
(3) Verify if your result $(7^a)^b \bmod p$ agrees to Weber and Denny's result, i.e., check if $(7^a)^b \equiv (7^b)^a \pmod{p}$.

2. Let the DHM parameters be as follows:

$$p = 10000000000000000000000000000000000000000000000000000000000000000000000000002047062703855328380597445351669742748036083943401234596957986745915265913726852295106528473397057976220755050698310434866651682889,$$

$$13^x \equiv 1085194592674893032153689778751160153629141155121596373579741375470500284577824376666678872677612280593569523266148125732037472098621361064920285476333105415813024411985737741571370874416352991514462 \pmod{p},$$

$$13^y \equiv 5220020840015652308048438724807676036219832225501701426725687374586670774992277718809198697784982872783584$$
$$83829459489565477648733256999972723227753686571233058$$
$$30747697800417855036551198719274264122371 \pmod p.$$

(1) Find the discrete logarithm x.
(2) Find the discrete logarithm y.
(3) Compute $(13^x)^y \pmod p$.
(4) Compute $(13^y)^x \pmod p$.

3. In ElGamal cryptosystem, Alice makes (p, g, g^a) public with p prime:

$$p = 1000000000000000000000000000000000000000000000000000000000000000000000002047062703855328380597445351669742748046083943401234596957986745915265913726852295106528473397057976220755050698310434866516832810,$$

$$g = 137,$$

$$g^a \equiv 152192663976681019592833161514263206836744518581110634576769050615795569256793550994428565649100694385549614388735928661950422196794512676225936419253780225375372526399843535000717745310900273315236760,$$

where $a \in \{1, 2, \cdots, p\}$ must be kept as a secret. Now Bob can send Alice an encrypted message $C = (g^b, Mg^{ab})$ to Alice by using her public-key information, where

$$g^b \equiv 5954767560145832230236560413372022069605274694047335504604974413791437414218363404323065365907081646746246663690438438200152876992521173008100665424935641282638988214669184221777907261184240637405125 9,$$

$$Mg^{ab} \equiv 4958786188281511383043041844766490753023726445360329447984952773672153355770786431468633064462459966056008783414765112903810620149108556012648495266834088333232637420655255354969816428652168170029597 60.$$

(1) Find the discrete logarithm a, and compute $(g^b)^a \bmod p$.
(2) Find the discrete logarithm b, and compute $(g^a)^b \bmod p$.
(3) Decode the ciphertext C by computer either

$$M \equiv Mg^{ab}/(g^b)^a \;(\bmod\; p),$$

or

$$M \equiv Mg^{ab}/(g^a)^b \;(\bmod\; p).$$

4. Let

$$p = 14197,$$
$$(e_A, d_A) = (13, 13105),$$
$$(e_B, d_B) = (17, 6681),$$
$$M = 1511 \;(\text{OK}).$$

Find

$$M^{e_A} \bmod p,$$
$$M^{e_A e_B} \bmod p,$$
$$M^{e_A e_B d_A} \bmod p,$$
$$M^{e_A e_B d_A d_B} \bmod p,$$

and check if $M \equiv M^{e_A e_B d_A d_B} \;(\bmod\; p)$.

5. Let

$$p = 2000000000000002559,$$
$$M = 201514042625151811 \;(\text{To New York}),$$
$$e_A = 6654873997,$$
$$e_B = 7658494001.$$

(1) Find

$$d_A \equiv 1/e_A \;(\bmod\; p-1),$$
$$d_B \equiv 1/e_B \;(\bmod\; p-1).$$

(2) Find

$$M^{e_A} \bmod p,$$
$$M^{e_A e_B} \bmod p,$$
$$M^{e_A e_B d_A} \bmod p,$$
$$M^{e_A e_B d_A d_B} \bmod p.$$

(3) Check if $M \equiv M^{e_A e_B d_A d_B} \;(\bmod\; p)$.

6. Suppose, in ElGamal cryptosystem, the random number k is chosen to sign two different messages. Let

$$b_1 \equiv k^{-1}(m_1 - xa) \ (\text{mod} \ (p-1)),$$

$$b_2 \equiv k^{-1}(m_2 - xa) \ (\text{mod} \ (p-1)),$$

where

$$a \equiv g^k \ (\text{mod} \ p).$$

(1) Show that k can be computed from

$$(b_1 - b_2)k \equiv (m_1 - m_2) \ (\text{mod} \ (p-1)).$$

(2) Show that the private key x can be determined from the knowledge of k.

7. Show that breaking DHM key-exchange scheme or any DLP-based cryptosystem is generally equivalent to solving the DLP problem.

4.3 Quantum Algorithms for Discrete Logarithms

4.3.1 Basic Ideas of Quantum Computing for DLP

Recall that in DLP, we wish to find r in

$$g^r \equiv x \ (\text{mod} \ p),$$

where g is a generator in the multiplicative group $\mathbb{Z}_p^*$. We assume the order of g in $\mathbb{Z}_p^*$ is known to be k, that is,

$$g^k \equiv 1 \ (\text{mod} \ p).$$

Notice first that in quantum factoring algorithm, we try to find r in

$$g^r \equiv 1 \ (\text{mod} \ p),$$

where r is the order of g in $\mathbb{F}_{p-1}$. In quantum discrete logarithm algorithm, we try to find

$$g^r \equiv x \ (\text{mod} \ p),$$

where r is discrete logarithm to the base g in $\mathbb{F}_{p-1}$. That is,

$$r \equiv \log_g x \ (\text{mod} \ p-1).$$

The definitions of r in the two quantum algorithms are different. However, since

$$g^r \equiv x \ (\text{mod} \ p),$$

we can define a 2-variable function (just the same as $f(a) = g^a \equiv 1 \pmod{p}$ in quantum algorithm):

$$f(a, b) = g^a x^{-b} \equiv 1 \pmod{p}$$

such that

$$a - br \equiv k \pmod{p - 1},$$

which can be so, because

$$
\begin{aligned}
g^a x^{-b} &\equiv g^a (g^r)^{-b} \\
&\equiv g^a g^{-br} \\
&\equiv g^{a-br} \\
&\equiv g^k \pmod{p}.
\end{aligned}
$$

Thus, in quantum discrete logarithm algorithm, we essentially need to solve r in

$$r \equiv (a - k)b^{-1} \pmod{p - 1},$$

which is, in turn, just an inverse problem. Shor [60] shows that the quantum algorithm can solve r in polynomial-time. Of course, if $p - 1$ is smooth (i.e., $p - 1$ must have small prime factors), then DLP in $\mathbb{Z}_p^*$ can already be solved in polynomial-time by Pohlig-Hellman algorithm [47] (we call this case as an easy case of DLP). However for general p, there is still no classical polynomial-time for DLP (we call this case as a hard case of DLP). In what follows, we shall first discuss the easy case and then the hard case of the quantum DLP attacks.

4.3.2 Easy Case of Quantum DLP Algorithm

The easy case of the quantum DLP attack is basically the quantum analog or quantum version of the Pohlig-Hellman method for DLP. Recall that to find the discrete logarithm r in

$$g^r \equiv x \pmod{p},$$

where g is a generator of the multiplicative group $\mathbb{Z}_p^*$ and p a prime with $p - 1$ smooth, Pohlig-Hellman method can solve the problem efficiently in polynomial-time on a classical computer. It looks no advantage to use quantum computers to solve this particular easy, smooth case of DLP. However, it is a good exercise to show that a quantum computer can solve a problem just the same as a classical computer.

Algorithm 4.8 (Quantum Algorithm for Easy Case of DLP). Given $g, x \in \mathbb{N}$ and p prime. This algorithm will find the integer r such that $g^r \equiv x \pmod{p}$ if r exists. It uses three quantum registers.

[1] Beginning with the initial state

$$|\Psi_0\rangle = |0\rangle|0\rangle|0\rangle,$$

choose numbers a and b modulo $p - 1$ uniformly, and perform a Fourier transform modulo $p - 1$, denoted by A_{p-1}. So the state of the machine after this step is

$$|\Psi_1\rangle = \frac{1}{\sqrt{p-1}} \sum_{a=0}^{p-2} |a\rangle \cdot \frac{1}{\sqrt{p-1}} \sum_{b=0}^{p-2} |b\rangle |0\rangle$$

$$= \frac{1}{p-1} \sum_{a=0}^{p-2} \sum_{b=0}^{p-2} |a, b, 0\rangle.$$

[2] Compute $g^a x^{-b} \pmod{p}$ reversibly the values of a and b must be kept on the tape (just memory, in terms of quantum Turing machine, we call tape). This leaves the quantum computer in the state $|\Psi_2\rangle$:

$$|\Psi_2\rangle = \frac{1}{p-1} \sum_{a=0}^{p-2} \sum_{b=0}^{p-2} |a, \ b, \ g^a x^{-b} \ (\mathrm{mod} \ p)\rangle.$$

[3] Use the Fourier transform A_{p-1} to map $|a\rangle \rightarrow |c\rangle$ with probability amplitude

$$\sqrt{\frac{1}{p-1}} \exp\left(\frac{2\pi i a c}{p-1}\right)$$

and $|b\rangle \rightarrow |d\rangle$ with probability amplitude

$$\sqrt{\frac{1}{p-1}} \exp\left(\frac{2\pi i b d}{p-1}\right).$$

Thus, the state $|a, b\rangle$ will be changed to the state:

$$\frac{1}{(p-1)^2} \sum_{a,c=0}^{p-2} \sum_{b,d=0}^{p-2} \exp\left(\frac{2\pi i}{p-1}(ac + bd)\right) |c, d\rangle.$$

This leaves the machine in the state $|\Psi_2\rangle$:

$$|\Psi_3\rangle = \frac{1}{(p-1)^2} \sum_{a,b,c,d=0}^{p-2} \exp\left(\frac{2\pi i}{p-1}(ac+bd)\right)|c,\ d,\ g^a x^{-b} \pmod{p}\rangle.$$

[4] Observe the state of the quantum computer and extract the required information. The probability of observing a state $|c,\ d,\ g^k \pmod{p}\rangle$ is

$$\text{Prob}(c,d,g^k) = \left| \frac{1}{(p-1)^2} \sum_{\substack{a,b \\ a-rb \equiv k \pmod{p-1}}} \exp\left(\frac{2\pi i}{p-1}(ac+bd)\right) \right|^2$$

where the sum is over all (a,b) such that

$$a - rb \equiv k \pmod{p-1}. \tag{4.10}$$

[5] Substitue

$$a \equiv k + rb \pmod{p-1}$$

in (4.10), we get

$$\text{Prob}(c,d,g^k) = \left| \frac{1}{(p-1)^2} \sum_{b}^{p-2} \exp\left(\frac{2\pi i}{p-1}(kc + b(d+rc))\right) \right|^2$$

Notice that if $d + rc \not\equiv 0 \pmod{p-1}$, then the probability is 0. Thus, the probability $\neq 0$ if and only if $d + rc \equiv 0 \pmod{p-1}$, that is,

$$r \equiv -dc^{-1} \pmod{p-1}.$$

[6] As our computation has produced a random c and the corresponding $d \equiv -rc \pmod{p-1}$. Thus if $\gcd(c, p-1) = 1$, then we can find r by finding the multiplicative inverse of c using Euclid'd algorithm. More importantly, the chance that $\gcd(c, p-1) = 1$ is

$$\frac{\phi(p-1)}{p-1} > \frac{1}{\log p},$$

in fact,

$$\liminf \frac{\phi(p-1)}{p-1} \approx \frac{e^{-\gamma}}{\log\log p}.$$

So, we only need a number of experiments that is polynomial in $\log p$ to obtain r with high probability.

4.3.3 General Case of Quantum DLP Algorithm

We have just showed that quantum computers can solve a computational problem, namely the special case of DLP, just the same as classical computer. However, a quantum computer may also be able to solve a computational problem efficiently in polynomial-time, namely the general case of DLP, that cannot be solve efficiently in polynomial-time on a classical computer. Here is the quantum algorithm.

Recall that the special case DLP is based on the fact that $p - 1$ is smooth. In the general case, we remove this restriction by choosing a random smooth q such that $p \leq q \leq 2p$; it can be shown that such a q can be found in polynomial-time such that no prime power larger than $c \log q$ divides q for some constant c independent of p.

Algorithm 4.9 (Quantum Algorithm for General Case of DLP). Let g be a generator of $\mathbb{Z}_p^*$, $x \in \mathbb{Z}_p$. This algorithm will find the integer r such that $g^r \equiv x \pmod{p}$.

[1] Choose a random smooth number q such that $p \leq q \leq 2p$. Note that we do not require $p - 1$ to be smooth.

[2] Just the same as the special case, choose numbers a and b modulo $p - 1$ uniformly and perform a Fourier transform modulo $p - 1$. This leaves the quantum computer in the state $| \Psi_1 \rangle$:

$$| \Psi_1 \rangle = \frac{1}{p-1} \sum_{a=0}^{p-2} \sum_{b=0}^{p-2} | a, \ b \ (\mathrm{mod} \ p) \rangle .$$

[2] Compute $g^a x^{-b} \bmod p$ reversibly. This leaves the quantum computer in the state $| \Psi_2 \rangle$:

$$| \Psi_2 \rangle = \frac{1}{p-1} \sum_{a=0}^{p-2} \sum_{b=0}^{p-2} | a, \ b, \ g^a x^{-b} \ (\mathrm{mod} \ p) \rangle .$$

[3] Use the Fourier transform A_q to map $|a\rangle \rightarrow |c\rangle$ with the probability amplitude

$$\frac{1}{\sqrt{q}} \exp \left(\frac{2\pi i a c}{q} \right)$$

and $|b\rangle \rightarrow |d\rangle$ with probability amplitude

$$\frac{1}{\sqrt{q}} \exp \left(\frac{2\pi i b d}{q} \right) .$$

Thus, the state $|a, b\rangle$ will be changed to the state:

$$\frac{1}{p-1} \sum_{c=0}^{p-2} \sum_{d=0}^{p-2} \exp \left(\frac{2\pi i}{q} (ac + bd) \right) |c, \ d\rangle .$$

This leaves the machine in the state $|\Psi_3\rangle$:

$$|\Psi_3\rangle = \frac{1}{(p-1)q} \sum_{a,b=0}^{p-2} \sum_{c,d=0}^{q-1} \exp\left(\frac{2\pi i}{q}(ac+bd)\right)|c,\,d,\,g^a x^{-b}\ (\mathrm{mod}\ p)\rangle.$$

[4] Observe the state of the quantum computer and extract the required information. The probability of observing a state $|c,\,d,\,g^k\ (\mathrm{mod}\ p)\rangle$ is almost the same as the special case:

$$\mathrm{Prob}(c,d,g^k) = \left| \frac{1}{(p-1)q} \sum_{\substack{a,b \\ a-rb\equiv k\ (\mathrm{mod}\ p-1)}} \exp\left(\frac{2\pi i}{q}(ac+bd)\right) \right|^2 \qquad (4.11)$$

where the sum is over all (a,b) such that

$$a - rb \equiv k\ (\mathrm{mod}\ p-1).$$

[5] Use the relation

$$a \equiv k + br - (p-1)\left\lfloor \frac{br+k}{p-1} \right\rfloor.$$

and substitute in (4.11) to obtain the amplitude:

$$\frac{1}{(p-1)q} \sum_{b=0}^{p-2} \exp\left(\frac{2\pi i}{q}\left(brc + kc + bd - c(p-1)\left\lfloor \frac{br+k}{p-1} \right\rfloor\right)\right),$$

so that the sum of (4.11) becomes:

$$\left| \frac{1}{(p-1)q} \sum_{b=0}^{p-2} \exp\left(\frac{2\pi i}{q}\left(brc + kc + bd - c(p-1)\left\lfloor \frac{br+k}{p-1} \right\rfloor\right)\right) \right|^2,$$

which is the probability of observing the state $|c,\,d,\,g^k\ (\mathrm{mod}\ p)\rangle$.

[6] It can be shown that certain pair of values of c,d occur with high probability and satisfy the bound

$$\left| rc + d - \frac{r}{p-1}(c(p-1)\ \mathrm{mod}\ q) \right| \leq \frac{1}{2}.$$

Once such a pair c,d can be found, r can be deduced, as r is the only unknown in

$$\left| d + \frac{r(c(p-1) - c(p-1)\ \mathrm{mod}\ q)}{p-1} \right| \leq \frac{1}{2}.$$

Notice also that

$$q \mid (c(p-1) - c(p-1) \bmod q).$$

Then dividing both sides by q, we get

$$\left| \frac{d}{q} - \frac{rl}{p-1} \right| \le \frac{1}{2q}.$$

To find r, just round $\frac{d}{q}$ to the closest multiple of $p-1$, denoted by $\frac{m}{p-1}$, and then compute r from

$$\frac{m}{p-1} = \frac{rl}{p-1}.$$

That is,

$$r = \frac{m}{l}.$$

4.3.4   *Variations of Quantum DLP Algorithms*

In this section, we give two variations of Shor's quantum algorithms for discrete logarithms [77]: the first one is for DLP in $\mathbb{F}_p$, the other for DLP in $\mathbb{Z}_n^*$.

Algorithm 4.10. Given g, x, p with p prime. This algorithm tries to find

$$k \equiv \log_g x \ (\bmod \ p-1),$$

such that

$$x \equiv g^k \ (\bmod \ p).$$

[1] Find a number q such that $p \le q = 2^t \le 2p$.
[2] Initialize the three quantum registers with zeroes:

$$|\Psi_0\rangle = |0\rangle |0\rangle |0\rangle.$$

[3] Perform a Hadamard transform on Reg1 and Reg2, we get

$$U_f : |\Psi_0\rangle \to |\Psi_1\rangle = \frac{1}{p-1} \sum_{a=0}^{p-2} \sum_{b=0}^{p-2} |a\rangle |b\rangle |0\rangle.$$

[4] Perform the modular exponentiations, we get

$$U_f : |\Psi_1\rangle \to |\Psi_2\rangle = \frac{1}{p-1} \sum_{a=0}^{p-2} \sum_{b=0}^{p-2} |a\rangle|b\rangle|f(a,b)\rangle$$

$$= \frac{1}{p-1} \sum_{a=0}^{p-2} \sum_{b=0}^{p-2} |a\rangle|b\rangle|g^a x^b \ (\mathrm{mod}\ p)\rangle.$$

[5] Measure Reg3, suppose we observe m satisfying $g^l \equiv m \ (\mathrm{mod}\ p)$, where $0 \le l \le p-2$, and the states collapse into a superposition. And $|a\rangle|b\rangle$ satisfy $g^a x^b = g^l \equiv m \ (\mathrm{mod}\ p)$, that is, $a + br \equiv l \ (\mathrm{mod}\ p-1)$, where, for fixed r, l, $p-1$ and any given b, there exists only one k_b such that $a = l - br - k_b(p-1)$. Now Reg1 and Reg2 are in the states $|\Psi_3\rangle$

$$|\Psi_3\rangle = \frac{1}{\sqrt{p-1}} \sum_{b=0}^{p-2} |l - br - k_b(p-1)\rangle|b\rangle.$$

[6] Perform QFT on Reg1, 2, we get

$$\mathrm{QFT} : |\Psi_3\rangle \to |\Psi_4\rangle = \frac{1}{q\sqrt{p-1}} \sum_{b=0}^{p-2} \sum_{\mu=0}^{q-1} \sum_{\nu=0}^{q-1} e^{\frac{2\pi i(l-br-k_b(p-1))\mu}{q}} e^{\frac{2\pi i b\nu}{q}} |\mu, \nu\rangle$$

$$= \frac{1}{q\sqrt{p-1}} \sum_{b=0}^{p-2} \sum_{\mu=0}^{q-1} \sum_{\nu=0}^{q-1} w_q^{(\nu-\mu r)b + l\mu - k_b(p-1)\mu} |\mu, \nu\rangle$$

$$= \frac{1}{q\sqrt{p-1}} \sum_{\nu \equiv \mu r \ \mathrm{mod}\ (p-1)} \sum_{b=0}^{p-2} w_q^{(\nu-\mu r)b} w_q^{l\mu} |\mu, \nu\rangle$$

$$= \frac{\sqrt{p-1}}{q} \sum_{\mu=0}^{q-1} w_q^{l\mu} |\mu, \mu r\rangle,$$

where $w_q = e^{\frac{2\pi i}{q}}$.

[7] Measure Reg1 and Reg2, we get $(\mu, \mu r)$. By the previous steps, we know $k \equiv \mu^{-1}(\mu r) \ (\mathrm{mod}\ (p-1))$.

Example 4.12. Let $g = 4, p = 13, x = 10$. We try to find

$$k \equiv \log_g 10 \ (\mathrm{mod}\ 12),$$

such that

$$10 \equiv 4^k \ (\mathrm{mod}\ 13).$$

[1] Find a number q such that $13 \leq q = 2^4 = 16 < 2 \cdot 13$.

[2] Initialize the three quantum registers with zeroes:

$$|\Psi_0\rangle = |0,0,0\rangle.$$

[3] Perform a Hadamard transform on Reg1 and Reg2, we get

$$H : |\Psi_0\rangle \rightarrow |\Psi_1\rangle = \frac{1}{p-1} \sum_{a=0}^{p-2} \sum_{b=0}^{p-2} |a\rangle|b\rangle|0\rangle$$

$$= \frac{1}{12} \sum_{a=0}^{11} \sum_{b=0}^{11} |a\rangle|b\rangle|0\rangle.$$

[4] Perform the modular exponentiations, we get

$$U_f : |\Psi_1\rangle \rightarrow |\Psi_2\rangle = \frac{1}{12} \sum_{a=0}^{11} \sum_{b=0}^{11} |a\rangle|b\rangle|4^a \cdot 10^b \ (\text{mod } 13)\rangle.$$

The relationship between $4^a \cdot 10^b$ (mod 13) and a, b, shown in the following table:

a\b	0	1	2	3	4	5	6	7	8	9	10	11
0	1	10	9	12	3	4	1	10	9	12	3	4
1	4	1	10	9	12	3	4	1	10	9	12	3
2	3	4	1	10	9	12	3	4	1	10	9	12
3	12	3	4	1	10	9	12	3	4	1	10	9
4	9	12	3	4	1	10	9	12	3	4	1	10
5	10	9	12	3	4	1	10	9	12	3	4	1
6	1	10	9	12	3	4	1	10	9	12	3	4
7	4	1	10	9	12	3	4	1	10	9	12	3
8	3	4	1	10	9	12	3	4	1	10	9	12
9	12	3	4	1	10	9	12	3	4	1	10	9
10	9	12	3	4	1	10	9	12	3	4	1	10
11	10	9	12	3	4	1	10	9	12	3	4	1

[5] Measure Reg3, suppose we observe 4 satisfying $4^l \equiv 4$ (mod 13), where $0 \leq l \leq 11$. Now Reg1 and Reg2 are in the states

$$\frac{1}{\sqrt{12}} (|0\rangle|5\rangle + |0\rangle|11\rangle + |1\rangle|0\rangle + |1\rangle|6\rangle + |2\rangle|1\rangle + |2\rangle|7\rangle + |3\rangle|2\rangle + |3\rangle|8\rangle +$$

$$|4\rangle|3\rangle + |4\rangle|9\rangle + |5\rangle|4\rangle + |5\rangle|10\rangle + |6\rangle|5\rangle + |6\rangle|11\rangle + |7\rangle|0\rangle + |7\rangle|6\rangle +$$

$$|8\rangle|1\rangle + |8\rangle|7\rangle + |9\rangle|2\rangle + |9\rangle|8\rangle + |10\rangle|3\rangle + |10\rangle|9\rangle + |11\rangle|4\rangle + |11\rangle|10\rangle).$$

[6] Perform QFT on Reg1 and Reg2, we get

$$\frac{\sqrt{12}}{16} \sum_{\mu=0}^{15} w_{16}^{3\mu} |\mu, \mu r\rangle$$

$$= \frac{\sqrt{12}}{16} (|0\rangle|0\rangle + |1\rangle|5\rangle + |2\rangle|10\rangle + |3\rangle|15\rangle + |4\rangle|4\rangle + |5\rangle|1\rangle +$$

$$|6\rangle|6\rangle + |7\rangle|11\rangle + |8\rangle|4\rangle + |9\rangle|9\rangle + |10\rangle|2\rangle + |11\rangle|7\rangle + |12\rangle|0\rangle +$$

$$|13\rangle|5\rangle + |14\rangle|10\rangle + |15\rangle|3\rangle).$$

where $w_{16} = e^{\frac{2\pi i}{16}}$.

[7] Measure Reg1 and Reg2, we get $(13, 5)$, thus $r \equiv 13^{-1} \cdot 5 \pmod{12} \equiv 5$.

Now we change the discrete logarithms in $\mathbb{F}_p$ to that in $\mathbb{Z}_n^*$.

Algorithm 4.11. Given $C = \langle g \rangle = \mathbb{Z}_n^*$, $y \in C$, $n \in Z^+$. This algorithm tries to find

$$k \equiv \log_g y \pmod{n},$$

such that

$$y \equiv g^k \pmod{n}.$$

[1] Let N be the order of group C.

[2] Initialize the three quantum registers with zeroes:

$$|\Psi_0\rangle = |0^s, 0^s, 0^t\rangle,$$

where $s = \lfloor \log N \rfloor + 1$, $t = \lfloor \log n \rfloor + 1$.

[3] Perform a Hadamard transform on Reg1 and Reg2, we get

$$U_f : |\Psi_0\rangle \to |\Psi_1\rangle = \frac{1}{N} \sum_{a=0}^{N-1} \sum_{b=0}^{N-1} |a\rangle|b\rangle|0\rangle.$$

[4] Perform the modular exponentiations, we get

$$U_f : |\Psi_1\rangle \to |\Psi_2\rangle = \frac{1}{N} \sum_{a=0}^{N-1} \sum_{b=0}^{N-1} |a\rangle|b\rangle|f(a,b)\rangle$$

$$= \frac{1}{N} \sum_{a=0}^{N-1} \sum_{b=0}^{N-1} |a\rangle|b\rangle|g^a y^b \pmod{n}\rangle.$$

[5] Measure Reg3, we will observe m satisfying $g^l \equiv m \pmod{n}$, where $0 \leq l \leq N - 1$, and the state will collapse into a superposition. And $|a\rangle|b\rangle$ satisfy $g^a y^b = g^l \equiv m \pmod{n}$, that is, $a + bx \equiv l \pmod{N}$, where, for fixed x, l, N and any given b, there exists only one k_b such that $a = l - bx - k_b N$. Now Reg1 and Reg2 are in the state $|\Psi_3\rangle$

$$|\Psi_3\rangle = \frac{1}{\sqrt{N}} \sum_{b=0}^{N-1} |l - bx - k_b N\rangle|b\rangle.$$

[6] Perform QFT on Reg1, 2, we get

$$QFT : |\Psi_3\rangle \to |\Psi_4\rangle = \frac{1}{N\sqrt{N}} \sum_{b=0}^{N-1}\sum_{\mu=0}^{N-1}\sum_{v=0}^{N-1} e^{\frac{2\pi i(l-bx-k_b N)\mu}{N}} e^{\frac{2\pi i bv}{N}} |\mu, v\rangle$$

$$= \frac{1}{N\sqrt{N}} \sum_{b=0}^{N-1}\sum_{\mu=0}^{N-1}\sum_{v=0}^{N-1} w_N^{(v-\mu x)b+l\mu-k_b N\mu} |\mu, v\rangle$$

$$= \frac{1}{N\sqrt{N}} \sum_{v \equiv \mu x \bmod N}\sum_{b=0}^{N-1} w_N^{(v-\mu x)b} w_N^{l\mu} |\mu, v\rangle$$

$$= \frac{1}{\sqrt{N}} \sum_{\mu=0}^{N-1} w_N^{l\mu} |\mu, \mu x\rangle,$$

where $w = e^{\frac{2\pi i}{N}}$.

[7] Measure Reg1 and Reg2, we get $(\mu, \mu x)$. By the previous step, we know $x \equiv \mu^{-1}(\mu x) \pmod{N}$.

Each step of above algorithm may be best illustrated by the following example.

Example 4.13. Let $C = \langle g = 105\rangle, y = 144, n = 221$.

[1] Compute the order of C: $N = |C| = 16$.

[2] Initialize the three quantum registers with zeroes:

$$|\Psi_0\rangle = |0, 0, 0\rangle.$$

[3] Perform a Hadamard transform on Reg1 and Reg2, we get

$$H : |\Psi_0\rangle \to |\Psi_1\rangle = \frac{1}{16} \sum_{a=0}^{15}\sum_{b=0}^{15} |a\rangle|b\rangle|0\rangle.$$

[4] Perform the modular exponentiations, we get

$$U_f : |\Psi_1\rangle \to |\Psi_2\rangle = \frac{1}{16} \sum_{a=0}^{15}\sum_{b=0}^{15} |a\rangle|b\rangle|105^a \cdot 144^b \pmod{221}\rangle.$$

The relationship between $105^a \cdot 144^b \pmod{221}$ and a, b, shown in the following table:

a \ b	0	1	2	3	4	5	6	7	8	9	10	11	12	13	14	15
0	1	144	183	53	118	196	157	66	1	144	183	53	118	196	157	66
1	105	92	209	40	14	27	131	79	105	92	209	40	14	27	131	79
2	196	157	66	1	144	183	53	118	196	157	66	1	144	183	53	118
3	27	131	79	105	92	209	40	14	27	131	79	105	92	209	40	14
4	183	53	118	196	157	66	1	144	183	53	118	196	157	66	1	144
5	209	40	14	27	131	79	105	92	209	40	14	27	131	79	105	92
6	66	1	144	183	53	118	196	157	66	1	144	183	53	118	196	157
7	79	105	92	209	40	14	27	131	79	105	92	209	40	14	27	131
8	118	196	157	66	1	144	183	53	118	196	157	66	1	144	183	53
9	14	27	131	79	105	92	209	40	14	27	131	79	105	92	209	40
10	144	183	53	118	196	157	66	1	144	183	53	118	196	157	66	1
11	92	209	118	14	27	131	79	105	92	209	118	14	27	131	79	105
12	157	66	1	144	183	53	118	196	157	66	1	144	183	53	118	196
13	131	79	105	92	209	40	14	27	131	79	105	92	209	40	14	27
14	53	118	196	157	66	1	144	183	53	118	196	157	66	1	144	183
15	40	14	27	131	79	105	92	209	40	14	27	131	79	105	92	209

[5] Measure Reg3, we will observe 27 satisfying $27 \equiv 105^3 \pmod{221}$. Now Reg1 and Reg2 are in the states as follows:

$$\frac{1}{\sqrt{16}}(|1\rangle|5\rangle + |1\rangle|3\rangle + |3\rangle|0\rangle + |3\rangle|8\rangle + |5\rangle|3\rangle + |5\rangle|11\rangle + |7\rangle|6\rangle +$$

$$|7\rangle|14\rangle + |9\rangle|1\rangle + |9\rangle|9\rangle + |11\rangle|4\rangle + |11\rangle|12\rangle + |13\rangle|7\rangle +$$

$$|13\rangle|15\rangle + |15\rangle|2\rangle + |15\rangle|10\rangle))$$

[6] Perform QFT on Reg1 and Reg2, we get

$$\frac{1}{\sqrt{16}} \sum_{\mu=0}^{15} w_{16}^{3\mu} |\mu, \mu x\rangle,$$

the following states:

$|0\rangle|0\rangle, |1\rangle|10\rangle, |2\rangle|4\rangle, |3\rangle|14\rangle, |4\rangle|8\rangle, |5\rangle|2\rangle, |6\rangle|12\rangle, |7\rangle|6\rangle, |8\rangle|0\rangle,$

$|9\rangle|10\rangle, |10\rangle|4\rangle, |11\rangle|14\rangle, |12\rangle|8\rangle, |13\rangle|2\rangle, |14\rangle|12\rangle, |15\rangle|6\rangle$

can be observed. Suppose the states $|9\rangle|10\rangle$ are observe. Then by computing

$$10 \equiv 9x \pmod{16},$$

we get $x = 10$.

Problems for Section 4.3

1. Show that the computational complexity of Algorithm 4.9 for solving DLP over $\mathbb{Z}_p^*$ is $\mathcal{O}((\log p)^{2+\epsilon})$, where $\log p$ is the number of bits of p.
2. The complexity of Algorithm 4.9 is currently in $\mathcal{BQP}$. Can this algorithm be improved to be in $\mathcal{QP}$? This is, can the randomness be removed from Algorithm 4.9?
3. In the general quantum DLP algorithm, the value of q is chosen to be in the range $p \leq q \leq 2p$. Can this value of q be reduced to a small number, so that the algorithm could be easy to implement on a small quantum computer?
4. Pollard's ρ and λ methods for DLP is very well suited for parallel computation, and in fact there are some novel parallel versions of the ρ and λ methods for DLP. Can the ρ and/or λ methods for DLP be implemented on a quantum computer? If so, develop a quantum version of the ρ or λ methods for DLP.
5. The NFS (Number Field Sieve) is currently the fastest method for solving DLP in $\mathbb{Z}_p^*$. Develop, if possible, a quantum version of the NFS for DLP.
6. The IFP and DLP can be generated to the HSP (Hidden Subgroup Problem). Let G be an Abelian group. We say that $f : G \to S$ (taking values in some set S) hides the subgroup $H \leq G$ if

$$f(x) = f(y) \Longleftrightarrow x - y \in H.$$

The Abelian HSP asks that given a device that computes f, find a generating set for H. Give a quantum algorithm to solve the more general HSP problem.

4.4 Chapter Notes and Further Reading

Logarithms were invented by the Scottish mathematician John Napier (1550–1617). Basically, logarithm is the inverse of the mathematical operation exponentiation. We say k is the logarithm of y to the base x, denoted by $k = \log_x y$, if $y = x^k$, where $x, y, k \in \mathbb{R}$. The Logarithm Problem (LP) is to find k given x, y. Apparently, it is an easy problem, that is,

$$\text{LP}: \{x, y = x^k\} \xrightarrow{\text{easy}} \{k\},$$

as we can always solve the problem by using the following formulas:

$$\log_x y = \frac{\ln y}{\ln x}$$

and

$$\ln x = \sum_{i=1}^{\infty}(-1)^{i+1}\frac{(x-1)^i}{i}.$$

For example,

$$\log_2 5 = \frac{\ln 5}{\ln 2} \approx \frac{1.609437912}{0.692147106} \approx 2.321928095.$$

The situation is, however, completely different from that of Discrete Logarithm Problem (DLP), say, e.g., over $\mathbb{Z}_p^*$ rather than over $\mathbb{R}$. Just the same as IFP, DLP is also an intractable computational number-theoretic problem and can be utilized to construct various public-key cryptosystems and protocols. There are many classical methods for solving DLP, say, e.g.,

1. Baby-step giant-step,
2. Pollard's ρ method,
3. Pollard's λ method,
4. Pohlig-Hellman method,
5. Index calculus (e.g., NFS),
6. Xedni calculus,
7. Function Field Sieve (FFS).

It is interesting to note that for both IFP and DLP, no efficient algorithms are known for non-quantum computers, but efficient quantum algorithms are known. Moreover, algorithms from one problem are often adapted to the other, making IFP and DLP twin sister problems. In this chapter, we have introduced some of the most popular attacks on the DLP problem, and some of the most widely used DLP-based cryptographic systems and protocols that are unbreakable by all classical attacks in polynomial-time. As mentioned, quantum computers can solve the DLP problem and break DLP-based cryptographic systems in polynomial-time, so in the last section of this chapter, quantum attacks on DLP and DLP-based cryptography are discussed and analyzed.

The Baby-Step and Giant-Step method for DLP was originally proposed by Shanks in 1971 [59]. Pohlig-hellman method for DLP was proposed in [47]. The ρ and λ methods for DLP were proposed by Pollard in [49]. The currently most powerful method, the index calculus, for DLP was discussed in many references such as [1, 25, 26, 56]. The Function Field Sieve is based on the algebraic function field which is just an analog of the number field. Same as NFS, FFS can be used for solving both IFP and DLP. Incidentally, FFS is more suitable for solving the discrete logarithm problem in finite fields of small characteristic. For more information on FFS, particularly for the recent progress in DLP in finite fields of small characteristic, see [3, 4, 6, 24, 31–33].

For general references on DLP and methods for solving DLP, readers are suggested to consult: [2, 5, 11, 14–16, 21, 27, 30, 35–37, 40, 41, 45, 46, 50–52, 54, 57, 65, 73, 75, 76].

DLP-based cryptography also forms an important class of cryptography, including cryptographic protocols and digital signatures. In the public literatures, the first public-key system, namely, the key-exchange scheme, was proposed by Diffie and Hellman in 1976 in [18], based on an idea of Merkle [42] (although published later). The first DLP-based cryptographic system and digital signature scheme were proposed by ElGamal in 1985 [21]. For general references on DLP-based cryptographic systems and digital signature schemes, readers are suggested to consult [1, 7–10, 12, 13, 17, 19, 20, 22, 23, 28, 29, 34, 38, 41, 43, 44, 47, 53, 55, 58, 66–73, 76].

The quantum algorithm for DLP was first proposed in 1994 by Shor [60] (see Shor's other papers [61–64] for more information).

References

1. L.M. Adleman, A subexponential algorithm for the discrete logarithm problem with applications to cryptography, in *Proceedings of the 20th Annual IEEE Symposium on Foundations of Computer Science* (IEEE Press, New York, 1979), pp. 55–60
2. L.M. Adleman, Algorithmic number theory—the complexity contribution, in *Proceedings of the 35th Annual IEEE Symposium on Foundations of Computer Science* (IEEE Press, New York, 1994), pp. 88–113
3. L.M. Adleman, The function field Sieve, in *Algorithmic Number Theory (ANTS I)*. Lecture Notes in Computer Science, vol. 877 (Springer, Berlin, 1994), pp. 108–121
4. L.M. Adleman, M.D.A. Huang, Function field sieve method for discrete logarithms over finite fields. Inform. Comput. **151**(1–2), 5–16 (1999)
5. S. Bai, R.P. Brent, On the efficiency of Pollard's Rho method for discrete logarithms, in *Proceedings of Fourteenth Computing: The Australasian Theory Symposium*, Wollongong, 22–25 January 2008, pp. 125–131, ed. by J. Harland, P. Manyem
6. R. Barbulescu, P. Gaudry, A. Joux, E. Thome, Heuristic quasi-polynomial algorithm for discrete logarithm in finite fields of small characteristic, in *Advances in Cryptology – EUROCRYPT 2014*. Lecture Notes in Computer Science, vol. 8441 (Springer, Berlin, 2014), pp. 1–16
7. T.H. Barr, *Invitation to Cryptology* (Prentice-Hall, Upper Saddle River, 2002)
8. F.L. Bauer, *Decrypted Secrets: Methods and Maxims of Cryptology*, 3rd edn. (Springer, Berlin, 2002)
9. D. Bishop, *Introduction to Cryptography with Java Applets* (Jones and Bartlett, Boston, 2003)
10. J.A. Buchmann, *Introduction to Cryptography*, 2nd edn. (Springer, New York, 2004)
11. J.A. Buchmann, D. Weber, Discrete logarithms: recent progress, in *Proceedings of an International Conference on Coding Theory, Cryptography and Related Areas*, ed. by J. Buchmann, T. Hoeholdt et al. (Springer, New York, 2000), pp. 42–56
12. CACAM, The digital signature standard proposed by NIST and responses to NIST's proposal. Commun. ACM **35**(7), 36–54 (1992)
13. W.L. Chang, S.C. Huang, K.W. Lin, M.S.H. Ho, Fast parallel dna-based algorithm for molecular computation: discrete logarithms. J. Supercomput. **56**(2), 129–163 (2011)

14. H. Cohen, *A Course in Computational Algebraic Number Theory*. Graduate Texts in Mathematics, vol. 138 (Springer, Heidelberg, 1993)
15. H. Cohen, G. Frey, *Handbook of Elliptic and Hyperelliptic Curve Cryptography* (CRC Press, Boca Raton, 2006)
16. R. Crandall, C. Pomerance, *Prime Numbers: A Computational Perspective*, 2nd edn. (Springer, New York, 2005)
17. W. Diffie, The first ten years of public-key cryptography. Proc. IEEE **76**(5), 560–577 (1988)
18. W. Diffie, M.E. Hellman, New directions in cryptography. IEEE Trans. Inform. Theory **22**(5), 644–654 (1976)
19. W. Diffie, M.E. Hellman, Privacy and authentication: an introduction to cryptography. Proc. IEEE **67**(3), 397–427 (1979)
20. A.J. Elbirt, *Understanding and Applying Cryptography and Data Security* (CRC Press, Boca Raton, 2009)
21. T. ElGamal, A public-key cryptosystem and a signature scheme based on discrete logarithms, in *Advances in Cryptology – Crypto 1984*. Lecture Notes in Computer Science, vol. 196 (Springer, Berlin, 1985), pp. 10–18
22. T. ElGamal, A subexponential-time algorithm for computing discrete logarithms over GF(p^2). IEEE Trans. Inform. Theory **31**(4), 473–481 (1985)
23. B.A. Forouzan, *Cryptography and Network Security* (McGraw-Hill, New York, 2008)
24. F. Gologlu, R. Granger, G. McGuire et al., On the function field Sieve and the impact of higher splitting probabilities: application to discrete logarithms in $\mathbb{F}_{2^{1971}}$ and $\mathbb{F}_{2^{3164}}$ in cryptology, Part II, in *Advances in Cryptology – CRYPTO 2013*. Lecture Notes in Computer Science, vol. 8043 (Springer, Heidelberg, 2014), pp. 109–128
25. D.M. Gordon, Discrete logarithms in GF(p) using the number field Sieve. SIAM J. Discret. Math. **6**(1), 124–138 (1993)
26. D.M. Gordon, K.S. McCurley, Massively parallel computation of discrete logarithms, in *Advances in Cryptology – Crypto 1992*. Lecture Notes in Computer Science, vol. 740 (Springer, New York, 1992), pp. 312–323
27. T. Hayashi, N. Shinohara, L. Wang et al., Solving a 676-Bit discrete logarithm problem in GF(3^{6n}), in *Public Key Cryptography – PKC 2010*. Lecture Notes in Computer Science, vol. 6056 (Springer, Berlin, 2010), pp. 351–367
28. M.E. Hellman, An overview of public-key cryptography. IEEE Commun. Mag. **5**, 42–49 (1976) [50th Anniversary Commemorative Issue]
29. J. Hoffstein, J. Pipher, J.H. Silverman, *An Introduction to Mathematical Cryptography* (Springer, New York, 2008)
30. M.D. Huang, W. Raskind, Signature calculus and discrete logarithm problems, in *Algorithmic Number Theory 2006*. Lecture Notes in Computer Science, vol. 4076 (Springer, Berlin, 2006), pp. 558–572
31. A. Joux, Faster index calculus for the medium prime case application to 1175-Bit and 1425-Bit finite fields, in *Advances in Cryptology – EUROCRYPT 2013*. Lecture Notes in Computer Science, vol. 7881 (Springer, Heidelberg, 2013), pp. 177–193
32. A. Joux, A new index calculus algorithm with complexity $L(1/4+o(1))$ in small characteristic, in *Selected Areas in Cryptography – SAC 2013*. Lecture Notes in Computer Science, vol. 8282 (Springer, Berlin, 2014), pp. 355–379
33. A. Joux, R. Lercier, The function field sieve in the medium prime case, in *Advances in Cryptology – EUROCRYPT 2006*. Lecture Notes in Computer Science, vol. 4004 (Springer, Berlin, 2006), pp. 254–270
34. J. Katz, Y. Lindell, *Introduction to Modern Cryptography* (CRC Press, Boca Raton, 2008)
35. N. Koblitz, *A Course in Number Theory and Cryptography*, 2nd edn. Graduate Texts in Mathematics, vol. 114 (Springer, New York, 1994)
36. N. Koblitz, *Algebraic Aspects of Cryptography*. Algorithms and Computation in Mathematics, vol. 3 (Springer, New York, 1998)
37. M.T. Lacey, *Cryptography, Cards, and Kangaroos* (Georgia Institute of Technology, Atlanta, 2008)

38. W. Mao, *Modern Cryptography* (Prentice-Hall, Upper Saddle River, 2004)
39. J.L. Massey, J.K. Omura, Method and apparatus for maintaining the privacy of digital message conveyed by public transmission, US Patent No 4677600, 28 Jan 1986
40. K.S. McCurley, The discrete logarithm problem, in *Cryptology and Computational Number Theory*, ed. by C. Pomerance. Proceedings of Symposia in Applied Mathematics, vol. 42 (American Mathematics Society, Providence, 1990), pp. 49–74
41. A. Menezes, P.C. van Oorschot, S.A. Vanstone, *Handbook of Applied Cryptosystems* (CRC Press, Boca Raton, 1996)
42. R.C. Merkle, Secure communications over insecure channels. Commun. ACM **21**(4), 294–299 (1978)
43. R.A. Mollin, *An Introduction to Cryptography*, 2nd edn. (Chapman & Hall/CRC Press, Boca Raton, 2006)
44. R. Motwani, P. Raghavan, *Randomized Algorithms* (Cambridge University Press, Cambridge, 1995)
45. A.M. Odlyzko, Discrete logarithms in finite fields and their cryptographic significance, in *Advances in Cryptography – EUROCRYPT 1984*. Lecture Notes in Computer Science, vol. 209 (Springer, Berlin, 1984), pp. 225–314
46. A.M. Odlyzko, Discrete logarithms: the past and the future. Des. Codes Crypt. **19**(2), 129–145 (2000)
47. S.C. Pohlig, M.E. Hellman, An improved algorithm for computing logarithms over GF(p) and its cryptographic significance. IEEE Trans. Inform. Theory **24**(1), 106–110 (1978)
48. J.M. Pollard, A Monte Carlo method for factorization. BIT **15**(3), 331–332 (1975)
49. J.M. Pollard, Monte Carlo methods for index computation (mod p). Math. Comput. **32**(143), 918–924 (1980)
50. J.M. Pollard, Kangaroos, monopoly and discrete logarithms. J. Cryptol. **13**(4), 437–447 (2000)
51. J.M. Pollard, Kruskal's card trick. Math. Gaz. **84**(500), 265–267 (2000)
52. C. Pomerance, Elementary thoughts on discrete logarithms, in *Algorithmic Number Theory*, ed. by J.P. Buhler, P. Stevenhagen (Cambridge University Press, Cambridge, 2008), pp. 385–395
53. M. Rabin, Digitalized signatures and public-key functions as intractable as factorization. Technical Report MIT/LCS/TR-212, MIT Laboratory for Computer Science (1979)
54. H. Riesel, *Prime Numbers and Computer Methods for Factorization* (Birkhäuser, Boston, 1990)
55. J. Rothe, *Complexity Theory and Cryptography* (Springer, Berlin, 2005)
56. O. Schirokauer, D. Weber, T. Denny, Discrete logarithms: the effectiveness of the index calculus method, in *Algorithmic Number Theory (ANTS-II)*. Lecture Notes in Computer Science, vol. 1122 (Springer, Berlin, 1996), pp. 337–362
57. O. Schirokauere, The impact of the number field sieve on the discrete logarithm problem in finite fields, in *Algorithmic Number Theory*, ed. by J.P. Buhler, P. Stevenhagen (Cambridge University Press, Cambridge, 2008), pp. 421–446
58. B. Schneier, *Applied Cryptography: Protocols, Algorithms, and Source Code in C*, 2nd edn. (Wiley, New York, 1996)
59. D. Shanks, Class number, a theory of factorization and Genera, in *Proceedings of Symposium of Pure Mathematics*, vol. 20 (American Mathematical Society, Providence, 1971), pp. 415–440
60. P. Shor, Algorithms for quantum computation: discrete logarithms and factoring, in *Proceedings of the 35th Annual Symposium on Foundations of Computer Science*, Santa Fe (IEEE Computer Society Press, New York, 1994), pp. 124–134
61. P. Shor, Polynomial-time algorithms for prime factorization and discrete logarithms on a quantum computer. SIAM J. Comput. **26**(5), 1484–1509 (1997)
62. P. Shor, Quantum computing. Doc. Math. Extra Volume ICM I, 467–486 (1998)
63. P. Shor, Polynomial-time algorithms for prime factorization and discrete logarithms on a quantum computer. SIAM Rev. **41**(2), 303–332 (1999)
64. P. Shor, Introduction to quantum algorithms. AMS Proc. Symp. Appl. Math. **58**, 143–159 (2002)

65. V. Shoup, *A Computational Introduction to Number Theory and Algebra* (Cambridge University Press, Cambridge, 2005)
66. N. Smart, *Cryptography: An Introduction* (McGraw-Hill, New York, 2003)
67. M. Stamp, R.M. Low, *Applied Cryptanalysis* (Wiley, New York, 2007)
68. A. Stanoyevitch, *Introduction to Cryptography* (CRC Press, Boca Raton, 2011)
69. D.R. Stinson, *Cryptography: Theory and Practice*, 3rd edn. (Chapman & Hall/CRC Press, Boca Raton, 2006)
70. C. Swenson, *Modern Cryptanalysis* (Wiley, New York, 2008)
71. W. Trappe, L. Washington, *Introduction to Cryptography with Coding Theory*, 2nd edn. (Prentice-Hall, Upper Saddle River, 2006)
72. H.C.A. van Tilborg, *Fundamentals of Cryptography* (Kluwer, Boston, 1999)
73. S.S. Wagstaff Jr., *Cryptanalysis of Number Theoretic Ciphers* (Chapman & Hall/CRC Press, Boca Raton, 2002)
74. D. Weber, T.F. Denny, The solution of McCurley's discrete log challenge, *Advances in Cryptology - CRYPTO 1998*. Lecture Notes in Computer Science, vol. 1462 (Springer, Berlin, 1998), pp. 458–471
75. S.Y. Yan, Computing prime factorization and discrete logarithms: from index calculus to Xedni calculus. Int. J. Comput. Math. **80**(5), 573–590 (2003)
76. S.Y. Yan, *Primality Testing and Integer Factorization in Public-Key Cryptography*, 2nd edn. Advances in Information Security, vol. 11 (Springer, New York, 2009)
77. S.Y. Yan, Y.H. Wang, *New Quantum Algorithms for Discrete Logarithm Problem* (Computer School, Wuhan University, Wuhan, 2015)

Chapter 5
Quantum Computing for Elliptic Curve Discrete Logarithms

The best way to predict the future is to invent it.

ALAN KAY
The 2003 Turing Award Recipient

In this chapter we shall first discuss the Elliptic Curve Discrete Logarithm Problem (ECDLP) and the classical solutions to ECDLP, then we shall present some quantum algorithms for solving the ECDLP problem and for attacking the ECDLP-based cryptography.

5.1 Classical Algorithms for Elliptic Curve Discrete Logarithms

5.1.1 Basic Concepts

The Elliptic Curve Discrete Logarithm Problem (ECDLP): Let E be an elliptic curve over the finite field $\mathbb{F}_p$, say, given by a Weierstrass equation

$$E : y^2 \equiv x^3 + ax + b \ (\mathrm{mod}\ p),$$

S and T the two points in the elliptic curve group $E(\mathbb{F}_p)$. Then the ECDLP is to find the integer k (assuming that such an integer k exists)

$$k = \log_T S \in \mathbb{Z}, \quad \text{or} \quad k \equiv \log_T S \ (\mathrm{mod}\ p)$$

such that

$$S = kT \in E(\mathbb{F}_p), \quad \text{or} \quad S \equiv kT \ (\mathrm{mod}\ p).$$

The ECDLP is a more difficult problem than the DLP, on which the Elliptic Curve Digital Signature Algorithm (ECDSA) is based on. Clearly, the ECDLP is the generalization of DLP, which extends the multiplicative group $\mathbb{F}_p^*$ to the elliptic curve group $E(\mathbb{F}_p)$.

5.1.2   Pohlig-Hellman Algorithm for ECDLP

The ECDLP problem is little bit more difficult than the DLP problem, on which the Elliptic Curve Digital Signature Algorithm/Elliptic Curve Digital Signature Standard (ECDSA/ECDSS) [27] is based. As ECDLP is the generalization of DLP, which extends, e.g., the multiplicative group $\mathbb{F}_p^*$ to the elliptic curve group $E(\mathbb{F}_p)$, many methods for DLP, even for IFP, can be extended to ECDLP, for example, the Baby-Step Giant-Step for DLP, Pollard's ρ and λ methods for IFP and DLP; Silver-Pohlig-Hellman method for DLP, can also be naturally extended to ECDLP. In what follows, we present an example of solving ECDLP by an analog of Silver-Pohlig-Hellman method for elliptic curves over $\mathbb{F}_p^*$.

Example 5.1. Let

$$Q \equiv kP \text{ (mod 1009)},$$

where

$$\begin{cases} E : \ y^2 \equiv x^3 + 71x + 602 \text{ (mod 1009)} \\ P = (1, 237) \\ Q = (190, 271) \\ \text{order}(E(\mathbb{F}_{1009})) = 1060 = 2^2 \cdot 5 \cdot 53 \\ \text{order}(P) = 530 = 2 \cdot 5 \cdot 53. \end{cases}$$

Find k. The detailed solution may be as follows.

[1] Find the individual logarithm modulo 2: as $(530/2) = 265$, we have

$$\begin{cases} P_2 = 265P = (50, 0) \\ Q_2 = 265Q = (50, 0) \\ Q_2 = P_2 \\ k \equiv 1 \text{ (mod 2)}. \end{cases}$$

[2] Find the individual logarithm modulo 5: as $530/5 = 106$, we have

$$\begin{cases} P_5 = 106P = (639, 160) \\ Q_5 = 106Q = (639, 849) \\ Q_5 = -P_5 \\ k \equiv 4 \ (\text{mod } 5). \end{cases}$$

[3] Find the individual logarithm modulo 53: as $530/53 = 10$, we have

$$\begin{cases} P_{53} = 10P = (32, 737) \\ Q_{53} = 10Q = (592, 97) \\ Q_{53} = 48P_{53} \\ k \equiv 48 \ (\text{mod } 53). \end{cases}$$

[4] Use the Chinese Remainder Theorem to combine the individual logarithms to get the final logarithm:

$$\text{CHREM}([1, 4, 48], [2, 5, 53]) = 419.$$

That is,

$$(190, 271) = 419(1, 237) \ (\text{mod } 1009),$$

or alternatively,

$$(190, 271) \equiv \underbrace{(1, 237) + \cdots + (1, 237)}_{419 \text{ summands}} \ (\text{mod } 1009).$$

5.1.3 Baby-Step Giant-Step Algorithm for ECDLP

The Shanks Baby-Step Giant-Step for DLP can be easily extended for ECDLP. To find k in $Q = kP$, the idea is to compute and store a list of points iP for $1 \leq i \leq m$ (Baby-Steps), then compute $Q - jmP$ (Giant-Steps) and try to find a match in the stored list. The algorithm may be described as follows.

Algorithm 5.1 (Baby-Step Giant-Step for ECDLP). Let E be an elliptic curve over $\mathbb{Z}_p$, $P, Q \in E(\mathbb{Z}_p)$. This algorithm tries to find k in $Q \equiv kP \ (\text{mod } p)$.

[1] Set $m = \lfloor p \rfloor$.
[2] For i from 1 to m, compute and store iP.
[3] For j from 1 to $m - 1$, compute $Q - jmP$ and check this against the list stored in Step [2].

[4] If a match is found then $Q - jmP = iP$ and hence $Q = (i + jm)P$.
[5] Output $k \equiv i + jm \pmod{p}$.

Example 5.2 (Baby-Step Giant-Step for ECDLP). Let $E\backslash \mathbb{F}_{719} :\ y^2 \equiv x^3 + 231x + 508 \pmod{719}$ be an elliptic curve over $\mathbb{F}_{719}$, $|E(\mathbb{F}_{719})| = 727$, $P = (513, 30), Q = (519, 681) \in E(\mathbb{F}_{719})$. We wish to find $k\ Q \equiv kP \pmod{719}$.

[1] Set $m = \lfloor 719 \rfloor = 27$ and compute $27P = (714, 469)$.
[2] For i from 1 to m, compute and store iP:

$$
\begin{aligned}
1P &= (513, 30) \\
2P &= (210, 538) \\
3P &= (525, 236) \\
4P &= (507, 58) \\
5P &= (427, 421) \\
6P &= (543, 327) \\
&\vdots \\
24P &= (487, 606) \\
25P &= (529, 253) \\
26P &= (239, 462) \\
27P &= (714, 469).
\end{aligned}
$$

[3] For j from 1 to $m - 1$, compute $Q - jmP$ and check this against the list stored in Step [2].

$$
\begin{aligned}
Q - (0 \cdot 27)P &= (511, 681) \\
Q - (1 \cdot 27)P &= (650, 450) \\
Q - (2 \cdot 27)P &= (95, 422) \\
&\vdots \\
Q - (19 \cdot 27)P &= (620, 407) \\
Q - (20 \cdot 27)P &= (143, 655) \\
Q - (21 \cdot 27)P &= (239, 462).
\end{aligned}
$$

[4] A match is found for $27P = (714, 469)$ and $Q - (21 \cdot 27)P = (239, 462)$. Thus, $Q = (26 + 21 \cdot 27)P$.
[5] Output $k \equiv 26 + 21 \cdot 27 \equiv 593 \pmod{719}$.

5.1.4 ρ Method for ECDLP

The fastest algorithm for solving ECDLP is Pollard's ρ method. Up to date, the largest ECDLP instance solved with ρ is still the ECC_p-109, for an elliptic curve over a 109-bit prime field. Recall that the ECDLP problem asks to find $k \in [1, r-1]$ such that

$$Q = kP,$$

where r is a prime number, P is a point of order r on an elliptic curve over a finite field $\mathbb{F}_p$, $Q \in G$ and $G = \langle P \rangle$. The main idea of ρ for ECDLP is to find distinct pairs (c', d') and (c'', d'') of integers modulo r such that

$$c'P + d'Q = c''P + d''Q.$$

Then

$$(c' - c'')P = (d'' - d')Q,$$

that is,

$$Q = \frac{c' - c''}{d'' - d'}P,$$

thus,

$$k \equiv \frac{c' - c''}{d'' - d'} \pmod{r}.$$

To implement the idea, we first choose a random iteration function $f : G \to G$, then start a random initial point P_0 and compute the iterations $P_{i+1} = f(P_i)$. Since G is finite, there will be some indices $i < j$ such that $P_i = P_j$. Then

$$P_{i+1} = f(P_i) = f(P_j) = P_{j+1},$$

and in fact

$$P_{i+l} = P_{j+l}, \text{ for all } l \geq 0.$$

Therefore, the sequence of points $\{P_i\}$ is periodic with period $j - i$ (see Figure 5.1). This is why we call it the ρ method; we may also called it the λ method, as the computation paths for $c'P + d'Q$ and $c''P + d''Q$ will eventually be met and traveled along on the same road, symbolized by the Greek letter λ. If f is a randomly chosen random function, then we expect to find a match (i.e., a collision) with j at most a constant times $\sqrt{r}$. In fact, by the birthday paradox, the expected number of iterations before a *collision* is obtained is approximately $\sqrt{\pi r/2} \approx 1.2533\sqrt{r}$. To quickly detect the collision, the Floyd cycle detection trick will be used. That is, just the same as ρ for IFP and DLP, we compute pairs (P_i, P_{2i}) for $i = 1, 2, \cdots$, until a match is found. Here is the algorithm and an example [19].

Algorithm 5.2 (Pollard's ρ Algorithm for ECDLP). Given $P \in E(\mathbb{F}_p)$ of prime order r, $Q \in \langle P \rangle$, this algorithm tries to find

$$k \equiv \log_P Q \pmod{p}$$

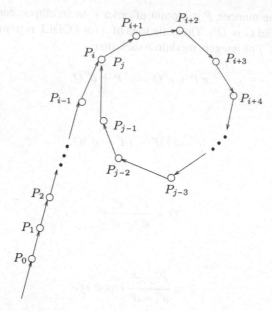

Figure 5.1 ρ for ECDLP

such that

$$Q \equiv kP \pmod{p},$$

via

$$k \equiv \frac{c' - c''}{d'' - d'} \pmod{r}.$$

[1] Initialization. Choose the number L of branches, and select a partition function $H : \langle P \rangle \to \{1, 2, \ldots, L\}$.

[2] Compute $a_i P + b_i Q$.

    for i from 1 to L do

        choose $a_i, b_i \in [0, r-1]$

        compute $R_i = a_i P + b_i Q$.

[3] Compute $c'P + d'Q$. Choose $c', d' \in [0, r-1]$, and compute $X' = c'P + d'Q$.

[4] Prepare for loop.

    Set $X'' \leftarrow X'$

    $c'' \leftarrow c'$

    $d'' \leftarrow d'$.

[5] Loop.

> Repeat
> Compute $j = H(X')$
> Set $X' \leftarrow X' + R_j$
> > $c' \leftarrow c' + a_j \bmod r$
> > $d' \leftarrow d' + b_j \bmod r$.
> for i from to 2 do
> > Compute $j = H(X'')$
> Set $X'' \leftarrow X'' + R_j$
> > $c'' \leftarrow c'' + a_j \bmod r$
> > $d'' \leftarrow d'' + b_j \bmod r$.
> Until $X' = X''$.

[6] Output and exit.

> If $d \neq d''$ then computer $k \equiv (c' - c'')(d'' - d')^{-1} \pmod{r}$.
> > otherwise return(failure), stop or startover again.

Example 5.3. Consider the elliptic curve

$$E \backslash \mathbb{F}_{229} : y^2 \equiv x^3 + x + 44 \pmod{229}.$$

The point $P = (5, 116) \in E(\mathbb{F}_{229})$ has prime order $r = 239$. Let $Q = (155, 166) \in \langle P \rangle$ (where $\langle P \rangle$ denotes the subgroup generated by the point P). We wish to find k such that

$$Q \equiv kP \pmod{229}.$$

That is,

$$k \equiv \log_P Q \pmod{229}.$$

We perform the following steps:

[1] Select the partition function $H : \langle P \rangle \to \{1, 2, 3, 4\}$ with 4 partitions:

$$H(x, y) = (x \bmod 4) = 1.$$

Let $R_i = a_i P + b_i Q$ with $i = 1, 2, 3, 4$. Then

$$(a_1, b_1, R_1) = (79, 163, (135, 117))$$
$$(a_2, b_2, R_2) = (206, 19, (96, 97))$$
$$(a_3, b_3, R_3) = (87, 109, (84, 62))$$
$$(a_4, b_4, R_4) = (219, 68, (72, 134)).$$

[2] Compute the iteration table until a mach (collision) is found.

Iteration	c'	d'	$c'P + d'Q$	c''	d''	$c''P + d''Q$
0	54	175	(39,159)	54	175	(39,159)
1	34	4	(160,9)	113	167	(130,182)
2	113	167	(130,182)	180	105	(36, 97)
3	200	37	(27,17)	0	97	(108,89)
4	180	105	(36,97)	46	40	(223,153)
5	20	29	(119,180)	232	127	(167,57)
6	0	97	(108,89)	192	24	(57,105)
7	79	21	(81,168)	139	111	(185,227)
8	46	40	(223,153)	193	0	(197,92)
9	26	108	(9,18)	140	87	(194,145)
10	232	127	(167,57)	67	120	(223,153)
11	212	195	(75,136)	14	207	(167,57)
12	192	24	**(57,105)**	213	104	**(57,105)**

[3] At the step $i = 12$, we find a match

$$192P + 24Q = 213P + 104Q = (57,105).$$

That is,

$$Q = \frac{192 - 213}{104 - 24}P \ (\text{mod } 229).$$

Thus, we have

$$k \equiv (192 - 213)(104 - 24)^{-1}$$

$$\equiv 176 \ (\text{mod } 239).$$

5.1.5 Xedni Calculus for ECDLP

The index calculus is the most powerful method for DLP in some groups including the multiplicative group $\mathbb{F}_q^*$ over a finite field, it is however generally not suitable for ECDLP as it is not for general groups. In what follows, we introduce a method, called xedni calculus for ECDLP.

The xedni calculus was first proposed by Joseph Silverman in 1998 [56], and analyzed in [25, 35, 58]. It is called *xedni calculus* because it "stands index calculus on its head". The xedni calculus is a new method that *might* be used to solve the

ECDLP, although it has not yet been tested in practice. It can be described as follows [56]:

[1] Choose points in $E(\mathbb{F}_p)$ and lift them to points in $\mathbb{Z}^2$.
[2] Choose a curve $E(\mathbb{Q})$ containing the lift points; use Mestre's method [45] (in reverse) to make rank $E(\mathbb{Q})$ small.

Whilst the index calculus works in reverse:

[1] Lift $E/\mathbb{F}_p$ to $E(\mathbb{Q})$; use Mestre's method to make rank $E(\mathbb{Q})$ large.
[2] Choose points in $E(\mathbb{F}_p)$ and try to lift them to points in $E(\mathbb{Q})$.

A brief description of the xedni algorithm is as follows (a complete description and justification of the algorithm can be found in [56]).

Algorithm 5.3 (Xedni Calculus for the ECDLP). Let $\mathbb{F}_p$ be a finite field with p elements (p prime), $E/\mathbb{F}_p$ an elliptic curve over $\mathbb{F}_p$, say, given by

$$E: \quad y^2 + a_{p,1}xy + a_{p,3}y = x^3 + a_{p,2}x^2 + a_{p,4}x + a_{p,6}.$$

N_p the number of points in $E(\mathbb{F}_p)$, S and T the two points in $E(\mathbb{F}_p)$. This algorithm tries to find an integer k

$$k = \log_T S$$

such that

$$S = kT \quad \text{in } E(\mathbb{F}_p).$$

[1] Fix an integer $4 \leq r \leq 9$ and an integer M which is a product of small primes.
[2] Choose r points:

$$P_{M,i} = [x_{M,i}, y_{M,i}, z_{M,i}], \quad 1 \leq i \leq r$$

having integer coefficients and satisfying

[2-1] the first 4 points are $[1, 0, 0]$, $[0, 1, 0]$, $[0, 0, 1]$ and $[1, 1, 1]$.
[2-2] For every prime $l \mid M$, the matrix $\mathbf{B}(P_{M,1}, \ldots, P_{M,r})$ has maximal rank modulo l.

Further choose coefficients $u_{M,1}, \ldots, u_{M,10}$ such that the points $P_{M,1}, \ldots, P_{M,r}$ satisfy the congruence:

$$u_{M,1}x^3 + u_{M,2}x^2y + u_{M,3}xy^2 + u_{M,4}y^3 + u_{M,5}x^2z + u_{M,6}xyz + u_{M,7}y^2z$$
$$+ u_{M,8}xz^2 + u_{M,9}yz^2 + u_{M,10}z^3 \equiv 0 \pmod{M}.$$

[3] Choose r random pair of integers (s_i, t_i) satisfying $1 \leq s_i, t_i < N_p$, and for each $1 \leq i \leq r$, compute the point $P_{p,i} = (x_{p,i}, y_{p,i})$ defined by

$$P_{p,i} = s_i S - t_i T \quad \text{in } E(\mathbb{F}_p).$$

[4] Make a change of variables in $\mathbb{P}^2$ of the form

$$
\begin{pmatrix} X' \\ Y' \\ Z' \end{pmatrix} = \begin{pmatrix} a_{11} & a_{12} & a_{13} \\ a_{21} & a_{22} & a_{23} \\ a_{31} & a_{32} & a_{33} \end{pmatrix} \begin{pmatrix} X \\ Y \\ Z \end{pmatrix}
$$

so that the first four points become

$$
P_{p,1} = [1,0,0], \ P_{p,2} = [0,1,0], \ P_{p,3} = [0,0,1], \ P_{p,4} = [1,1,1].
$$

The equation for E will then have the form:

$$
u_{p,1}x^3 + u_{p,2}x^2y + u_{p,3}xy^2 + u_{p,4}y^3 + u_{p,5}x^2z + u_{p,6}xyz
$$
$$
+u_{p,7}y^2z + u_{p,8}xz^2 + u_{p,9}yz^2 + u_{p,10}z^3 = 0.
$$

[5] Use the Chinese Remainder Theorem to find integers $u'_1, \ldots, u'_{10}$ satisfying

$$
u'_i \equiv u_{p,i} \pmod{p} \text{ and } u'_i \equiv u_{M,i} \pmod{M} \text{ for all } 1 \le i \le 10.
$$

[6] Lift the chosen points to $\mathbb{P}^2(\mathbb{Q})$. That is, choose points

$$
P_i = [x_i, y_i, z_i], \quad 1 \le i \le r,
$$

with integer coordinates satisfying

$$
P_i \equiv P_{p,i} \pmod{p} \text{ and } P_i \equiv P_{M,i} \pmod{M} \text{ for all } 1 \le i \le r.
$$

In particular, take $P_1 = [1,0,0], P_2 = [0,1,0], P_3 = [0,0,1], P_4 = [1,1,1].$

[7] Let $\mathbf{B} = \mathbf{B}(P_1, \ldots, P_r)$ be the matrix of cubic monomials defined earlier. Consider the system of linear equations:

$$
\mathbf{Bu} = 0. \tag{5.1}
$$

Find a small integer solution $\mathbf{u} = [u_1, \ldots, u_{10}]$ to (5.1) which has the additional property

$$
\mathbf{u} \equiv [u'_1, \ldots, u'_{10}] \pmod{M_p},
$$

where $u'_1, \ldots, u'_{10}$ are the coefficients computed in Step [5]. Let $C_{\mathbf{u}}$ denote the associated cubic curve:

$$
C_{\mathbf{u}} : u_1x^3 + u_2x^2y + u_3xy^2 + u_4y^3 + u_5x^2z + u_6xyz
$$
$$
+u_7y^2z + u_8xz^2 + u_9yz^2 + u_{10}z^3 = 0.
$$

[8] Make a change of coordinates to put $C_{\mathbf{u}}$ into standard minimal Weierstrass form with the point $P_1 = [1, 0, 0]$ the point at infinity, $\mathcal{O}$. Write the resulting equation as

$$E_{\mathbf{u}} : y^2 + a_1 xy + a_3 y = x^3 + a_2 x^2 + a_4 x + a_6 \qquad (5.2)$$

with $a_1, \ldots, a_6 \in \mathbb{Z}$, and let $Q_1, Q_2, \ldots, Q_r$ denote the images of $P_1, P_2, \ldots, P_r$ under this change of coordinates (so in particular, $Q_1 = \mathcal{O}$). Let $c_4(\mathbf{u})$, $c_6(\mathbf{u})$, and $\Delta(\mathbf{u})$ be the usual quantities in [56] associated to the Eq. (5.2).

[9] Check if the points $Q_1, Q_2, \ldots, Q_r \in E_{\mathbf{u}}(\mathbb{Q})$ are independent. If they are, return to Step [2] or [3]. Otherwise compute a relation of dependence

$$n_2 Q_2 + n_3 Q_3 + \cdots + n_r Q_r = \mathcal{O},$$

set

$$n_1 = -n_2 - n_3 - \cdots - n_r,$$

and continue with the next step.

[10] Compute

$$s = \sum_{i=1}^{r} n_i s_i \quad \text{and} \quad t = \sum_{i=1}^{r} n_i t_i.$$

If $\gcd(s, n_p) > 1$, go to Step [2] or [3]. Otherwise compute an inverse $ss' \equiv 1 \pmod{N_p}$. Then

$$\log_T S \equiv s' t \pmod{N_p},$$

and the ECDLP is solved.

As can be seen, the basic idea in the above algorithm is that we first choose points $P_1, P_2, \ldots, P_r$ in $E(\mathbb{F}_p)$ and lift them to points $Q_1, Q_2, \ldots, Q_r$ having integer coordinates, then we choose an elliptic curve $E(\mathbb{Q})$ that goes through the points $Q_1, Q_2, \ldots, Q_r$, finally, check if the points $Q_1, Q_2, \ldots, Q_r$ are *dependent*. If they are, the ECDLP is almost solved. Thus, the goal of the xedni calculus is to find an instance where an elliptic curve has *smaller* than expected rank. Unfortunately, a set of points $Q_1, Q_2, \ldots, Q_r$ as constructed above will usually be *independent*. So, it will not work. To make it work, a congruence method, due to Mestre [45], is used *in reverse* to produce the lifted curve E having smaller than expected rank.[1] Again unfortunately, Mestre's method is based on some deep ideas and unproved

---

[1]Mestre's original method is to produce elliptic curves of large rank.

Table 5.1 Algorithms for IFP, DLP and ECDLP

IFP	DLP	ECDLP
Trial divisions		
	Baby-step giant-step	Baby-step giant-step
	Pohlig-Hellman	Pohlig-Hellman
ρ	ρ	ρ
CFRAC/MPQS	Index calculus	
NFS	NFS	
Xedni calculus	Xedni calculus	Xedni calculus
Quantum algorithm	Quantum algorithms	Quantum algorithms

conjectures in analytic number theory and arithmetic algebraic geometry, it is not possible for us at present to give even a rough estimate of the running time of the algorithm. So, virtually we know nothing about the complexity of the xedni calculus. We also do not know if the xedni calculus will be practically useful; it may be completely useless from a practical point of view. Much needs to be done before we can have a better understanding of the xedni calculus.

The index calculus is probabilistic, subexponential-time algorithm applicable for IFP and DLP. However, there is no known subexponential-time algorithm for ECDLP; the index calculus will not work for ECDLP. The *xedni calculus*, on the other hand, is applicable to ECDLP (it is in fact also applicable to IFP and DLP), but unfortunately its complexity is essentially unknown. From a computability point of view, xedni calculus is applicable to IFP, DLP and ECDLP, but from a complexity point of view, the xedni calculus may turn out to be not useful. As for quantum algorithms, we now know that IFP, DLP and ECDLP can all be solved in polynomial-time if a quantum computer is available for use. However, the problem with quantum algorithms is that a practical quantum computer is out of reach in today's technology. We summarise various algorithms for IFP, DLP and ECDLP in Table 5.1.

Finally, we conclude that we do have algorithms to solve IFP, DLP and ECDLP; the only problem is that we do not have an efficient algorithm, nor does any one proved that no such an efficient algorithm exists. From a computational complexity point of view, a $\mathcal{P}$-type problem is easy to solve, whereas an $\mathcal{NP}$-type problem is easy to verify [18], so IFP, DLP and ECDLP are clearly in $\mathcal{NP}$. For example, it might be difficult (indeed, it is difficult at present) to factor a large integer, but it is easy to verify whether or not a given factorization is correct. If $\mathcal{P} = \mathcal{NP}$, then the two types of the problems are the same, the factorization is difficult only because no one has been clever enough to find an easy/efficient algorithm yet (it may turn out that the integer factorization problem is indeed $\mathcal{NP}$-Hard, regardless of the cleverness of the human beings). Whether or not $\mathcal{P} = \mathcal{NP}$ is one of the biggest open problems in both mathematics and computer science, and it is listed in the first of the seven Millennium Prize Problems by the Clay Mathematics Institute in

Boston on 24 May 2000 [12]. The struggle continues and more research needs to be done before we can say anything about whether or not $\mathcal{P} = \mathcal{NP}$!

5.1.6 Recent Progress in ECDLP

In November 1997, Certicom, a computer security company in Waterloo, Canada, introduced the Elliptic Curve Cryptosystem (ECC) challenge, consisting of a series of elliptic curve discrete logarithm problems (see the official webpage of the challenge problems):

http://www.certicom.com/index.php?action=ecc,ecc_challenge.

These problems aim at increasing industry understanding and appreciation for the difficulty of ECDLP and encouraging and stimulating further research in the

Table 5.2 Elliptic curves over $\mathbb{F}_{2^m}$

Curve	Field size (in bits)	Estimated number of machine days	Prize in US dollars	Status
ECC2K-95	97	8637	$5000	May 1998
ECC2-97	97	180,448	$5000	Sept 1999
ECC2K-108	108	1.3×10^6	$10,000	April 2000
ECC2-109	109	2.1×10^7	$10,000	April 2004
ECC2K-130	131	2.7×10^9	$20,000	?
ECC2-131	131	6.6×10^{10}	$20,000	?
ECC2-163	163	2.9×10^{15}	$30,000	?
ECC2K-163	163	4.6×10^{14}	$30,000	?
ECC2-191	191	1.4×10^{20}	$40,000	?
ECC2-238	239	3.0×10^{27}	$50,000	?
ECC2K-238	239	1.3×10^{26}	$50,000	?
ECC2-353	359	1.4×10^{45}	$100,000	?
ECC2K-358	359	2.8×10^{44}	$100,000	?

Table 5.3 Elliptic curves over $\mathbb{F}_p$

Curve	Field size (in bits)	Estimated number of machine days	Prize in US dollars	Status
ECCp-97	97	71,982	$5000	March 1998
ECCp-109	109	9×10^7	$10,000	Nov 2002
ECCp-131	131	2.3×10^{10}	$20,000	?
ECCp-163	163	2.3×10^{15}	$30,000	?
ECCp-191	191	4.8×10^{19}	$40,000	?
ECCp-239	239	1.4×10^{27}	$50,000	?
ECCp-359	359	3.7×10^{45}	$100,000	?

security analysis of ECC. The challenge is to compute the ECC private keys from the given list of ECC public keys and associated system parameters. It is the type of problem facing an adversary who wishes to attack ECC. These problems are defined on curves either over $\mathbb{F}_{2^m}$ or over $\mathbb{F}_p$ with p prime (see Tables 5.2 and 5.3). Also there are three levels of difficulty associated to the curves: exercise level (with bits less than 109), rather easy level (with bits in 109–131), and very hard level (with bits in 163–359). Readers who are interested in solving real-world ECDLP problems are suggested to try to solve the problems listed in Tables 5.2 and 5.3, particularly those with the question mark "?", as they are still open to date.

Note from the two tables that no progress has been made for problems with question mark "?" since 2004. There are however some progress for some other ECDLP problems. In what follows, we present three recent ECDLP records.

1. In 2009 Bos and Kaihara et al. [5] solved the following 112-bit prime ECDLP problem: For elliptic curve

$$E : y^2 = x^3 + ax + b$$

over the finite field $\mathbb{F}_p$, where

$$p = \frac{2^{128} - 3}{11 \cdot 6949}$$

$$= 4451685225093714772084598273548427,$$

$$a = 4451685225093714772084598273548424,$$

$$b = 2061118396808653202902996166388514,$$

$$x_P = 188281465057972534892223778713752,$$

$$y_P = 3419875491033170827167861896082688,$$

$$x_Q = 1415926535897932384626433832795028,$$

$$y_Q = 3846759606494706724286139623885544,$$

with $P(x_P, y_P)$ and $Q(x_Q, y_Q)$ the two points on E, they found the required logarithm to be

$$k = 312521636014772477161767351856699,$$

such that

$$Q = kP.$$

2. Wenger and Wolger [68] solved in 2014 the following 113-bit ECDLP. For elliptic curve (Koblitz Curve)

$$E : y^2 + xy = x^3 + ax^2 + b$$

in $\mathbb{F}_{2^{113}}$, where

$$a = 1,$$
$$b = 1,$$
$$x_P = 3295120575173384136238266668942876,$$
$$y_P = 4333847502504860461181278233187993,$$
$$x_Q = 7971264128558500679984293536799342,$$
$$y_Q = 2895866652148624507420637092 87836,$$

with $P(x_P, y_P)$ and $Q(x_Q, y_Q)$ the two points on E, they found the required logarithm to be

$$k = 7995815148664371298369425364 65990,$$

such that

$$Q = kP.$$

3. Wenger and Wolfger (see [69, 70]) announced in Jan 2015 a discrete logarithm record in finite field $\mathbb{F}_{2^{113}}$. More specifically, for elliptic curve E over $\mathbb{F}_{2^{113}}$:

$$y^2 + xy = x^3 + ax^2 + b,$$

where

$$a = 984342157317881800509153672175863,$$
$$b = 4720643197658441292834747278018339,$$
$$x_P = 8611161909599329818310188302308875,$$
$$y_P = 7062592440118670058899979569784381,$$
$$x_Q = 6484392715773238573436200651832265,$$
$$y_Q = 7466851312800339937981984969376306,$$

with $P(x_P, y_P)$ and $Q(x_Q, y_Q)$ the two points on E, they found the required logarithm to be

$$k = 2760361941865110448921065488991383,$$

such that

$$Q = kP.$$

Problems for Section 5.1

1. As Shanks' Baby-Step Giant-Step method works for arbitrary groups, it can be extended, of course, to elliptic curve groups.

   (1) Develop an elliptic curve analog of Shanks' algorithm to solve the ECDLP problem.
   (2) Use the analog algorithm to solve the following ECDLP problem, that is, to find k such that

   $$Q \equiv kP \pmod{41},$$

   where $E/\mathbb{F}_{41} : y^2 \equiv x^3 + 2x + 1 \pmod{41}$, $P = (0, 1)$ and $Q = (30, 40)$.

2. Poland's ρ and λ methods for IFP/DLP can also be extended to ECDLP.

   (1) Develop an elliptic curve analog of Poland ρ algorithm to solve the ECDLP problem.
   (2) Use the ρ algorithm to solve the following ECDLP problem: find k such that

   $$Q \equiv kP \pmod{p},$$

   where $E\backslash\mathbb{F}_{1093} : y^2 \equiv x^3 + x + 1 \pmod{1093}$, $P = (0, 1)$ and $Q = (413, 959)$.

3. (Extend the Silver-Pohlig-Hellman method)

   (1) Develop an elliptic curve analog of Silver-Pohlig-Hellman method for ECDLP.
   (2) Use this analog method to solve the following ECDLP problem: find k such that

   $$Q \equiv kP \pmod{p},$$

   where $E\backslash\mathbb{F}_{599} : y^2 \equiv x^3 + 1 \pmod{1093}$, $P = (60, 19)$ and $Q = (277, 239)$.

4. In 1993, Menezes, Okamota and Vanstone developed an algorithm for ECDLP over $\mathbb{F}_{p^m}$ with p^m prime power. Give a description and complexity analysis of this algorithm.

5. Let $E\backslash\mathbb{F}_p$ be the elliptic curve E over $\mathbb{F}_p$ with p prime, where E is defined by

   $$y^2 = x^3 + ax + b.$$

   (1) Let $P, Q \in E$ with $P \neq \pm Q$ are two points on E. Find the addition formula for computing $P + Q$.
   (2) Let $P \in E$ with $P \neq -P$. Find the addition formula for computing $2P$.

(3) Let $E\backslash\mathbb{F}_{23}$ be as follows:

$$E\backslash\mathbb{F}_{23} : y^2 \equiv x^3 + x + 4 \pmod{23}.$$

Find all the points, $E(\mathbb{F}_{23})$, including the point at infinity, on the E.
(4) Let $P = (7, 20)$ and $Q = (17, 14)$ be in $E\backslash\mathbb{F}_{23}$ defined above, find $P + Q$ and $2P$.
(5) Let $Q = (13, 11)$ and $P = (0, 2)$ such that $Q \equiv kP \pmod{23}$. Find $k = \log_P Q \pmod{23}$, the discrete logarithm over $E(\mathbb{F}_{23})$.

6. Let the elliptic curve be as follows:

$$E\backslash\mathbb{F}_{151} : y^2 \equiv x^3 + 2x \pmod{151}$$

with order 152. A point $P = (97, 26)$ with order 19 is given. Let also $Q = (43, 4)$ such that

$$Q \equiv kP \pmod{151}.$$

Find $k = \log_P Q \pmod{151}$, the discrete logarithm over $E(\mathbb{F}_{151})$.
7. Let the elliptic curve be as follows:

$$E\backslash\mathbb{F}_{43} : y^2 \equiv x^3 + 39x^2 + x + 41 \pmod{43}$$

with order 43. Find the ECDLP

$$k = \log_P Q \pmod{43},$$

where $P = (0, 16)$ and $Q = (42, 32)$.
8. Let the elliptic curve be as follows:

$$E\backslash\mathbb{F}_{1009} : y^2 \equiv x^3 + 71x + 602 \pmod{1009}.$$

Find the ECDLP

$$k' = \log'_P Q' \pmod{1009}$$

in

$$Q' = (529, 97) = k'(32, 737) = k'P'$$

in the subgroup of order 53 generated by $P' = (32, 737)$.

9. In ECCp-109, given

$$E \backslash \mathbb{F}_p : y^2 \equiv x^3 + ax + b \pmod{p},$$
$$\{P(x_1, y_1), Q(x_2, y_2)\} \in E(\mathbb{F}_p),$$
$$p = 564538252084441556247016902735257,$$
$$a = 321094768129147601892514872825668,$$
$$b = 430782315140218274262276694323197,$$
$$x_1 = 973390109870590665231561339089335,$$
$$y_1 = 149670372846169285760682371978898,$$
$$x_2 = 446467696974058610576308618 84284,$$
$$y_2 = 522968098895785888047540374779097,$$

show that the following value of k

$$k = 281183840311601949668207954530684$$

is the correct value satisfying

$$Q(x_2, y_2) \equiv k \cdot P(x_1, y_1) \pmod{p}.$$

10. In ECCp-121, given

$$E \backslash \mathbb{F}_p : y^2 \equiv x^3 + ax + b \pmod{p},$$
$$\{P(x_1, y_1), Q(x_2, y_2)\} \in E(\mathbb{F}_p),$$
$$p = 4451685225093714772084598273548427,$$
$$a = 4451685225093714772084598273548424,$$
$$b = 2061118396808653202902996166388514,$$
$$x_1 = 1882814650579725348922237787137 52,$$

$$y_1 = 3419875491033170827167861896082688,$$
$$x_2 = 1415926535897932384626433832795028,$$
$$y_2 = 3846759606494706724286139623885544,$$

show that the following value of k

$$k = 312521636014772477161767351856699$$

is the correct value satisfying

$$Q(x_2, y_2) \equiv k \cdot P(x_1, y_1) \pmod{p}.$$

11. In ECCp-131, given

$$E\backslash\mathbb{F}_p : y^2 \equiv x^3 + ax + b \pmod{p},$$
$$\{P(x_1, y_1), Q(x_2, y_2)\} \in E(\mathbb{F}_p),$$
$$p = 1550031797834347859248576414813139942411,$$
$$a = 1399267573763578815877905235971153316710,$$
$$b = 1009296542191532464076260367525816293976,$$
$$x_1 = 1317953763239595888465524145589872695690,$$
$$y_1 = 434829348619031278460656303481105428081,$$
$$x_2 = 1247392211317907151303247721489640699240,$$
$$y_2 = 207534858442090452193999571026315995117,$$

find the correct value of k such that

$$Q(x_2, y_2) \equiv k \cdot P(x_1, y_1) \pmod{p}.$$

5.2 ECDLP-Based Cryptography

5.2.1 Basic Ideas in ECDLP-Based Cryptography

Since ECDLP is also computationally infeasible in polynomial-time, it can thus be used to construct unbreakable cryptographic systems:

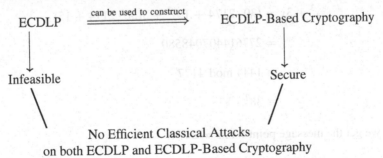

The first two people to use ECDLP to construct cryptographic systems, now widely known as Elliptic Curve Cryptography were Miller [47] and Koblitz [32] in the 1980s. Since then, ECDLP and ECC have been studied extensively, and many practical elliptic curve cryptographic systems and protocols have been development. Today, Elliptic Curve Cryptography is a standard term in the field.

5.2.2 Precomputations of Elliptic Curve Cryptography

To implement elliptic curve cryptography, we need to do the following precomputations:

[1] Embed Messages on Elliptic Curves: Our aim here is to do cryptography with elliptic curve groups in place of $\mathbb{F}_q$. More specifically, we wish to embed plain-text messages as points on an elliptic curve defined over a finite field $\mathbb{F}_q$, with $q = p^r$ and $p \in$ Primes. Let our message units m be integers $0 \le m \le M$, let also κ be a large enough integer for us to be satisfied with an error probability of $2^{-\kappa}$ when we attempt to embed a plain-text message m. In practice, $30 \le \kappa \le 50$. Now let us take $\kappa = 30$ and an elliptic curve $E : y^2 = x^3 + ax + b$ over $\mathbb{F}_q$. Given a message number m, we compute a set of values for x:

$$x = \{m\kappa + j, j = 0, 1, 2, \ldots\} = \{30m,\ 30m + 1,\ 30m + 2,\ \cdots\}$$

until we find $x^3 + ax + b$ is a square modulo p, giving us a point $(x, \sqrt{x^3 + ax + b})$ on E. To convert a point (x, y) on E back to a message number m, we just compute $m = \lfloor x/30 \rfloor$. Since $x^3 + ax + b$ is a square for approximately 50 % of all x, there is only about a $2^{-\kappa}$ probability that this method will fail to produce a point on E over $\mathbb{F}_q$. In what follows, we shall give a simple example of how to embed a message number by a point on an elliptic curve. Let E be $y^2 = x^3 + 3x$, $m = 2174$ and $p = 4177$ (in practice, we select $p > 30m$). Then we calculate $x = \{30 \cdot 2174 + j, j = 0, 1, 2, \ldots\}$ until $x^3 + 3x$ is a square modulo 4177. We find that when $j = 15$:

$$x = 30 \cdot 2174 + 15$$

$$= 65235,$$

$$x^3 + 3x = (30 \cdot 2174 + 15)^3 + 3(30 \cdot 2174 + 15)$$

$$= 277614407048580$$

$$\equiv 1444 \bmod 4177$$

$$\equiv 38^2.$$

So we get the message point for $m = 2174$:

$$(x,\ \sqrt{x^3 + ax + b}) = (65235, 38).$$

To convert the message point $(65235, 38)$ on E back to its original message number m, we just compute

$$m = \lfloor 65235/30 \rfloor = \lfloor 2174.5 \rfloor = 2174.$$

[2] Multiply Points on Elliptic Curves over $\mathbb{F}_q$: We have discussed the calculation of $kP \in E$ over $\mathbb{Z}/q\mathbb{Z}$. In elliptic curve public-key cryptography, we are now interested in the calculation of $kP \in E$ over $\mathbb{F}_q$, which can be done in $\mathcal{O}(\log k (\log q)^3)$ bit operations by the *repeated doubling method*. If we happen to know N, the number of points on our elliptic curve E and if $k > N$, then the coordinates of kP on E can be computed in $\mathcal{O}((\log q)^4)$ bit operations; recall that the number N of points on E satisfies $N \le q + 1 + 2\sqrt{q} = \mathcal{O}(q)$ and can be computed by René Schoof's algorithm in $\mathcal{O}((\log q)^8)$ bit operations.

[3] Compute Elliptic Curve Discrete Logarithms: Let E be an elliptic curve over $\mathbb{F}_q$, and B a point on E. Then the *discrete logarithm* on E is the problem, given a point $P \in E$, find an integer $x \in \mathbb{Z}$ such that $xB = P$ if such an integer x exists. It is likely that the discrete logarithm problem on elliptic curves over $\mathbb{F}_q$ is more intractable than the discrete logarithm problem in $\mathbb{F}_q$. It is this feature that makes cryptographic systems based on elliptic curves even more secure than that based on the discrete logarithm problem. In the rest of this section, we shall discuss elliptic curve analogues of some important public-key cryptosystems.

In what follows, we shall present some elliptic curve analogues of four widely used public-key cryptosystems, namely the elliptic curve DHM, the elliptic curve Massey–Omura, the elliptic curve ElGamal, the elliptic curve RSA and elliptic curve digital signature algorithm.

5.2.3 Elliptic Curve DHM

The Diffie-Hellman-Merkle key-exchange scheme over a finite field $\mathbb{F}_p$ can be easily extended to elliptic curve E over a finite field $\mathbb{F}_p$ (denoted by $E\backslash(\mathbb{F}_p)$); such an elliptic curve analog may be described as follows (see Figure 5.2).

[1] Alice and Bob publicly choose a finite field $\mathbb{F}_q$ with $q = p^r$ and $p \in$ Primes, an elliptic curve E over $\mathbb{F}_q$, and a random *base* point $P \in E$ such that P generates a large subgroup of E, preferably of the same size as that of E itself. All of this is public information.

[2] To agree on a secret key, Alice and Bob choose two secret random integers a and b. Alice computes $aP \in E$ and sends aP to Bob; Bob computes $bP \in E$ and sends bP to Alice. Both aP and bP are, of course, public but a and b are not.

[3] Now both Alice and Bob compute the secret key $abP \in E$, and use it for further secure communications.

[4] Cryptanalysis: For the eavesdropper Eve to get abP, she has to either to find a from (abP, P) or b from (bP, P).

As everybody knows, there is no known fast way to compute abP if one only knows P, aP and bP—this is the infeasible Elliptic Curve Discrete Logarithm Problem.

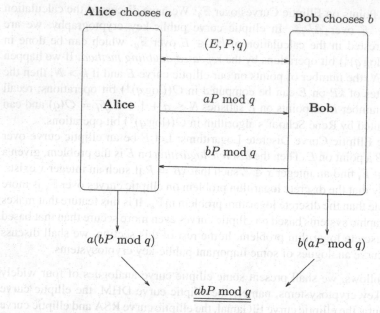

Figure 5.2 Elliptic curve DHM key-exchange scheme

Example 5.4. The following is an elliptic curve analog of the DHM scheme. Let

$$E\backslash\mathbb{F}_{199} : y^2 \equiv x^3 + x - 3,$$
$$P = (1, 76) \in E(\mathbb{F}_{199}),$$
$$a = 23,$$
$$b = 86.$$

Then

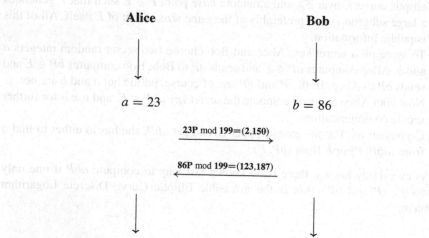

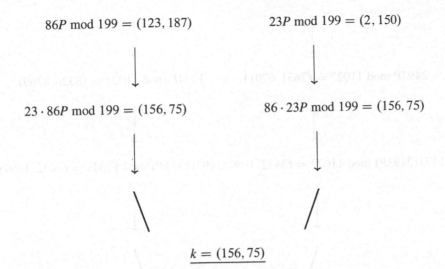

$$86P \bmod 199 = (123, 187) \qquad 23P \bmod 199 = (2, 150)$$

$$23 \cdot 86P \bmod 199 = (156, 75) \qquad 86 \cdot 23P \bmod 199 = (156, 75)$$

$$k = (156, 75)$$

Clearly, anyone who can find the discrete logarithm a or b such that

$$(2, 150) \equiv a(1, 76) \ (\bmod \ 199), \quad (123, 187) \equiv b(1, 76) \ (\bmod \ 199)$$

can get the key $abP \equiv (156, 75) \ (\bmod \ 199)$.

Example 5.5. We illustrate another example of the elliptic curve analog of the DHM scheme. Let

$E \backslash \mathbb{F}_{11027} : y^2 \equiv x^3 + 4601x + 548,$

$P = (9954, 8879) \in E(\mathbb{F}_{11027}),$

$a = 1374,$

$b = 2493.$

Then

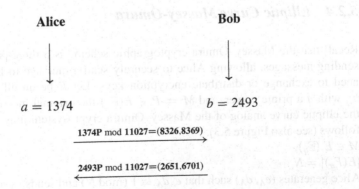

Alice   **Bob**

$a = 1374$ $b = 2493$

$$\xrightarrow{\quad 1374P \bmod 11027=(8326,8369) \quad}$$

$$\xleftarrow{\quad 2493P \bmod 11027=(2651,6701) \quad}$$

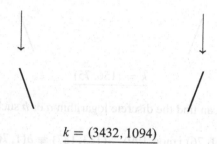

$2493P \bmod 11027 = (2651, 6701)$ $1374P \bmod 11027 = (8326, 8369)$

$1374(2493P) \bmod 11027 = (3432, 1094) \quad 2493(1374P) \bmod 11027 = (3432, 1094)$

$$k = (3432, 1094)$$

Anyone who can find the discrete logarithm a or b such that

$$(8326, 8369) \equiv a(9954, 8879) \ (\mathrm{mod}\ 11027),$$

or

$$(2651, 6701) \equiv b(9954, 8879) \ (\mathrm{mod}\ 11027)$$

can get the key $abP \equiv (3432, 1094) \ (\mathrm{mod}\ 11027)$.

5.2.4   Elliptic Curve Massey-Omura

Recall that the Massey–Omura cryptographic scheme is a three-pass protocol for sending messages, allowing Alice to securely send a message to Bob without the need to exchange or distribute encryption keys. Let E be an elliptic curve over $\mathbb{F}_q$ with q a prime power, and $M = P \in E(\mathbb{F}_q)$ the original message point. Then the elliptic curve analog of the Massey–Omura cryptosystem may be described as follows (see also Figure 5.3).

$M \in E.(\mathbb{F}_q)$,

$|E(F_q)| = N$

Alice generates (e_A, d_A) such that $e_A d_A \equiv 1 \ (\mathrm{mod}\ N)$ and sends e_A to Bob

Bob generates (e_B, d_B) such that $e_B d_B \equiv 1 \ (\mathrm{mod}\ N)$ and sends e_B to Alice

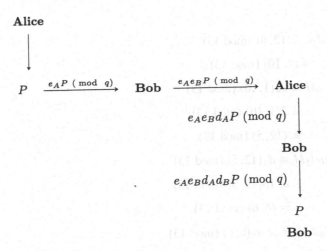

Figure 5.3 The elliptic curve Massey-Omura cryptography

[1] Alice and Bob publicly choose an elliptic curve E over $\mathbb{F}_q$ with $q = p^r$, a large prime power; as usual, we assume $q = p$ and we suppose also that the number of points on $E\backslash\mathbb{F}_q$ (denoted by N) is publicly known.

[2] Alice chooses a secret pair of numbers (e_A, d_A) such that $d_A e_A \equiv 1 \pmod{N}$. Similarly, Bob chooses (e_B, d_B) such that $d_B e_B \equiv 1 \pmod{N}$.

[3] If Alice wants to send a secret message-point $P \in E$ to Bob, then the procedure should be as follows:

[3–1] Alice sends $e_A P \bmod q$ to Bob,

[3–2] Bob sends $e_B e_A P \bmod q$ to Alice,

[3–3] Alice sends $d_A e_B e_A P \bmod q = e_B P$ to Bob,

[3–4] Bob computes $d_B e_B P = P$ and hence recovers the original message point.

Note that an eavesdropper would know $e_A P$, $e_B e_A P$, and $e_B P$. So if he could solve the elliptic curve discrete logarithm problem on E, he could determine e_B from the first two points and then compute $d_B = e_B^{-1} \bmod q$ and hence get $P = d_B(e_B P)$.

Example 5.6. We follow closely the steps in the above discussed elliptic curve Massey-Omura cryptography. Let

$$p = 13,$$

$$E\backslash\mathbb{F}_{13} : y^2 \equiv x^3 + 4x + 4 \pmod{13},$$

$$|E(\mathbb{F}_{13})| = 15,$$

$$M = (12, 8)),$$

$$(e_A, d_A) \equiv (7, 13) \pmod{15},$$

$$(e_B, d_B) \equiv (2, 8) \pmod{15}.$$

Then

$$e_A M \equiv 7(12, 8) \pmod{13}$$
$$\equiv (1, 10) \pmod{13},$$
$$e_A e_B M \equiv e_B(1, 10) \pmod{13}$$
$$\equiv 2(1, 10) \pmod{13}$$
$$\equiv (12, 5) \pmod{13},$$
$$e_A e_B d_A M \equiv d_A(12, 5) \pmod{13}$$
$$\equiv 13(12, 5) \pmod{13}$$
$$\equiv (6, 6) \pmod{13},$$
$$e_A e_B d_A d_B M \equiv d_B(6, 6) \pmod{13}$$
$$\equiv 8(6, 6) \pmod{13}$$
$$\equiv (12, 8) \pmod{13}.$$
$$\downarrow$$
$$M.$$

Example 5.7. Let

$$p = 13,$$
$$E \backslash \mathbb{F}_{13} : y^2 \equiv x^3 + x \pmod{13},$$
$$|E(\mathbb{F}_{13})| = 20,$$
$$M = (11, 9),$$
$$(e_A, d_A) \equiv (3, 7) \pmod{20},$$
$$(e_B, d_B) \equiv (13, 17) \pmod{20}.$$

Then

$$e_A M \equiv 3(11, 9) \pmod{13}$$
$$\equiv (7, 5) \pmod{13},$$
$$e_A e_B M \equiv e_B(7, 5) \pmod{13}$$
$$\equiv 13(7, 5) \pmod{13}$$
$$\equiv (11, 4) \pmod{13},$$
$$e_A e_B d_A M \equiv d_A(11, 4) \pmod{13}$$
$$\equiv 17(11, 4) \pmod{13}$$
$$\equiv (7, 5) \pmod{13},$$

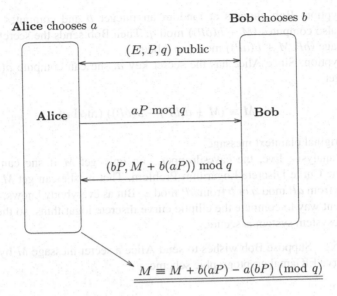

Figure 5.4 Elliptic curve ElGamal cryptography

$$e_A e_B d_A d_B M \equiv d_B(7, 5) \pmod{13}$$
$$\equiv 17(7, 5) \pmod{13}$$
$$\equiv (11, 9) \pmod{13}.$$
$$\downarrow$$
$$M.$$

5.2.5 *Elliptic Curve ElGamal*

Just the same as many other public-key cryptosystems, the famous ElGamal cryptosystem also has a very straightforward elliptic curve analog, which may be described as follows (see also Figure 5.4).

[1] Suppose Bob wishes to send a secret message to Alice:

$$\text{Bob} \xrightarrow{\text{secrete message}} \text{Alice}.$$

Alice and Bob publicly choose an elliptic curve E over $\mathbb{F}_q$ with $q = p^r$ a prime power, and a random *base* point $P \in E$. Suppose they also know the number of points on E, i.e., they know $|E(\mathbb{F}_q)| = N$.

[2] Alice chooses a random integer a, computes $aP \mod q$ and sends it to Bob.

[3] Encryption: Bob chooses at random an integer b and computes bP mod q. Bob also computes $(M + b(aP))$ mod q. Then Bob sends the secret encrypted message $(bP, M + b(aP))$ mod q to Alice.

[4] Decryption: Since Alice has the secret key a, she can compute $a(bP)$ mod q and get

$$M \equiv (M + a(bP) - b(aP)) \ (\text{mod } q),$$

the original plaintext message.

[5] Cryptanalysis: Eve, the eavesdropper, can only get M if she can solve the Elliptic Curve Discrete Logarithm Problem. That is, she can get M if she can find a from aP mod q or b from bP mod q. But as everybody knows, there is no efficient way to compute the elliptic curve discrete logarithms, so the ElGamal cryptosystem system is secure.

Example 5.8. Suppose Bob wishes to send Alice a secret message M by using the elliptic curve ElGamal cryptographic scheme.

[1] Set-up;

$$E \backslash \mathbb{F}_{29} : \ y^2 \equiv x^3 - x + 16 \ (\text{mod } 29),$$

$$N = |E(\mathbb{F}_{29})| = 31,$$

$$P = (5, 7) \in E(\mathbb{F}_{29}),$$

$$M = (28, 25).$$

[2] Public-key generation: Assume Bob sends the secret message M to Alice, so Alice:

> chooses a random secret integer $a = 23$,
>
> computes $aP = 23P = (21, 18) \ (\text{mod } 29)$,
>
> sends $aP = (21, 18) \ (\text{mod } 29)$ to Bob.

[3] Encryption: Bob

> chooses a random secret integer $b = 25$,
>
> computes $bP = 25P = (13, 24) \ (\text{mod } 29)$,
>
> $\qquad b(aP) = 17(23P) = 17(21, 18) = (1, 25) \ (\text{mod } 29)$,
>
> $\qquad M + b(aP) = (28, 25) + (1, 25) = (0, 4) \ (\text{mod } 29)$,
>
> sends $(bP = (1, 25), \ M + b(aP) = (0, 4))$ to Alice.

[4] Decryption: Alice computes

> $a(bP) = 23(25P) = 23(13, 24) = (1, 25)$,
>
> $M = M + b(aP) - a(bP)$

$$= (0, 4) - (1, 25)$$
$$= (0, 4) + (1, -25)$$
$$= (28, 25).$$

So, Alice recovers the original secret message $M = (28, 25)$.

Example 5.9. Now we give one more example on elliptic curve ElGamal cryptosystem.

[1] Set-up;

$$E \backslash \mathbb{F}_{523} : y^2 \equiv x^3 + 22x + 153 \pmod{523},$$

$$P = (167, 118) \in E(\mathbb{F}_{523}),$$

$$M = (220, 287) \text{ is the plaintext.}$$

[2] Public-key generation: Assume Bob sends the secret message M to Alice, so Alice:

> chooses a random secret integer $a = 97$,
>
> computes $aP = 97(167, 118) = (167, 405) \pmod{523}$,
>
> sends $aP = (167, 405) \pmod{523}$ to Bob.

[3] Encryption: Bob

> chooses a random secret integer $b = 263$,
> computes $bP = 263(167, 118) = (5, 503) \pmod{523}$,
>
> $$b(aP) = 263(167, 405) = (5, 20) \pmod{523},$$
>
> $$M + b(aP) = (220, 287) + (5, 20)$$
> $$= (36, 158) \pmod{523},$$
>
> sends $(bP = (5, 503), M + b(aP) = (36, 158))$ to Alice.

[4] Decryption: Alice computes

$$a(bP) = 97(5, 503) = (5, 20),$$
$$M = M + b(aP) - a(bP)$$
$$= (36, 158) - (5, 20)$$
$$= (36, 158) + (5, 503)$$
$$= (220, 287).$$

So, Alice recovers the original secret message $M = (220, 287)$.

The above are some elliptic curve analogues of certain public-key cryptosystems. It should be noted that almost every public-key cryptosystem has an elliptic curve analogue; it is of course possible to develop new elliptic curve cryptosystems which do not rely on the existing cryptosystems.

It should be also noted that the digital signature schemes can also be analogued by elliptic curves over $\mathbb{F}_q$ or over $\mathbb{Z}/n\mathbb{Z}$ with $n = pq$ and $p, q \in$ Primes in exactly the same way as that for public-key cryptography; several elliptic curve analogues of digital signature schemes have already been proposed, say, e.g., [46].

5.2.6 Menezes-Vanstone ECC

A serious problem with all above mentioned elliptic curve cryptosystems is that the plaintext message units m lie on the elliptic curve E, and there is no convenient method known of deterministically generating such points on E. Fortunately, Menezes and Vanstone had discovered a more efficient variation [42]; in this variation which we shall describe below, the elliptic curve is used for "masking", and the plaintext and cipher-text pairs are allowed to be in $\mathbb{F}_p^* \times \mathbb{F}_p^*$ rather than on the elliptic curve.

[1] Key generation: Alice and Bob publicly choose an elliptic curve E over $\mathbb{F}_p$ with $p > 3$ is prime and a random *base* point $P \in E(\mathbb{F}_p)$ such that P generates a large subgroup H of $E(\mathbb{F}_p)$, preferably of the same size as that of $E(\mathbb{F}_p)$ itself. Assume that randomly chosen $k \in \mathbb{Z}_{|H|}$ and $a \in \mathbb{N}$ are secret.

[2] Encryption: Suppose now Alice wants to sent message

$$m = (m_1, m_2) \in (\mathbb{Z}/p\mathbb{Z})^* \times (\mathbb{Z}/p\mathbb{Z})^*$$

to Bob, then she does the following:

[2–1] $\beta = aP$, where P and β are public;
[2–2] $(y_1, y_2) = k\beta$;
[2–3] $c_0 = kP$;
[2–4] $c_j \equiv y_j m_j \pmod{p}$ for $j = 1, 2$;
[2–5] Alice sends the encrypted message c of m to Bob:

$$c = (c_0, c_1, c_2).$$

[3] Decryption: Upon receiving Alice's encrypted message c, Bob calculates the following to recover m:

[3–1] $ac_0 = (y_1, y_2)$;
[3–2] $m = \left(c_1 y_1^{-1} \pmod{p}, \ c_2 y_2^{-1} \pmod{p}\right)$.

Example 5.10. The following is a nice example of Menezes-Vanstone cryptosystem [48].

[1] Key generation: Let E be the elliptic curve given by $y^2 = x^3 + 4x + 4$ over $\mathbb{F}_{13}$, and $P = (1, 3)$ be a point on E. Choose $E(\mathbb{F}_{13}) = H$ which is cyclic of order 15, generated by P. Let also the private keys $k = 5$ and $a = 2$, and the plain-text $m = (12, 7) = (m_1, m_2)$.

[2] Encryption: Alice computes:

$$\beta = aP = 2(1,3) = (12,8),$$
$$(y_1, y_2) = k\beta = 5(12,8) = (10,11),$$
$$c_0 = kP = 5(1,3) = (10,2),$$
$$c_1 \equiv y_1 m_1 \equiv 10 \cdot 2 \equiv 3 \pmod{13},$$
$$c_2 \equiv y_2 m_2 \equiv 11 \cdot 7 \equiv 12 \pmod{13}.$$

Then Alice sends

$$c = (c_0, c_1, c_2) = ((10,2), 3, 12)$$

to Bob.

[3] Decryption: Upon receiving Alice's message, Bob computes:

$$ac_0 = 2(10,2) = (10,11) = (y_1, y_2),$$
$$m_1 \equiv c_1 y_1^{-1} \equiv 12 \pmod{13},$$
$$m_2 \equiv c_2 y_2^{-1} \equiv 7 \pmod{13}.$$

Thus, Bob recovers the message $m = (12,7)$.

5.2.7 Elliptic Curve DSA

We have already noted that almost every public-key cryptosystem has an elliptic curve analogue. It should also be noted that digital signature schemes can also be represented by elliptic curves over $\mathbb{F}_q$ with q a prime power or over $\mathbb{Z}/n\mathbb{Z}$ with $n = pq$ and $p, q \in$ Primes. In exactly the same way as that for public-key cryptography, several elliptic curve analogues of digital signature schemes have already been proposed (see, for example, Meyer and Müller [46]). In what follows we shall describe an elliptic curve analogue of the DSA/DSS, called ECDSA [27].

Algorithm 5.4 (Elliptic Curve Digital Signature Algorithm). Let E be an elliptic curve over $\mathbb{F}_p$ with p prime, and let P be a point of prime order q (note that the q here is just a prime number, not a prime power) in $E(\mathbb{F}_p)$. Suppose Alice wishes to send a signed message to Bob.

[1] [ECDSA key generation] Alice does the following:

   [1–1] select a random integer $x \in [1, \ q - 1]$,
   [1–2] compute $Q = xP$,
   [1–3] make Q public, but keep x as a secret.

Now Alice has generated the public key Q and the private key x.

[2] [ECDSA signature generation] To sign a message m, Alice does the following:

[2–1] select a random integer $k \in [1, q - 1]$,

[2–2] compute $kP = (x_1, y_1)$, and $r \equiv x_1$ (mod q). If $r = 0$, go to step [2–1],

[2–3] compute k^{-1} mod q,

[2–4] compute $s \equiv k^{-1}(H(m) + xr)$ (mod q), where $H(m)$ is the hash value of the message. If $s = 0$, go to step [2–1].

The signature for the message m is the pair of integers (r, s).

[3] [ECDSA signature verification] To verify Alice's signature (r, s) of the message m, Bob should do the following:

[3–1] obtain an authenticated copy of Alice's public key Q,

[3–2] verify that (r, s) are integers in the interval $[1, q - 1]$, computes $kP = (x_1, y_1)$, and $r \equiv x_1$ (mod q),

[3–3] compute $w \equiv s^{-1}$ (mod q) and $H(m)$,

[3–4] compute $u_1 \equiv H(m)w$ (mod q) and $u_2 \equiv rw$ (mod q),

[3–5] compute $u_1 P + u_2 Q = (x_0, y_0)$ and $v \equiv x_0$ (mod q),

[3–6] accept the signature if and only if $v = r$.

As a conclusion to Elliptic Curve Cryptography, we provide two remarks about the comparison of ECC and other types of cryptography, particularly the famous and widely used RSA cryptography.

Remark 5.1. ECC provides a high level of security using smaller keys than that used in RSA. A comparison between the key sizes for an equivalent level of security for RSA and ECC is given in the following Table 5.4.

Remark 5.2. Just the same that there are weak keys for RSA, there are also weak keys for ECC, say, for example, as an acceptable elliptic curve for cryptography, it must satisfy the following conditions:

1. If N is the number of integer coordinates, it must be divisible by a large prime r such that $N = kr$ for some integer k.
2. It the curve has order r modulo p, then r must not be divisible by $p^i - 1$ for a small set of i, say, $0 \leq i \leq 20$.
3. Let N be the number of integer coordinates and $E(\mathbb{F}_p)$, then N must not equal to p. The curve that satisfies the condition $p = N$ is called the anomalous curve.

Table 5.4 Key size comparison between RSA and ECC

Security level	RSA	ECC
Low	512 bits	112 bits
Medium	1024 bits	161 bits
High	3027 bits	256 bits
Very high	15,360 bits	512 bits

Problems for Section 5.2

1. Describe the advantages of Elliptic Curve Cryptography (ECC) over integer factoring based and discrete logarithm based cryptography.
2. Give the complexity measures for the fastest known general algorithms for

   (1) Integer Factorization Problem (IFP).
   (2) Discrete Logarithm Problem (DLP).
   (3) Elliptic Curve Discrete Logarithm Problem (ECDLP).

3. Give the complexity measures for

   (1) Integer Factorization Problem (IFP) based cryptosytems.
   (2) Discrete Logarithm Problem (DLP) based cryptosytems.
   (3) Elliptic Curve Discrete Logarithm Problem (ECDLP) based cryptosytems.

4. The exponential cipher, invented by Pohlig and Hellman in 1978 and based on the mod p arithmetic, is a secret-key cryptosystem, but it is very close to the RSA public-key cryptosystem based on mod n arithmetic, where $n = pq$ with p, q prime numbers. In essence, the Pohlig-Hellman cryptosystem works as follows:

   [1] Choose a large prime number p and the encryption key k such that $0 < k < p$ and $\gcd(k, p - 1) = 1$.
   [2] Compute the decryption key k' such that $k \cdot k' \equiv 1 \pmod{p - 1}$.
   [3] Encryption: $C \equiv M^k \pmod{p}$.
   [4] Decryption: $M \equiv C^{k'} \pmod{p}$.

   Clearly, if you change the modulo p to modulo $n = pq$, then the Pohlig-Hellman cryptosystem is just the RSA cryptosystem.

   (1) Design an elliptic curve analog of the Pohlig-Hellman cryptosystem.
   (2) Explain why the original Pohlig-Hellman cryptosystem is easy to break whereas the elliptic curve Pohlig-Hellman cryptosystem is hard to break.

5. Koyama et al. [37] proposed three trap-door one-way functions; one of the functions claimed to be applicable to zero-knowledge identification protocols. Give an implementation of the elliptic curve trap-door one-way function to the zero-knowledge identification protocol.
6. Suppose that Alice and Bob want to establish a secret key for future encryption in ECDHM key-exchange. Both Alice and Bob perform as follows:

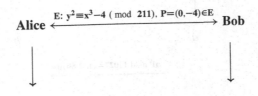

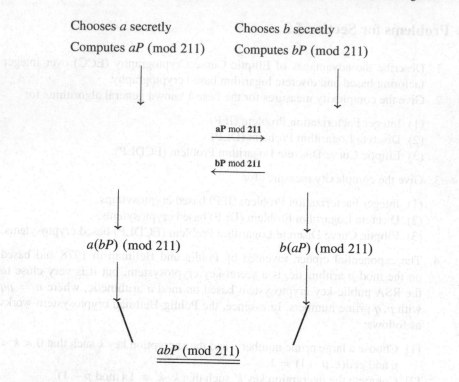

Chooses a secretly   Chooses b secretly

Computes aP (mod 211)   Computes bP (mod 211)

aP mod 211

bP mod 211

$a(bP)$ (mod 211) $b(aP)$ (mod 211)

abP (mod 211)

Find the actual values for

(1) aP mod 211.
(2) bP mod 211.
(3) abP mod 211.
(4) baP mod 211.

Verify $abP \equiv baP$ (mod 211).

7. Let the elliptic curve analog of a DHM scheme be as follows.

$$E \backslash \mathbb{F}_{11027} : y^2 \equiv x^3 + 4601x + 548,$$

$$P = (2651, 6701) \in E(\mathbb{F}_{11027}),$$

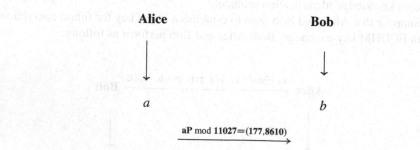

Alice   **Bob**

a b

aP mod $11027 = (177, 8610)$

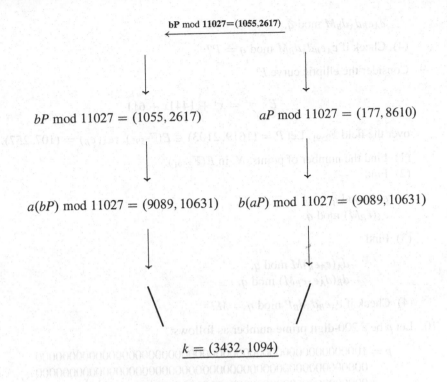

(1) Find the discrete logarithm a such that

$$aP \bmod 11027 = (177, 8610).$$

(2) Find the discrete logarithm b such that

$$bP \bmod 11027 = (1055, 2617).$$

8. Consider the elliptic curve E

$$E : y^2 = x^3 + x - 3$$

over the field $\mathbb{F}_{199}$. Let $M = (1, 76) \in E(\mathbb{F}_{199})$ and $(e_A, e_B) = (23, 71)$.

(1) Find the number of points, N, in $E(\mathbb{F}_{199})$.

(2) Find

$e_A P \bmod q$,

$e_A e_B M \bmod q$.

(3) Find

$e_A e_B d_A M \bmod q$,

$e_A e_B d_A d_B M \bmod q$.

(4) Check if $e_A e_B d_A d_B M \bmod q = P$?

9. Consider the elliptic curve E

$$E : y^2 = x^3 + 1441x + 611$$

over the field $\mathbb{F}_{2591}$. Let $P = (1619, 2103) \in E(\mathbb{F}_{2591})$, $(e_A, e_B) = (107, 257)$.

(1) Find the number of points, N, in $E(\mathbb{F}_{2591})$.
(2) Find

$e_A P \bmod q$,
$e_A (e_B M) \bmod q$.

(3) Find

$$d_A (e_A e_B) M \bmod q,$$
$$d_B (d_A e_A e_B M) \bmod q.$$

(4) Check if $e_A e_B d_A d_B P \bmod q = M$?

10. Let p be a 200-digit prime number as follows:

$p = 10000000000000000000000000000000000000000000000000000$
$00000000000000000000000000000000000000000000000000000$
$00000000000000000000000000000000000000000000000000000$
$00000000000000000000000000000000000000000000000153.$

Let the elliptic curve over $\mathbb{F}_p$ be as follows:

$$E \backslash \mathbb{F}_p : y^2 \equiv x^3 + 105x + 78153 \ (\bmod \ p),$$

with a point order:

$N = 10000000000000000000000000000000000000000000000000000$
$00000000000000000000000000000000000000000000000000000$
$0678975028800422411808031436546027764192804964188 8$
$3999159139296003221063056176002905085861368963175 3.$

(1) Let $e_A = 179$, compute $d_A \equiv \dfrac{1}{e_A} \bmod N$.
(2) Let $e_B = 983$, compute $d_B \equiv \dfrac{1}{e_B} \bmod N$.

11. Let p be a prime number

$p = 12345678901234567890123456789065483337452508596673$
$7125236501.$

Let also the elliptic curve over $\mathbb{F}_p$ be as follows:
$y^2 \equiv x^3 +$

1125079135286236108376138855036822306988688835725996813843335x
−1125079135286236108376138855036822306988688835725996813843335
(mod p).
with order $|E(\mathbb{F}_p)| = N$ as follows:

12345678901234567890123456789012345678901234567890123456789012345668197.

Suppose
(76429892329752928953563517549032780298048602232844063315749,
100181741322448105444520871614464053169400529776945655771441)
is the plaintext point M, and Alice wishes to send M to Bob.
Assume

$e_A = 3$,
$d_A = 823045260082304526008230452600823045260082304526008823045465$,
$e_B = 7$,
$d_B = 1763668414462081127160493827001763668414462081127160493844314$,

all modulo p. Compute:

(1) $e_A M \bmod p$.
(2) $e_B(e_A M) \bmod p$.
(3) $d_A(e_B e_A M) \bmod p$.
(4) $d_B(d_A e_B e_A M) \bmod p$.
(5) Check if $d_B(d_A e_B e_A M) \bmod p = M$?

12. Suppose that Alice wants to send Bob a secret massage $M = (10, 9)$ using elliptic curve ElGamal cryptography. Both Alice and Bob perform as follows;

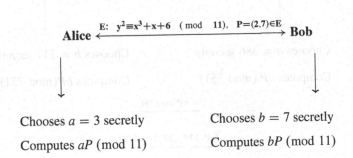

Alice $\xleftarrow{\text{E: } y^2 \equiv x^3 + x + 6 \ (\bmod \ 11), \ P = (2,7) \in E}$ Bob

Chooses $a = 3$ secretly   Chooses $b = 7$ secretly

Computes aP (mod 11)   Computes bP (mod 11)

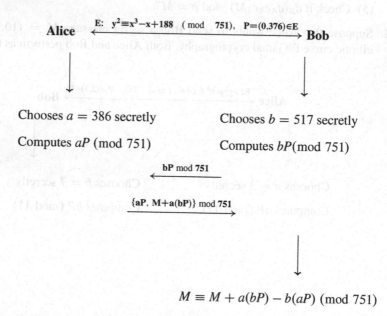

$$M \equiv M + a(bP) - b(aP) \pmod{11}$$

Compute the actual values for

(1) aP mod 11.
(2) bP mod 11.
(3) $b(aP)$ mod 11.
(4) $a(bP)$ mod 11.
(5) $(M + a(bP))$ mod 11.
(6) $(M + a(bP) - b(aP))$ mod 11.

Check if $(M + a(bP) - b(aP))$ mod 11 = (10, 9)?

13. Suppose that Alice wants to send Bob a secret massage $M = (562, 201)$ in elliptic curve ElGamal cryptography. Both Alice and Bob performs the following:

$$\text{Alice} \xleftarrow{\quad E:\ \ y^2 \equiv x^3 - x + 188 \ \ (\text{mod} \quad 751),\ \ P = (0, 376) \in E \quad} \text{Bob}$$

Chooses $a = 386$ secretly

Computes aP (mod 751)

Chooses $b = 517$ secretly

Computes bP (mod 751)

bP mod 751

{aP, M+a(bP)} mod 751

$$M \equiv M + a(bP) - b(aP) \pmod{751}$$

Compute the actual values for

(1) $aP \bmod 751$.

(2) $bP \bmod 751$.

(3) $a(bP) \bmod 751$.

(4) $b(aP) \bmod 751$.

(5) $(M + a(bP)) \bmod 751$.

(6) $(M + a(bP) - b(aP)) \bmod 751$.

Check if $(M + a(bP) - b(aP)) \bmod 751 = (562, 201)$?

14. Suppose that Alice wants to send Bob a secret massage $M = (316, 521)$ in elliptic curve ElGamal cryptography. Both Alice and Bob performs the following:

$$\text{Alice} \xleftarrow{\quad \text{E: } y^2 \equiv x^3 + 6x + 167 \ (\bmod\ 547), \quad P = (61, 440) \in E \quad} \text{Bob}$$

Chooses a secretly

Computes $aP \ (\bmod\ 547)$

$$= (483, 59)$$

Chooses b secretly

Computes $bP (\bmod\ 547)$

$$= (168, 341)$$

$$\xleftarrow{\quad bP \bmod 547 = (168, 341) \quad}$$

$$\xrightarrow{\quad \{aP, \ M + a(bP)\} \bmod 547 = \{(483, 59), (49, 178)\} \quad}$$

$$M \equiv M + a(bP) - b(aP) \ (\bmod\ 547)$$

$$\equiv (49, 178) + (143, -443) \ (\bmod\ 547)$$

$$\equiv (316, 521) \ (\bmod\ 547).$$

Find

(1) a such that $aP \bmod 547 = (483, 59)$.

(2) b such that $bP \bmod 547 = (168, 341)$.

(3) $a(bP) \bmod 547$.

(4) $b(aP) \bmod 547$.

(5) Check if $a(bP) \equiv b(aP) \ (\bmod\ 547)$?

15. Let $E\backslash\mathbb{F}_{2^m}$ be the elliptic curve E over $\mathbb{F}_{2^m}$ with $m > 1$, where E is defined be

$$y^2 + xy = x^3 + ax^2 + b.$$

(1) Let $P, Q \in E$ with $P \neq \pm Q$ are two points on E. Find the addition formula for computing $P + Q$.
(2) Let $P \in E$ with $P \neq -P$. Find the addition formula for computing $2P$.
(3) Let $E\backslash\mathbb{F}_{2^m}$ be as follows:

$$E\backslash\mathbb{F}_{2^4} : y^2 \equiv x^3 + \alpha^4 x^2 + 1 \pmod{2^4}.$$

Find all the points, $E(\mathbb{F}_{2^4})$, including the point at infinity, on the E.
(4) Let $P = (\alpha^6, \alpha^8)$ and $Q = (\alpha^3, \alpha^{13})$ be in $E\backslash\mathbb{F}_{2^4}$ defined above, find $P + Q$ and $2P$.

16. Show that breaking ECC or any ECDLP-base cryptography is generally equivalent to solving the ECDLP problem.

5.3 Quantum Algorithms for Elliptic Curve Discrete Logarithms

5.3.1 Basic Idea for Quantum Attacking on ECDLP/ECDLP-Based Cryptography

Shor's quantum algorithms for discrete logarithms can be used to solve the elliptic curve discrete logarithms in $\mathcal{BQP}$.

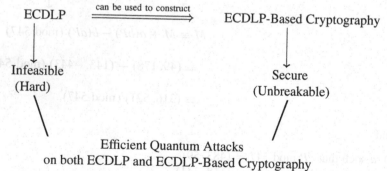

Surprisingly,

Quantum Period Finding Algorithm

Quantum ECDLP Algorithm

$$\downarrow$$

Quantum Attacks on ECDLP-Based Cryptography

As we mentioned earlier, the DLP problem is just the inverse problem-finding the multiplicative inverse in $\mathbb{Z}_p^*$. Remarkably enough, the ECDLP problem is also an inverse problem-finding the additive inverse in $E(\mathbb{F}_p)$. More importantly, the method for solving such an inverse problem is till the Euclid's algorithm, but an elliptic curve version of the old Euclid's and efficient algorithm. Let us first review how Euclid's algorithm can be used to solve (x, y) in the following congruence:

$$ax - by = 1.$$

To be more specific, we show how to use the Euclid's algorithm to find x, y in

$$7x - 26y = 1.$$

which is equivalent to find x in

$$\frac{1}{7} \equiv x \pmod{26}.$$

$$
\begin{aligned}
26 = 7 \cdot 3 + 5 \;\; &\rightarrow\; 5 = 26 - 7 \cdot 3 \\
7 = 5 \cdot 1 + 2 \;\; &\rightarrow\; 2 = 7 - 5 \cdot 1 \\
5 = 2 \cdot 2 + 1 \;\; &\rightarrow\; 1 = 5 - 2 \cdot 2 \\
&\quad\quad\;\; = 5 - 2(7 - 5 \cdot 1) \\
&\quad\quad\;\; = 3 \cdot 5 - 2 \cdot 7 \\
&\quad\quad\;\; = 3 \cdot (26 - 7 \cdot 3) - 2 \cdot 7 \\
&\quad\quad\;\; = 3 \cdot 26 - 7 \cdot 11 \\
&\quad\quad\;\; = 7(-11) - 26(-3)
\end{aligned}
$$

$$
\begin{array}{cc}
\downarrow & \downarrow \\
x & y
\end{array}
$$

So, we find

$$(x, y) = (-11, -3).$$

The quantum algorithms, say e.g., the Proos-Zalka's algorithm [51] and Eicherfor-Opoku's algorithm [15] for ECDLP, aim at finding (a, b) in

$$aP + bQ = 1.$$

Recall that the ECDLP problem asks to find r such that

$$Q = rP,$$

where P is a point of order m on an elliptic curve over a finite field $\mathbb{F}_p$, $Q \in G$ and $G = \langle P \rangle$. A way to find r is to find distinct pairs (a', b') and (a'', b'') of integers modulo r such that

$$a'P + b' = a''P + b''Q.$$

Then

$$(a' - a'')P = (b'' - b')Q,$$

that is,

$$Q = \frac{a' - a''}{b'' - b'}P,$$

or alternatively,

$$r \equiv \frac{a' - a''}{b'' - b'} \ (\mathrm{mod}\ m).$$

The computation to find say e.g., aP can be done efficiently as follows. Let $e_{\beta-1}e_{\beta-2}\cdots e_1 e_0$ be the binary representation of a. Then for i starting from $e_{\beta-1}$ down to e_0 ($e_{\beta-1}$ is always 1 and used for initialization), check whether or not $e_i = 1$. If $e_i = 1$, then perform a doubling and an addition group operation; otherwise, just perform a doubling operation. For example, to compute $89P$, since $89 = 1011001$, we have:

The following algorithm implements this idea of *repeated doubling and addition* for computing kP.

e_6	1	P	initialization
e_5	0	$2P$	doubling
e_4	1	$2(2P) + P$	doubling and addition
e_3	1	$2(2(2P) + P) + P$	doubling and addition
e_2	0	$2(2(2(2P) + P) + P)$	doubling
e_1	0	$2(2(2(2(2P) + P) + P))$	doubling
e_0	1	$2(2(2(2(2(2P) + P) + P))) + P$	doubling and addition

$$\|$$
$$89P$$

Algorithm 5.5 (Fast Group Operations kP on Elliptic Curves). This algorithm computes aP, where a is a large integer and P is assumed to be a point on an elliptic curve $E : y^2 = x^3 + ax + b$.

[1] Write a in the binary expansion form $a = e_{\beta-1}e_{\beta-2}\cdots e_1 e_0$, where each e_i is either 1 or 0. (Assume a has β bits.)

[2] Set $c \leftarrow 0$.

[3] Compute aP:

> for i from $\beta - 1$ down to 0 do
> $\quad c \leftarrow 2c$ (doubling);
> $\quad$ if $e_i = 1$ then $c \leftarrow c + P$; (addition)

[4] Print c; (now $c = aP$)

Note that Algorithm 5.5 does not actually calculate the coordinates (x, y) of kP on an elliptic curve

$$E\backslash \mathbb{F}_p : y^2 \equiv x^3 + ax + b \pmod{p}.$$

To make Algorithm 5.5 a practically useful algorithm for point additions on an elliptic curve E, we must incorporate the actual coordinate addition $P_3(x_3, y_3) = P_1(x_1, y_1) + P_2(x_2, y_2)$ on E into the algorithm. To do this, we use the following formulas to compute x_3 and y_3 for P_3:

$$(x_3, y_3) = (\lambda^2 - x_1 - x_2, \ \lambda(x_1 - x_3) - y_1),$$

where

$$\lambda = \begin{cases} \dfrac{3x_1^2 + a}{2y_1} & \text{if } P_1 = P_2, \\[2ex] \dfrac{y_2 - y_1}{x_2 - x_1} & \text{otherwise.} \end{cases}$$

For curves of the form

$$E\backslash \mathbb{F}_{2^m} : y^2 + xy \equiv x^3 + ax + b \pmod{2^m},$$

if $P_1 \neq P_2$, then

$$(x_3, y_3) = (\lambda^2 + \lambda + x_1 + x_2 + a, \ \lambda(x_1 + x_3) + x_3 + y_1),$$

where

$$\lambda = \frac{y_1 + y_2}{x_1 + x_2}.$$

If $P_1 = P_2$, then

$$(x_3, y_3) = (\lambda^2 + \lambda + a, \; x_1^2 + \lambda x_3 + x_3),$$

where

$$\lambda = \frac{x_1 + y_1}{x_1}.$$

Also for curves of the form

$$E \backslash \mathbb{F}_{2^m} : \; y^2 + cy \equiv x^3 + ax + b \pmod{2^m},$$

if $P_1 \neq P_2$, then

$$(x_3, y_3) = (\lambda^2 + x_1 + x_2, \; \lambda(x_1 + x_3) + y_1 + c),$$

where

$$\lambda = \frac{y_1 + y_2}{x_1 + x_2}.$$

If $P_1 = P_2$, then

$$(x_3, y_3) = (\lambda^2, \; \lambda(x_1 + x_3) + y_1 + c),$$

where

$$\lambda = \frac{x_1^2 + a}{c}.$$

In what follows, we shall mainly introduce three types of the quantum attacks on ECDLP/ECC:

1. Eicher-Opoku's Quantum Attack on ECDLP.
2. Proos-Zalka's Quantum Attack on ECDLP.
3. CMMP Quantum Attack on Elliptic Curve Cryptography.

5.3.2 Eicher-Opoku's Quantum Algorithm for ECDLP

It is quite straightforward to use Shor's quantum algorithm for DLP [54], discussed in the previous chapter, to solve ECDLP in $\mathcal{BQP}$. The following is a modified version of Shor's algorithm to solve the ECDLP problem over $\mathbb{F}_p$ with p prime (we assume that N is the order of the point P in $E(\mathbb{F}_p)$), based on Eicher and Opoku [15].

Algorithm 5.6 (Eicher-Opoku's Quantum Algorithm for ECDLP). The quantum algorithm tries to find

$$r \equiv \log_P Q \pmod{p}$$

such that

$$Q \equiv rP \pmod{p},$$

where $P, Q \in E(\mathbb{F}_p)$, and N is the is the order of the point P in $E(\mathbb{F}_p)$.

[1] Initialize three required quantum registers as follows:

$$|\Psi_1\rangle = |\mathcal{O}, \mathcal{O}, \mathcal{O}\rangle,$$

where $\mathcal{O}$ denotes the point at infinity, as defined in the elliptic curve group $E(\mathbb{F}_p)$.

[2] Choose q with $p \leq q \leq 2p$.

[3] Put in the first two registers of the quantum computer the uniform superposition of all $|a\rangle$ and $|b\rangle$ (mod p), and compute $aP + bQ$ (mod p) in the third register. This leaves the quantum computer in the state $|\Psi_2\rangle$:

$$|\Psi_1\rangle = \frac{1}{q} \sum_{a=0}^{q-1} \sum_{b=0}^{q-1} |a, b, aP + bQ \pmod{p}\rangle$$

Note that $aP + bQ$ (mod p) can be done efficiently by classical *doubling-addition* method [73].

[4] Use the Fourier transform A_q to map $|a\rangle \rightarrow |c\rangle$ and $|b\rangle \rightarrow |d\rangle$ with probability amplitude

$$\frac{1}{q} \exp\left(\frac{2\pi i}{q}(ac + bd)\right).$$

Thus, the state $|a, b\rangle$ will be changed to the state:

$$\frac{1}{q} \sum_{c=0}^{q-1} \sum_{d=0}^{q-1} \exp\left(\frac{2\pi i}{q}(ac + bd)\right) |c, d\rangle.$$

This leaves the machine in the state $|\Psi_3\rangle$:

$$|\Psi_3\rangle = \frac{1}{q} \sum_{a,b=0}^{q-1} \sum_{c,d=0}^{q-1} \exp\left(\frac{2\pi i}{q}(ac + bd)\right) |c, d, aP + bQ \pmod{p}\rangle.$$

[5] Observe the state of the quantum computer and extract the required information. The probability of observing a state $|c, d, kP \pmod{p}\rangle$ is

$$\text{Prob}(c, d, kP) = \left| \frac{1}{q} \sum_{\substack{a,b \\ a - rb \equiv k \,(\text{mod } p-1)}} \exp\left(\frac{2\pi i}{q}(ac + bd) \right) \right|^2 \tag{5.3}$$

where the sum is over all (a, b) such that

$$aP + bQ \equiv kP \pmod{p}.$$

[6] Just the same as the quantum algorithm for the DLP problem, use the relation

$$a = rb + k - (p - 1)\left\lfloor \frac{br + k}{p - 1} \right\rfloor. \tag{5.4}$$

to substitute in (5.3) to get the amplitude on $|c, d, kP \pmod{p}\rangle$:

$$\frac{1}{q} \sum_{b=0}^{p-1} \exp\left(\frac{2\pi i}{q}\left(brc + kc + bd - c(p-1)\left\lfloor \frac{br + k}{p - 1} \right\rfloor \right) \right). \tag{5.5}$$

This leaves finally the machine in the state $|\Psi_3\rangle$:

$$\frac{1}{q} \sum_{b=0}^{p-1} \exp\left(\frac{2\pi i}{q}\left(brc + kc + bd - c(p-1)\left\lfloor \frac{br + k}{p - 1} \right\rfloor \right) \right)$$

$$|c, d, kP \pmod{p}\rangle. \tag{5.6}$$

The probability of observing the above state $|c, d, kP \pmod{p}\rangle$ is thus:

$$\left| \frac{1}{q} \sum_{b=0}^{N-1} \exp\left(\frac{2\pi i}{q}\left(brc + kc + bd - c(p-1)\left\lfloor \frac{br + k}{p - 1} \right\rfloor \right) \right) \right|^2. \tag{5.7}$$

Since $\exp(2\pi i kc/q)$ does not change the probability, (5.5) can be rewrite algebraically as follows:

$$\left| \frac{1}{q} \sum_{b=0}^{p-1} \exp\left(\frac{2\pi i}{q}bT \right) \exp\left(\frac{2\pi i}{q}V \right) \right|^2, \tag{5.8}$$

where

$$T = rc + d - \frac{r}{p-1}\{cp)\}_q,$$

$$V = \left(\frac{br}{p} - \left\lfloor \frac{br+k}{p} \right\rfloor\right)\{cp)\}_q.$$

The notation $\{\alpha\}_q$ here denotes $\alpha \bmod q$ with $-q/2 < \{\alpha\}_q < q/2$.
[7] Finally, deduce r from (c, d). Let j be the closest integer to T/q and $b \in [0, p-2]$, then

$$|\{T\}_q| = \left| rc + d - \frac{r}{p-1}\{cp\}_q - jq \right| \le \frac{1}{2}.$$

Further, if

$$|\{cp\}_q| \le \frac{q}{12},$$

then

$$|V| \le \frac{q}{12}.$$

Therefore, given (c, d), r can be easily calculated with a high probability.

Remark 5.3. Eicher and Opoku also showed in [15] an example of using the algorithm to break a particular elliptic curve Massey-Omurra cryptographic system. More specifically, assume that

$E \backslash \mathbb{F}_{2^5} : y^2 + y \equiv x^3 \pmod{33}$,

$\mathbb{F}_{2^5} = \{0, 1, \omega, \omega^2, \omega^3, \ldots, \omega^{30}\}$,

$N = |\mathbb{F}_{2^5}| = 33$,

$P_m = \{\omega^{15}, \omega^{10}\}$,

$e_A P_m = \{\omega^9, \omega^{14}\}$,

$e_A e_B P_m = \{\omega^{29}, \omega^{16}\}$,

$e_A e_B d_A P_m = e_B P_m = \{\omega^{18}, \omega^{20}\}$.

They then give a demonstration of how to use the quantum algorithm to find e_A, since once e_A can be found, $d_B \equiv e_A^{-1} \pmod{33}$ can be found, therefore, $P_m = d_A e_A P_m$, the original message point, can be found.

5.3.3 Proos-Zalka's Quantum Algorithm for ECDLP

Proos and Zalka [51] proposed a quantum algorithm for solving the ECDLP problem over the finite field $\mathbb{F}_p$ with p prime (not equally important to that over the finite field $\mathbb{F}_{2^m}$ or other finite fields). Their experience showed that a smaller quantum computer can break an ECDLP-based cryptographic system with the same level of security of an IFP-based cryptographic system that would need a large computer. More specifically, A 160-bit ECC key could be broken on a quantum computer with about 1000 qubits whereas factoring the security equivalent 1024-bit RSA modulus would need about 2000 qubits. This means that in classical computation, ECC provides a high level of security using smaller keys than that used in RSA, say for example, for the same level of security, if a RSA key is about 15,360 bits, an ECC key would only need 512 bits . However, in quantum computation, the situation is completely opposite, ECDLP-based cryptography is easy to break than IFP-based cryptography.

In Proos-Zalka's modification of Shor's DLP quantum algorithm, they first replace the quantum Fourier transform A_q with A_{2^n} with $q \approx 2^n$, for the easy implementation purpose as follows.

$$| \Psi_1 \rangle = | \mathcal{O}, \mathcal{O}, \mathcal{O} \rangle ,$$

$$= \frac{1}{2^n} \sum_{a=0}^{2^n-1} \sum_{b=0}^{2^n-1} | a, b, \mathcal{O} \rangle$$

$$= \frac{1}{2^n} \sum_{a=0}^{2^n-1} \sum_{b=0}^{2^n-1} | a, b, aP + bQ \rangle$$

where

$$aP + bQ = \sum_i b_i P + \sum_i b_i Q$$

with

$$a = \sum_i a_i 2^i,$$

$$b = \sum_i b_i 2^i,$$

$$P_i = 2^i P,$$

$$Q_i = 2^i Q$$

can be performed efficient by classical Algorithm 5.5. However, in their implementation, Proos and Zalka have made some interesting modifications over Shor's original algorithm, as follows.

1. Eliminate the input registers $|a, b\rangle$. Only one accumulator register is needed for adding a fixed point P_i (with respect to Q_i) to a superposition of points (called *group shift*), and two unitary transforms U_{P_i} and U_{Q_i} which acts on any basis state $|S\rangle$ representing a point on E are needed:

$$U_{P_i} : |S\rangle \rightarrow |S + P_i\rangle \quad \text{and} \quad U_{Q_i} : |S\rangle \rightarrow |S + Q_i\rangle.$$

2. Decompose the group shift. The ECDLP can be decomposed into a sequence of group shifts by constant classically known elements:

$$U_A : |S\rangle \rightarrow |S + A\rangle \quad S, A \in E, \quad A \text{ is fixed.}$$

In term of the coordinators (x, y) of the points on E, the group shift is:

$$|S\rangle = |(x, y)| \quad \rightarrow \quad |S + A\rangle = |(x, y) + (\alpha, \beta)\rangle = |(x', y')\rangle.$$

So the formulas for the group addition may be as follows:

$$\lambda \quad = \quad \frac{y - \beta}{x - \alpha} = \frac{y' + \beta}{x' - \alpha}, \quad x' = \lambda^2 - (x + \alpha)$$

$$x, y \quad \longleftrightarrow \quad x, \lambda$$

$$\longleftrightarrow \quad x', \lambda$$

$$\longleftrightarrow \quad x', y'$$

$$x, y \quad \longleftrightarrow \quad x - \alpha, y - \beta$$

$$\longleftrightarrow \quad x - \alpha, \lambda = \frac{y - \beta}{x - \alpha}$$

$$\longleftrightarrow \quad x' - \alpha, \lambda = \frac{y' + \beta}{x' - \alpha}$$

$$\longleftrightarrow \quad x' - \alpha, y' + \beta$$

$$\longleftrightarrow \quad x', y'$$

where $\longleftrightarrow$ denotes the reversible operation.

3. Decompose the divisions. The divisions of the form $x, y \longleftrightarrow x, y/x$ may be decomposed into the following forms:

$$x, y \xleftrightarrow{\text{Modular inverse}} 1/x, y$$

$$\xleftrightarrow{\text{Multiplication}} 1/x, y, y/x$$

$$\xleftrightarrow{\text{Multiplicative inverse}} x, y, y/x$$

$$\xleftrightarrow{\text{Multiplication}} x, 0, y/x.$$

4. Modular multiplication. The modular multiplication of the form

$$x, y \longleftrightarrow x, y, x \cdot y$$

in

$$|x, y\rangle \to |x, y, x \cdot y \bmod p\rangle$$

may be decomposed into a sequence of modular additions and modular doublings as follows:

$$x \cdot y = \sum_{i=0}^{n-1} x_i 2^i y$$

$$\equiv x_0 y + 2(x_i y + 2(x_2 y + 2(x_3 y + \cdots))) \pmod{p}$$

whereas the following series operations are performed in the third register:

$$A \quad \longleftrightarrow \quad 2A$$

$$\longleftrightarrow \quad 2A + x_i y \pmod{p}, \ i = n - 1, n - 2, \ldots, 0.$$

5. Modular inverse. The modular inverse is the most difficult operation in the quantum implementation. However, this can be done efficiently on classical computers by Euclid's algorithm. So, we suggest to use a classical computer, rather than a quantum computer to solve the problem, making quantum and classical computations complimentary. Readers who are interested in the detailed quantum implementation of the modular inverse should consult [51] for more information.

Remark 5.4. The algorithm runs in time $\mathcal{O}(\lambda^3)$ and in space $\mathcal{O}(\lambda)$ using roughly 6λ qubits, where λ is the input length in bits.

Table 5.5 Comparison between quantum IFP and ECDLP algorithms

Quantum IFP			Quantum ECDLP			Classical
	Qubits	Time		Qubits	Time	
λ	2λ	$4\lambda^3$	λ	7λ	$360\lambda^3$	Time
512	1024	$0.54 \cdot 10^9$	110	700	$0.5 \cdot 10^9$	c
1024	2048	$4.3 \cdot 10^9$	163	1000	$1.6 \cdot 10^9$	$c \cdot 10^8$
2048	4096	$34 \cdot 10^9$	224	1300	$4.0 \cdot 10^9$	$c \cdot 10^{17}$
3072	6144	$120 \cdot 10^9$	256	1500	$6.0 \cdot 10^9$	$c \cdot 10^{22}$
15360	30720	$1.5 \cdot 10^{13}$	512	2800	$50 \cdot 10^9$	$c \cdot 10^{60}$

Remark 5.5. One of the most important advantages of quantum algorithms for ECDLP over quantum IFP is that for breaking the same level of security cryptographic systems, namely RSA and ECC, quantum algorithms for ECDLP use less qubits than that for IFP, as given in Table 5.5.

5.3.4 Optimized Quantum Algorithm on ECDLP/ECC

As can be seen, the Proos-Zalka algorithm [51] is only applicable to the ECDLP over finite field $\mathbb{F}_p$. However, in practice, elliptic curve cryptographic systems often use curves over the binary finite field $\mathbb{F}_{2^m}$. So later on, Kaye and Zalka [31] extended the Proos-Zalka algorithm applicable for $\mathbb{F}_{2^m}$. More specifically, they use the Euclid's algorithm for polynomials to compute inverses in $\mathbb{F}_{2^m}$.

Remarkably enough, Cheung et al. [10] proposed a quantum algorithm for attacking the ECDLP/ECC over $\mathbb{F}_{2^m}$ such as $\mathbb{F}_{2^{255}}$. More specifically, they improved an earlier algorithms by constructing an efficient quantum circuit (see e.g., Figure 5.5 for a particular example) elements in binary finite fields and by representing elliptic curve points in projective coordinators. The depth of their circuit implementation is $\mathcal{O}(m^2)$, while the previous bound is $\mathcal{O}(m^3)$.

Problems for Section 5.3

1. Give a complete algorithmic description of the Kaye-Zalka quantum ECDLP algorithm [31] for $E(\mathbb{F}_{2^m})$.
2. Give a complete complexity analysis of the attack given in [10] on ECDLP/ECC over $E(\mathbb{F}_{2^m})$.
3. Design a quantum circuit to implement the Kaye-Zalka algorithm [31] for breaking ECDLP/ECC in $E(\mathbb{F}_{2^m})$.

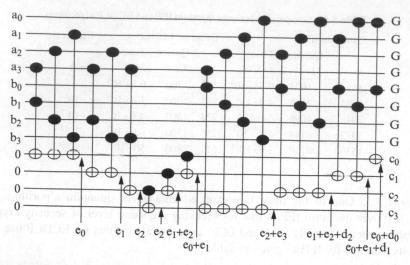

Figure 5.5 $\mathbb{F}_{2^4}$ multiplier with $P(x) = x^4 + x + 1$

4. Van Meter and Itoh [64] developed a fast quantum modular exponentiation algorithm. Extend van Meter-Otoh's quantum modular exponentiation algorithm to fast quantum elliptic curve group operation.
5. Euclid's algorithm is suitable to compute gcd for both integers and polynomials, and more importantly, it can be performed in polynomial-time even on a classical computer. What is the advantage to implement the quantum Euclid's algorithm?
6. The fastest known (classical) algorithm for solving the Elliptic Curve Discrete Logarithm Problem in $F(\mathbb{F}_p)$ is Pollard's ρ method, runs in $\mathcal{O}(\sqrt{p})$ steps. As the periodicity lives at the very heart of the ρ method, it might (or should) be possible to implement a quantum version of the ρ method for ECDLP. Thus, give, if possible, a quantum implementation of the ρ algorithm for ECDLP.

5.4 Chapter Notes and Further Reading

In the DLP problem, we aim to find the discrete logarithm k such that

$$y \equiv x^k \pmod{p},$$

where x, y, p are given and p prime, whereas in ECDLP. We aim to find the elliptic curve discrete logarithm k such that

$$Q \equiv kP \pmod{p},$$

where P is a point of order r on the elliptic curve

$$E\backslash\mathbb{F}_p : y^2 \equiv x^2 + ax + b \ (\mathrm{mod}\ p),$$

$Q \in \langle P \rangle$, p is a prime. From a group-theoretic point of view, the computation of DLP is basically in the multiplicative group $\mathbb{Z}_p^*$, whereas the computation of ECDLP is mainly in the additive group $E(\mathbb{Z}_p)$. Compared to DLP, the computation of ECDLP is more difficult that of DLP; the fastest general-purpose algorithm known for solving ECDLP is Pollard's ρ method, which has full-exponential expected running time of $\sqrt{\pi r/2} = \mathcal{O}(\sqrt{p})$. As for the same level of security, the key length of DCDLP-based cryptography is shorter than that of IFP or DLP based cryptography. Thus, ECDLP-based cryptography is more useful in wireless security, where the key size is limited. However, this advantage of ECDLP-based cryptography is actually a serious disadvantage against the quantum attacks, as for the same level of security, ECC is easy to break than e.g., RSA. In this chapter, same as the previous two chapters, the ECDLP problem and the classical solutions to the ECDLP problem are discussed, followed by an introduction to the ECDLP-based cryptographic systems. Finally, various quantum attacks on ECDLP and ECDLP-based cryptographic systems are discussed.

The search for efficient classical solutions to ECDLP and ECDLP-based cryptography, and practical quantum attacks on ECDLP and ECDLP-based cryptography is one of the most active on-going research areas in mathematics, physics, computer science and cryptography. Readers who wish to know more about ECDLP and methods for solving ECDLP are suggested to consult, e.g., [3, 4, 6, 7, 11, 13, 16, 17, 19, 21, 27, 28, 33, 34, 43, 57, 58, 67]. In particular, the Xedni calculus for ECDLP was proposed in [56] and analysed in [25].

The security of Elliptic Curve Cryptography and Elliptic Curve Digital Signature Algorithm, are based on the infeasibility of the Elliptic Curve Discrete Logarithm Problem. The idea to use elliptic curves, more specifically the Elliptic Curve Discrete Logarithm Problem as the basis to construct cryptographic systems were independently proposed by Miller [47] and Koblitz [32]. The following references provide more information on elliptic curves and elliptic curve (ECDLP-based) cryptography: [1–4, 9, 11, 13, 14, 19–22, 24, 33, 34, 36, 38, 39, 41, 44, 46, 48, 49, 52, 53, 56–63, 65–67, 73, 74].

Related literatures on quantum attacks on ECDLP and ECDLP-based cryptography may be found in [8, 10, 15, 26, 30, 31, 50, 51, 54, 55, 71, 72].

For recent research progress on molecular DNA computation for ECDLP, readers are suggested to consult the following references and reference therein: [23, 29, 40].

References

1. G. Agnew, R. Mullin, S.A. Vanstone, An implementation of elliptic curve cryptosystems over $\mathbb{F}_{2^{155}}$. IEEE J. Sel. Areas Commun. **11**, 804–813 (1993)
2. R.M. Avanzi, *Development of Curve Based Cryptography* (Ruhr-Universität, Bochum, 2007), 12 p.

3. I. Blake, G. Seroussi, N. Smart, *Elliptic Curves in Cryptography* (Cambridge University Press, Cambridge, 1999)
4. I. Blake, G. Seroussi, N. Smart, *Advances in Elliptic Curves Cryptography* (Cambridge University Press, Cambridge, 2005)
5. J.W. Bos, M.E. Kaihara, T. Kleinjung et al., PlayStation 3 computing breaks 2^{60} barrier 112-Bit prime ECDLP solved. Laboratory for Cryptographic Algorithms, EPFL IC LACAL, CH-1015 Lausanne (2009)
6. J.W. Bos, M.E. Kaihara, T. Kleinjung et al., On the security of 1024-Bit RSA and 160-Bit elliptic curve cryptography. IACR Cryptol. 19 p. (2009) [ePrint Archive]
7. J.W. Bos, M.E. Kaihara, T. Kleinjung et al., Solving a 112-Bit prime elliptic curve discrete logarithm problem on game consoles using sloppy reduction. Int. J. Appl. Cryptogr. **2**(3), 212–228 (2012)
8. D.E. Browne, Efficient classical simulation of the quantum fourier transform. New J. Phys. **9**(146), 1–7 (2007)
9. Certicom Research, *Certicom ECC Challenge*, 10 November 2009, 47 p. www.certicom.com
10. D. Cheung, D. Maslo et al., On the design and optimization of a quantum polynomial-time attack on elliptic curve cryptography, in *Theory of Quantum Computation, Communication, and Cryptography Third Workshop, Theory of Quantum Computing 2008*. Lecture Notes in Computer Science, vol. 5106 (Springer, New York, 2008), pp. 96–104
11. H. Cohen, G. Frey, *Handbook of Elliptic and Hyperelliptic Curve Cryptography* (CRC Press, Boca Raton, 2006)
12. S. Cook, *The P versus NP problem*, in The Millennium Prize Problems, ed. by J. Carlson, A. Jaffe, A. Wiles. (Clay Mathematics Institute/American Mathematical Society, Providence, 2006), pp. 87–104
13. R. Crandall, C. Pomerance, *Prime Numbers: A Computational Perspective*, 2nd edn. (Springer, Berlin, 2005)
14. N. Demytko, A new elliptic curve based analogue of RSA, in *Advances in Cryptology – EUROCRYPT 1993*. Lecture Notes in Computer Science, vol. 765 (Springer, Berlin, 1994), pp. 40–49
15. J. Eicher, Y. Opoku, *Using the Quantum Computer to Break Elliptic Curve Cryptosystems* (University of Richmond, Richmond, 1997), 28 p.
16. G. Frey, The arithmetic behind cryptography. Not. AMS **57**(3), 366–374 (2010)
17. G. Frey, M. Müller, H.G. Rück, *The Tate Pairing and the Discrete Logarithm Applied to Elliptic Curve Cryptosystems* (University of Seen, Germany, 1998), 5 p.
18. M.R. Garey, D.S. Johnson, *Computers and Intractability: A Guide to the Theory of NP-Completeness* (W.H. Freeman and Company, New York, 1979)
19. D. Hankerson, A.J. Menezes, S. Vanstone, *Guide to Elliptic Curve Cryptography* (Springer, New York, 2004)
20. G.H. Hardy, E.M. Wright, *An Introduction to Theory of Numbers*, 6th edn. (Oxford University Press, Oxford, 2008)
21. J. Hoffstein, J. Pipher, J.H. Silverman, *An Introduction to Mathematical Cryptography* (Springer, New York, 2008)
22. D. Husemöller, *Elliptic Curves*. Graduate Texts in Mathematics, vol. 111 (Springer, New York, 1987)
23. G. Iaccarino, T. Mazza, Fast parallel molecular algorithms for the elliptic curve logarithm problem over $GF(2^n)$, in *Proceedings of the 2009 Workshop on Bio-inspired Algorithms for Distributed Systems* (ACM Press, New York, 2008), pp. 95–104
24. K. Ireland, M. Rosen, *A Classical Introduction to Modern Number Theory*, 2nd edn. Graduate Texts in Mathematics, vol. 84 (Springer, New York, 1990)
25. M.J. Jacobson, N. Koblitz, J.H. Silverman et al., Analysis of the Xedni calculus attack. Des. Codes Crypt. **20**(1), 41–64 (2000)
26. R. Jain, Z. Ji et al., QIP = PSPACE. Commun. ACM **53**(9), 102–109 (2010)
27. D. Johnson, A. Menezes, S. Vanstone, The elliptic curve digital signatures algorithm (ECDSA). Int. J. Inf. Secur. **1**(1), 36–63 (2001)

28. O. Johnston, A discrete logarithm attack on elliptic curves. IACR Cryptol. **575**, 14 (2010) [ePrint Archive]
29. K. Karabina, A. Menezes, C. Pomerance, I.E. Shparlinski, On the asymptotic effectiveness of Weil descent attacks. J. Math. Cryptol. **4**(2), 175–191 (2010)
30. P. Kaye, Techniques for quantum computing, Ph.D. Thesis, University of Waterloo, 2007, 151 p.
31. P. Kaye, C. Zalka, Optimized quantum implementation of elliptic curve arithmetic over binary fields. Quantum Inf. Comput. **5**(6), 474–491 (2006)
32. N. Koblitz, Elliptic curve cryptography. Math. Comput. **48**, 203–209 (1987)
33. N. Koblitz, *A Course in Number Theory and Cryptography*, 2nd edn. Graduate Texts in Mathematics, vol. 114 (Springer, New York, 1994)
34. N. Koblitz, *Algebraic Aspects of Cryptography*. Algorithms and Computation in Mathematics, vol. 3 (Springer, New York, 1998)
35. N. Koblitz, Cryptography, in *Mathematics Unlimited – 2001 and Beyond*, ed. by B. Enguist, W. Schmid (Springer, New York, 2001), pp. 749–769
36. N. Koblitz, A. Menezes, S.A. Vanstone, The state of elliptic curve cryptography. Des. Codes Crypt. **19**(2), 173–193 (2000)
37. K. Koyama, U.M. Maurer, T. Okamoto, S.A. Vanstone, *New Public-Key Schemes Based on Elliptic Curves over the Ring* $\mathbb{Z}_n$ (NTT Laboratories, Kyoto, 1991)
38. K. Lauter, The advantages of elliptic curve cryptography for wireless security. IEEE Wireless Commun. **2**, 62–67 (2004)
39. H.W. Lenstra Jr., *Elliptic Curves and Number-Theoretic Algorithms* (Mathematisch Instituut, Universiteit van Amsterdam, Amsterdam, 1986)
40. K. Li, S. Zou, J. Xv, Fast parallel molecular algorithms for DNA-based computationl solving the elliptic curve logarithm problem over GF(2^n). J. Biomed. Biotechnol. **2008**, Article ID 518093, 10 p. (2008)
41. A.J. Menezes, *Elliptic Curve Public Key Cryptography* (Kluwer, Boston, 1993)
42. A. Menezes, S.A. Vanstone, Elliptic curve cryptosystems and their implementation. J. Cryptol. **6**(4), 209–224 (1993)
43. A. Menezes, T. Okamoto, S.A. Vanstone, Reducing elliptic curve logarithms in a finite field. IEEE Trans. Inf. Theory **39**(5), 1639–1646 (1993)
44. A. Menezes, P.C. van Oorschot, S.A. Vanstone, *Handbook of Applied Cryptography* (CRC Press, Boca Raton, 1996)
45. J.F. Mestre, Formules Explicites et Minoration de Conducteurs de Variétés algébriques. Compos. Math. **58**, 209–232 (1986)
46. B. Meyer, V. Müller, A public-key cryptosystem based on elliptic curves over $\mathbb{Z}/n\mathbb{Z}$ equivalent to factoring, in *Advances in Cryptology – EUROCRYPT 1996*. Lecture Notes in Computer Science, vol. 1070 (Springer, Berlin, 1996), pp. 49–59
47. V. Miller, Uses of elliptic curves in cryptography. Lecture Notes in Computer Science, vol. 218 (Springer, Berlin, 1986), pp. 417–426
48. R.A. Mollin, *An Introduction to Cryptography*, 2nd edn. (Chapman & Hall/CRC, Boca Raton, 2006)
49. R.A. Mollin, *Algebraic Number Theory*, 2nd edn. (Chapman & Hall/CRC, Boca Raton, 2011)
50. M.A. Nielson, I.L. Chuang, *Quantum Computation and Quantum Information*, 10th Anniversary Edition (Cambridge University Press, Cambridge, 2010)
51. J. Proos, C. Zalka, Shor's discrete logarithm quantum algorithm for elliptic curves. Quantum Inf. Comput. **3**(4), 317–344 (2003)
52. M. Rosing, *Implementing Elliptic Curve Cryptography* (Manning, Greenwich, 1999)
53. R. Schoof, Elliptic curves over finite fields and the computation of square roots mod p. Math. Comput. **44**, 483–494 (1985)
54. P. Shor, Algorithms for quantum computation: discrete logarithms and factoring, in *Proceedings of 35th Annual Symposium on Foundations of Computer Science* (IEEE Computer Society Press, New York, 1994), pp. 124–134

55. P. Shor, Polynomial-time algorithms for prime factorization and discrete logarithms on a quantum computer. SIAM J. Comput. **26**(5), 1484–1509 (1997)
56. J.H. Silverman, The Xedni calculus and the elliptic curve discrete logarithm problem. Des. Codes Crypt. **20**(1), 5–40 (2000)
57. J.H. Silverman, *The Arithmetic of Elliptic Curves*, 2nd edn. Graduate Texts in Mathematics, vol. 106 (Springer, New York, 2010)
58. J.H. Silverman, J. Suzuki, Elliptic curve discrete logarithms and the index calculus, in *Advances in Cryptology – ASIACRYPT 1998*. Lecture Notes in Computer Science, vol. 1514 (Springer, New York, 1998), pp. 110–12
59. N. Smart, *Cryptography: An Introduction* (McGraw-Hill, New York, 2003)
60. M. Stamp, R.M. Low, *Applied Cryptanalysis* (Wiley, New York, 2007)
61. A. Stanoyevitch, *Introduction to Cryptography* (CRC Press, Boca Raton, 2011)
62. D.R. Stinson, *Cryptography: Theory and Practice*, 2nd edn. (Chapman & Hall/CRC Press, Boca Raton, 2002)
63. W. Trappe, L. Washington, *Introduction to Cryptography with Coding Theory*, 2nd edn. (Prentice-Hall, Upper Saddle River, 2006)
64. R. van Meter, K.M. Itoh, Fast quantum modular exponentiation. Phys. Rev. A. **71**(5), 052320 1–12 (2005)
65. H.C.A. van Tilborg, *Fundamentals of Cryptography* (Kluwer, Boston, 1999)
66. S.S. Wagstaff Jr., *Cryptanalysis of Number Theoretic Ciphers* (Chapman & Hall/CRC, Boca Raton, 2002)
67. L. Washington, *Elliptic Curves: Number Theory and Cryptography*, 2nd edn. (Chapman & Hall/CRC, Boca Raton, 2008)
68. E. Wenger, P. Wolfger, Solving the discrete logarithm of a 113-Bit Koblitz curve with an FPGA cluster, in *Selected Areas in Cryptography – SAC 2014*. Lecture Notes in Computer Science, vol. 8781 (Springer, Heidelberg, 2014), pp. 363–379
69. E. Wenger, P. Wolfger, New 113-Bit ECDLP Record, in *NUMTHRY List*, 27 January 2015 listserv.nodak.edu
70. E. Wenger, P. Wolfger, Harder, Better, Faster, Stronger – Elliptic Curve Discrete Logarithm Computations on FPGAs. ePrint.iaer.org/2015/143.pdf (2015)
71. C.P. Williams, *Explorations in Quantum Computation*, 2nd edn. (Springer, New York, 2011)
72. C.P. Williams, S.H. Clearwater, *Ultimate Zero and One: Computing at the Quantum Frontier* (Copernicus, New York, 2000)
73. S.Y. Yan, *Number Theory for Computing*, 2nd edn. (Springer, New York, 2002)
74. S.Y. Yan, *Primality Testing and Integer Factorization in Public-Key Cryptography*, 2nd edn. Advances in Information Security, vol. 11 (Springer, New York, 2009)

Chapter 6
Miscellaneous Quantum Algorithms

Any noun can be verbed.

ALAN PERLIS (1922–1990)
The First (1966) Turing Award Recipient

So far, we have discussed classical and particularly quantum algorithms for integer factoring, discrete logarithms and elliptic curve discrete logarithms. This does not mean quantum algorithms can only be used to solve integer factorization problem, discrete logarithm problem and elliptic curve discrete logarithm problem. In fact, quantum algorithms and quantum computers in general can solve other problems with either superpolynomially (exponentially) speedup or polynomially speedup. In this last and short chapter, we shall discuss some various other quantum algorithms and methods for more number-theoretic problems. Unlike the previous chapters, we will not emphasize on the introduction of the details quantum algorithms for number-theoretic problems, rather we shall concentrated on new ideas and new developments in quantum algorithms for number-theoretic problems.

6.1 Solving Pell's Equation

By solving Pell's equation, we mean to find the positive integer solution (x, y) to any one of the following equations

$$x^2 - dy^2 = \pm 1,$$

$$x^2 - dy^2 = \pm c,$$

where d is a positive square-free integer and c is a positive integer less than $\sqrt{d}$. Mathematically speaking, the solution to Pell's equation can be easily obtained in terms of the continued fraction of $\sqrt{d}$. In what follows, we present some theoretical results for solving Pell's equation without proving (the complete proofs may be found in [53]).

© Springer International Publishing Switzerland 2015
S.Y. Yan, *Quantum Computational Number Theory*,
DOI 10.1007/978-3-319-25823-2_6

Pell's equation may be informally defined as follows.

$$
\text{PellEqn} \overset{\text{def}}{=} \begin{cases} \text{Input}: \begin{cases} d, & \text{square free positive integer,} \\ c, & \text{positive integer less than } \sqrt{d}. \end{cases} \\ \\ \text{Output}: \begin{cases} (x_0, y_0), \text{ smallest positive integer solution to} \\ \qquad\qquad x^2 - dy^2 = \pm c. \end{cases} \end{cases}
$$

In most cases, we consider the equation of the form

$$
x^2 - dy^2 = \pm 1,
$$

or simply just

$$
x^2 - dy^2 = 1.
$$

Theorem 6.1. *Let α be an irrational number. If a/b is a rational number in lowest terms, where a and b are integers $b > 0$, such that*

$$
\left| \alpha - \frac{a}{b} \right| < \frac{1}{2b^2},
$$

then a/b is a convergent of the simple continued fraction expansion of α.

Theorem 6.2. *Let α be an irrational number greater than 1. The $(k + 1)$th convergent to $1/\alpha$ is the reciprocal of the kth convergent to α, for $k = 1, 2, \cdots$.*

Theorem 6.3. *Let d be a positive integer other than a perfect square. If (x_0, y_0) is a positive integral solution of $x^2 - dy^2 = \pm 1$, then $x_0 = P_n$ and $y_0 = Q_n$, where $\dfrac{P_n}{Q_n}$ is one of the convergents of $\sqrt{d}$.*

Theorem 6.4. *Let d be a positive integer other than a perfect square, and m the period of the expansion of $\sqrt{d}$ as a simple continued fraction. Then we have:*

1. *m is even*

  (1) *The positive integer solutions of $x^2 - dy^2 = 1$ are*

$$
\left. \begin{array}{l} x = P_{km-1}, \\ y = Q_{km-1}, \end{array} \right\}
$$

   for $k = 1, 2, 3, \cdots$, with

$$
\left. \begin{array}{l} x = P_{m-1}, \\ y = Q_{m-1}, \end{array} \right\}
$$

as the smallest *positive integer solution.*

(2) *The equation* $x^2 - dy^2 = -1$ *has no integer solution.*

2. *m is odd*

(1) *The positive integer solutions of* $x^2 - dy^2 = 1$ *are*

$$\left. \begin{array}{l} x = P_{km-1}, \\ y = Q_{km-1}, \end{array} \right\}$$

for $k = 2, 4, 6, \cdots$, *with*

$$\left. \begin{array}{l} x = P_{2m-1}, \\ y = Q_{2m-1}, \end{array} \right\}$$

as the smallest *positive integer solution.*

(2) *The positive integer solutions of* $x^2 - dy^2 = -1$ *are*

$$\left. \begin{array}{l} x = P_{km-1}, \\ y = Q_{km-1}, \end{array} \right\}$$

for $k = 1, 3, 5, \cdots$, *with*

$$\left. \begin{array}{l} x = P_{m-1}, \\ y = Q_{m-1}, \end{array} \right\}$$

as the smallest *positive integer solution.*

Example 6.1. Find the integer solutions of $x^2 - 73y^2 = 1$. Note first that

$$\sqrt{73} = [8, \overline{1, 1, 5, 5, 1, 1, 16}].$$

So the period $m = 7$ and of course m is odd. Thus, the equation is soluble and its smallest positive integral solution is

$$\left. \begin{array}{l} x = P_{km-1} = P_{2 \cdot 7 - 1} = P_{13} = 2281249, \\ y = Q_{km-1} = Q_{2 \cdot 7 - 1} = Q_{13} = 267000. \end{array} \right\}$$

That is, $2281249^2 - 73 \cdot 267000^2 = 1$.

Example 6.2. Find the integer solutions of $x^2 - 97y^2 = 1$. Note first that

$$\sqrt{97} = [9, \overline{1, 5, 1, 1, 1, 1, 1, 1, 5, 1, 18}].$$

So the period $m = 11$ is odd. Thus, the equation is soluble and its smallest positive integral solution is

$$x = P_{2m-1} = P_{2 \cdot 11 - 1} = P_{21} = 62809633,$$
$$y = Q_{2m-1} = Q_{2 \cdot 11 - 1} = Q_{21} = 6377352.$$

That is, $62809633^2 - 97 \cdot 6377352^2 = 1$.

Remark 6.1. Incidentally, the continued fraction for $\sqrt{d}$, with d not a perfect square, always has the form

$$\sqrt{d} = [q_0, \overline{q_1, q_2, q_3, \cdots, q_3, q_2, q_1, 2q_0}],$$

as can be seen in Table 6.1.

Table 6.1 Continued fractions for $\sqrt{d}$ with $d \leq 50$ and not perfect square

$\sqrt{2} = [1, \overline{2}]$	$\sqrt{3} = [1, \overline{1, 2}]$
$\sqrt{5} = [2, \overline{4}]$	$\sqrt{6} = [2, \overline{2, 4}]$
$\sqrt{7} = [2, \overline{1, 1, 1, 4}]$	$\sqrt{8} = [2, \overline{1, 4}]$
$\sqrt{10} = [3, \overline{6}]$	$\sqrt{11} = [3, \overline{3, 6}]$
$\sqrt{12} = [3, \overline{2, 6}]$	$\sqrt{13} = [3, \overline{1, 1, 1, 1, 6}]$
$\sqrt{14} = [3, \overline{1, 2, 1, 6}]$	$\sqrt{15} = [3, \overline{1, 6}]$
$\sqrt{17} = [4, \overline{8}]$	$\sqrt{18} = [4, \overline{4, 8}]$
$\sqrt{19} = [4, \overline{2, 1, 3, 1, 2, 8}]$	$\sqrt{20} = [4, \overline{2, 8}]$
$\sqrt{21} = [4, \overline{1, 1, 2, 1, 1, 8}]$	$\sqrt{22} = [4, \overline{1, 2, 4, 2, 1, 8}]$
$\sqrt{23} = [4, \overline{1, 3, 1, 8}]$	$\sqrt{24} = [4, \overline{1, 8}]$
$\sqrt{26} = [5, \overline{10}]$	$\sqrt{27} = [5, \overline{5, 10}]$
$\sqrt{28} = [5, \overline{3, 2, 3, 10}]$	$\sqrt{29} = [5, \overline{2, 1, 1, 2, 10}]$
$\sqrt{30} = [5, \overline{2, 10}]$	$\sqrt{31} = [5, \overline{1, 1, 3, 5, 3, 1, 1, 10}]$
$\sqrt{32} = [5, \overline{1, 1, 1, 10}]$	$\sqrt{33} = [5, \overline{1, 2, 1, 10}]$
$\sqrt{34} = [5, \overline{1, 4, 1, 10}]$	$\sqrt{35} = [5, \overline{1, 10}]$
$\sqrt{37} = [6, \overline{12}]$	$\sqrt{38} = [6, \overline{6, 12}]$
$\sqrt{39} = [6, \overline{4, 12}]$	$\sqrt{40} = [6, \overline{3, 12}]$
$\sqrt{41} = [6, \overline{2, 2, 12}]$	$\sqrt{42} = [6, \overline{2, 12}]$
$\sqrt{43} = [6, \overline{1, 1, 3, 1, 5, 1, 3, 1, 1, 12}]$	$\sqrt{44} = [6, \overline{1, 1, 1, 2, 1, 1, 1, 12}]$
$\sqrt{45} = [6, \overline{1, 2, 2, 2, 1, 12}]$	$\sqrt{46} = [6, \overline{1, 3, 1, 1, 2, 6, 2, 1, 1, 3, 1, 12}]$
$\sqrt{47} = [6, \overline{1, 5, 1, 12}]$	$\sqrt{48} = [6, \overline{1, 12}]$
$\sqrt{50} = [7, \overline{14}]$	

Tables 6.2 and 6.3 show the smallest positive integer solutions (x, y) to Pell's equations $x^2 - dy^2 = 1$ and $x^2 - Ny^2 = -1$ for $1 < d < 100$ (except the perfect squares), respectively.

The following is actually a corollary of Theorem 6.4.

Corollary 6.1. *Let d be a positive integer other than a perfect square, m the period of the expansion of $\sqrt{d}$ as a simple continued fraction, and $\dfrac{P_n}{Q_n}$, $n = 1, 2, \cdots$ the convergents to $\sqrt{d}$. Then the complete set of all solutions, including positive and negative (if any) of Pell's equation are:*

1. *m even*

   (1) $x^2 - dy^2 = 1$: *For $i = 0, 1, 2, 3, \cdots$,*

Table 6.2 The smallest solution to $x^2 - dy^2 = 1$ for $d \leq 100$

d	x	y	d	x	y
2	3	2	3	2	1
5	9	4	6	5	2
7	8	3	8	3	1
10	19	6	11	10	3
12	7	2	13	649	180
14	15	4	15	4	1
17	33	8	18	17	4
19	170	39	20	9	2
21	55	12	22	197	42
23	24	5	24	5	1
26	51	10	27	26	5
28	127	24	29	9801	1820
30	11	2	31	1520	273
32	17	3	33	23	4
34	35	6	35	6	1
37	73	12	38	37	6
39	25	4	40	19	3
41	2049	320	42	13	2
43	3482	531	44	199	30
45	161	24	46	24335	3588
47	48	7	48	7	1
50	99	14	51	50	7
52	649	90	53	66249	9100
54	485	66	55	89	12
56	15	2	57	151	20
58	19603	2574	59	530	69
60	31	4	61	1766319049	226153980

(continued)

Table 6.2 (continued)

d	x	y	d	x	y
62	63	8	63	8	1
65	129	16	66	65	8
67	48842	5967	68	33	4
69	7775	936	70	251	30
71	3480	413	72	17	2
73	2281249	267000	74	3699	430
75	26	3	76	57799	6630
77	351	40	78	53	6
79	80	9	80	9	1
82	163	18	83	82	9
84	55	6	85	285769	30996
86	10405	1122	87	28	3
88	197	21	89	500001	53000
90	19	2	91	1574	165
92	1151	120	93	12151	1260
94	2143295	221064	95	39	4
96	49	5	97	62809633	6377352
98	99	10	99	10	1

Table 6.3 The smallest solution to $x^2 - dy^2 = -1$ for $d \leq 100$

d	x	y	d	x	y	d	x	y
2	1	1	5	2	1	10	3	1
13	18	5	17	4	1	26	5	1
29	70	13	37	6	1	41	32	5
50	7	1	53	182	25	58	99	13
61	29718	3805	65	8	1	73	1068	125
74	43	5	82	9	1	85	378	41
89	500	53	97	5604	569			

$$x + y\sqrt{d} = \pm(P_{m-1} \pm \sqrt{d}Q_{m-1})^i.$$

(2) $x^2 - dy^2 = -1$: *No solutions.*

2. *m odd*

(1) $x^2 - dy^2 = 1$: *For $i = 1, 3, 5, \cdots$,*

$$x + y\sqrt{d} = \pm(P_{m-1} \pm \sqrt{d}Q_{m-1})^i.$$

(2) $x^2 - dy^2 = -1$: *For $i = 0, 2, 4, \cdots$,*

$$x + y\sqrt{d} = \pm(P_{m-1} \pm \sqrt{d}Q_{m-1})^i.$$

The solutions to the more general equation

$$x^2 - dy^2 = \pm c$$

are also related to the continued fraction of $\sqrt{d}$. It can be shown that every solution of such equation comes from some convergent in the continued fraction for $\sqrt{d}$.

It is well-known that the continued fraction of $\sqrt{d}$ can be computed by Euclid's algorithm which can be executed in polynomial-time. However, the smallest positive (i.e., the fundamental) solution (x_0, y_0) to the equation, say. e.g., $x^2 - dy^2 = 1$ may have exponentially many bits in general in terms of the input size d, namely, $\log d$. So, finding the fundamental solution using the continued fraction method, together with the aid of the Schönhage Strassen algorithm for fast integer multiplication cannot be done in polynomial-time [30]. Of course, a much faster method, namely, the quadratic sieve, but this is still not a polynomial-times algorithm as it runs in subexponential-time $\mathcal{O}(\exp(\log d \log \log d)^{1/2})$ (see [46, 52]). To resolve this difficulty, the computational problem is recast as computing the integer closest to the regulator $R = \log(x_0 + y_0\sqrt{d})$, which identifies (x_0, y_0). In this representation, solutions of Pell's equation are positive integer multiples of R. Hallgren [25] showed that a quantum computer can find the above representation for the solution to Pell's equation in polynomial-time. That is,

Theorem 6.5. *There is a polynomial-time quantum algorithm that solves Pell's equation.*

Remark 6.2. Hallgren's algorithm for Pell's equation, which can be interpreted as an algorithm for finding the *group of units of a real quadratic number field*, was later extended to more general fields by Schmidt and Völlmer [40].

Computing the unit group, computing the class number and class group and solving the principal ideal problems are the main problems of computational algebraic number theory [12]. Incidentally, all these problems can be solved in quantum polynomial-time.

Theorem 6.6. *All the following computational algebraic number-theoretic problems:*

1. *the unit group of a real quadratic number field,*
2. *the principal ideal problem in real quadratic number fields,*
3. *the class group of a real quadratic number field (assuming GRH),*
4. *the class number of a real quadratic number field (assuming GRH),*

can be solved in quantum polynomial-time.

Corollary 6.2. *Any cryptographic scheme based on the above problems if any, say, e.g., the Buchmann-Williams key-exchange protocol in real quadratic number fields [7], can be broken in quantum polynomial-time.*

Fast quantum algorithms for computing unit group, class group and class number of more general number fields and function fields are also known, interested readers are suggested to consult, say, e.g., [14, 15, 24].

Problems for Section 6.1

1. Design a continued fraction algorithm for solving Pell's equation $x^2 - dy^2 = \pm c$, where d is a square-free positive integer and $c < \sqrt{d}$ a positive integer, and give a complete complexity analysis of the algorithm. Develop a quantum version, if possible, of the classical continued fraction method discussed in the section for solving Pell's equation.

2. Apply Grover's quantum search algorithm to integer factoring by fast searching all possible prime factors of n. Check or verify if this search algorithm for factoring can be done in polynomial-time.

3. In [39], Shanks proposed an exponential-time complexity, $\mathcal{O}(n^{1/5+\epsilon})$, algorithm based on class group for integer factorization. Design, if possible, an exponentially speedup quantum version of Shanks' class group factoring algorithm.

4. Whether or not there is a polynomial-time classical algorithm for factoring is open. Prove of disprove that integer factorization cannot be done in polynomial-time classically. There are problems which are harder than factoring such as finding the unit group of an arbitrary degree number field for which no efficient quantum algorithm has been found yet. Extend, if possible, Hallgren's quantum algorithm [24] for computing the unit group and class group of constant degree number fields to that of arbitrary degree number fields.

6.2   Verifying Number-Theoretic Conjectures

Verifying unproved conjectures is important task in number theory [45], as number theory bounds in many conjectures opened for many years. In this section we study some important conjectures for which quantum computing may have a play, since if these conjectures are wrong, then quantum computing may be able to find a counterexample quickly than classical computing.

6.2.1   Verifying Riemann's Hypothesis

Recall that the Riemann ζ-function is defined by

$$\zeta(s) = \sum_{n=1}^{\infty} \frac{1}{n^s},$$

where

$$\begin{cases} s = \sigma + it, \\ \{\sigma, t\} \in \mathbb{R}, \\ i = \sqrt{-1}. \end{cases}$$

Note that σ is the real part of s, denoted by $\text{Re}(s)$, whereas it is the imaginary part of s, and denoted by $\text{Im}(s)$. The Riemann hypothesis states that all the nontrivial (complex) zeros ρ of the ζ function lying in the critical strip $0 < \text{Re}(s) < 1$ must lie on the critical line $\text{Re}(s) = 1/2$, that is, $\rho = 1/2 + it$, where ρ denotes a nontrivial zero of $\zeta(s)$. Riemann himself calculated the first five nontrivial zeros of $\zeta(s)$ and found that they all lie on the critical line, he then conjectured that all the nontrivial zeros of $\zeta(s)$ are on the critical line. Riemann's conjecture may be true and also may be false, unless one can prove it is true or one can find a counter-example to show it is false. Up to date, more than 10^{24} complex zeroes of the ζ-function have been calculated; all of them are indeed lying on the vertical line of $\sigma = 1/2$. We know that there are infinitely many complex zeroes in the critical stripe $0 < \sigma < 1$, but we do not know if these infinitely many complex zeroes are all lying on the critical line $\sigma = 1/2$. If we can find one of the complex zeroes is in the critical stripe $0 < \sigma < 1$, but not on the critical line $\sigma = 1/2$, then Riemann's hypothesis is showing to be *false*. Given the exponentially parallelism, quantum computers seems to be very suitable for verifying number-theoretic conjectures by counter-examples. So, developing an efficient quantum algorithm for calculating the nontrivial zeroes of $\zeta(s)$ is an interesting research topic in quantum computational number theory [47].

Of course, to verify Riemann's hypothesis, we may not need to calculate the zeroes of the $\zeta(s)$ function, rather, we could calculate the values for the prime counting function $\pi(x)$, since if Riemann's hypothesis is true, then there is a refinement of the Prime Number Theorem

$$\pi(x) = \int_2^x \frac{dt}{\log t} + \mathcal{O}\left(xe^{-c\sqrt{\log x}}\right)$$

to the effect that

$$\pi(x) = \int_2^x \frac{dt}{\log t} + \mathcal{O}\left(\sqrt{x}\log x\right).$$

That is,

Riemann's hypothesis is true

$$\Updownarrow$$

$$\pi(x) = \int_2^x \frac{dt}{\log t} + \mathcal{O}\left(\sqrt{x}\log x\right).$$

Latorre and Sierra (see [31, 32]) developed some quantum algorithms for computing $\pi(x)$ and $\pi_2(x)$, as well as primality testing, in order to verify the Riemann hypothesis and the twin prime number conjecture.

Theorem 6.7. *There are efficient quantum algorithms for verifying or determine*

1. *the Riemann hypothesis,*
2. *the Twin prime number conjecture,*
3. *the Skewes number.*

For example, if we can find a counter example of Riemann's hypothesis (i.e., a complex zero that is not lying on the vertical line of $\sigma = 1/2$), then Riemann's hypothesis is showing to be false. In this section, we discuss some potential conjectures that might be verified by quantum computers.

Of course we do not know if the Riemann hypothesis is true. Whether or not the Riemann hypothesis is true is one of the most important open problems in mathematics, and in fact it is one of the seven Millennium Prize Problems proposed by the Clay Mathematics Institute in Boston in 2000, each with one million US dollars (see [8, 9]).

6.2.2 Verifying BSD Conjecture

Now we move on to the introduce to the Birch and Swinnerton-Dyer (BSD) conjecture. The problem of determining the group of rational points on an elliptic curve $E : y^2 = x^3 + ax + b$ over $\mathbb{Q}$, denoted by $E(\mathbb{Q})$, is one of the oldest and most intractable problems in mathematics, and it remains unsolved to this day, although vast numerical evidences exist. In 1922, Mordell showed that $E(\mathbb{Q})$ is a finitely generated (Abelian) group. That is, $E(\mathbb{Q}) \approx E(\mathbb{Q})_{\text{tors}} \oplus \mathbb{Z}^r$, where $r \geq 0$, $E(\mathbb{Q})_{\text{tors}}$ is a finite Abelian group (called torsion group). The integer r is called the *rank* of the elliptic curve E over $\mathbb{Q}$, denoted by rank($E(\mathbb{Q})$). Is there an algorithm to compute $E(\mathbb{Q})$ given an arbitrary elliptic curve E? The answer is not known, although $E(\mathbb{Q})_{\text{tors}}$ can be found easily, due to a theorem of Mazur in 1978: $\#(E(\mathbb{Q})_{\text{tors}}) \leq 16$. The famous Birch and Swinnerton-Dyer conjecture (or BSD conjecture, in short), asserts that the size of the group of rational points on E over $\mathbb{Q}$, denoted by $\#(E(\mathbb{Q}))$, is related to the behavior of an associated zeta function $\zeta(s)$, called the Hasse-Weil L-function $L(E, s)$, near the point $s = 1$. That is, if we define the *incomplete* L-function $L(E, s)$ (we called it *incomplete* because we omit the set of "bad" primes $p \mid 2\Delta$) as follows:

$$L(E, s) := \prod_{p \nmid 2\Delta} (1 - a_p p^{-s} + p^{1-2s})^{-1},$$

where $\Delta = -16(4a^3 + 27b^2)$ is the discriminant of E, $N_p :=$ #{rational solutions of $y^2 \equiv x^3 + ax + b \pmod{p}$} with p prime and $a_p = p - N_p$.

This L-function converges for $\text{Re}(s) > \frac{3}{2}$, and can be analytically continued to an entire function [5]. It was conjectured by Birch and Swinnerton-Dyer in the 1960's that the *rank* of the Abelian group of points over a number field of an elliptic curve E is related to the order of the zero of the associated L-function $L(E, s)$ at $s = 1$:

BSD Conjecture (Version 1): $\text{ord}_{s=1}L(E, s) = \text{rank}(E(\mathbb{Q}))$.

This amazing conjecture asserts particularly that $L(E, 1) = 0 \iff E(\mathbb{Q})$ is infinite. Conversely, if $L(E, 1) \neq 0$, then the set $E(\mathbb{Q})$ is finite. An alternative version of BSD, in term of Taylor expansion of $L(E, s)$ at $s = 1$, is as follows:

BSD Conjecture (Version 2): $L(E, s) \sim c(s - 1)^r$, where $c \neq 0$ and $r = \text{rank}(E(\mathbb{Q}))$.

There is also a refined version of BSD for the *complete* L-function $L^*(E, s)$:

$$L^*(E, s) := \prod_{p|2\Delta}(1 - a_pp^{-s})^{-1} \cdot \prod_{p \nmid 2\Delta}(1 - a_pp^{-s} + p^{1-2s})^{-1}.$$

In this case, we have:

BSD Conjecture (Version 3): $L^*(E, s) \sim c^*(s - 1)^r$, with

$$c^* = |\text{III}_E|R_\infty w_\infty \prod_{p|\Delta} w_p / |E(\mathbb{Q})_{\text{tors}}|^2,$$

where $|\text{III}_E|$ is the order of the Tate-Shafarevich group of elliptic curve E, the term R_∞ is an $r \times r$ determinant whose matrix entries are given by a height pairing applied to a system of generators of $E(\mathbb{Q})/E(\mathbb{Q})_{\text{tors}}$, the w_p are elementary local factors and w_∞ is a simple multiple of the real period of E.

The eminent American mathematician, John Tate commented BSD in 1974 that "$\cdots$ this remarkable conjecture relates the behaviour of a function L at a point where it is at present not known to be defined to the order of a group III which is not known to be finite." So it hoped that a proof of the conjecture would yield a proof of the finiteness of III_E. Using the idea of Kurt Heegner (1893–1965), Birch and his former PhD student Stephens established, in the first time, the existence of rational points of infinite order on certain elliptic curves over $\mathbb{Q}$, without actually writing down the coordinates of these points and naively verifying that they satisfy the equation of the curves. These points are now called *Heegner points* on elliptic curves (a Heegner point is a point on modular elliptic curves that is the image of a quadratic imaginary point of the upper half-plane). Based on Birch and Stephens' work, particular based on their massive computation of the Heegner points on modular elliptic curves, Gross at Harvard obtained a deep result in 1986 [17], jointly with Zagier at Maryland/Bonn, now called the Gross-Zagier theorem [17], which describes the height of Heegner points in terms of a derivative of the L-function of the elliptic curve at the point $s = 1$. That is, if $L(E, 1) = 0$, then there is a closed formula to relate $L'(E, 1)$ and the height of the Heegner points on E. More generally, together with Kohnen, Gross and Zagier showed in 1987 [18] that Heegner points could be used to construct rational points on the curve for each positive integer n, and the heights of these points were the coefficients of a modular form of weight $3/2$. Later, in 1989, the Russian mathematician Kolyvagin [29] further used Heegner points to construct Euler systems, and used this to prove much of the Birch-Swinnerton-Dyer conjecture for rank 1 elliptic curves. More specifically, he showed that if the Heegner points is of infinite order, then $\text{rank}(E(\mathbb{Q})) = 1$. Other notable results in BSD also include S.W. Zhang's generalization of Gross-Zagier theorem for elliptic curves to Abelian varieties, and M.L. Brown's proof of BSD for most rank 1 elliptic curves over global fields of positive characteristic [6]. Of course, all these resolutions are far away from the complete settlement of BSD. Just the same as Riemann's hypothesis, the BSD conjecture is also chosen to be one of the seven Millennium Prize Problems [51]. Despite some progress, it basically does not know how to prove the Riemann hypothesis, the Goldbach conjecture and the BSD conjecture. So, it is a good chance for quantum computing to have a play in this research field, as it may well be possible to find a counter-example in one of the three open conjectures, giving the parallel computing power of quantum computers.

Problems for Section 6.2

1. Design a polynomial or exponential time quantum algorithm to calculate the values of $\pi(x)$ and $\pi_2(x)$.
2. Design a polynomial or exponential time quantum algorithm for calculating the zeroes of $\zeta(s)$.
3. Develop a polynomial or exponential time quantum algorithm for computing the elliptic curve L function $L(E, s)$.
4. Design a polynomial or exponential time quantum algorithm for verifying Riemann's hypothesis.
5. Design a polynomial or exponential time quantum algorithm for verifying Goldbach's conjecture.
6. Design a polynomial or exponential time quantum algorithm for verifying the Birch and Swinnerton-Dyer conjecture.

6.3 More Quantum Algorithms

Up to date, all know quantum algorithms offering substantial (particularly exponential, i.e., superpolynomial[1]) speedup over classical algorithms for the same problems fall into one of the following categories (see [26, 43, 50]).

1. Use the quantum Fourier transform to find the periodicity of the problems, these include:

---

[1]A typical superpolynomial complexity is $\mathcal{O}((\log n)^{\log \log \log n})$, as $n \to \infty$, where $\log n$ is the input length. Note that superpolynomial is exponential not polynomial. Thus, e.g., $\mathcal{O}((\log n)^{11})$ is polynomial, whereas $\mathcal{O}(n^{0.1})$ is exponential.

(1) The Deutsch–Jozsa algorithm for a black-box function decision problem (see [10, 13]). It is one of the first examples of a quantum algorithm that is exponentially faster than any possible *deterministic* classical algorithm, but not for classical *random* algorithm, since this problem is easy to be solved by a classical random algorithm in polynomial-time $\mathcal{RP}$.

(2) Simon's quantum algorithm for a black-box function distinguishing problem [44]. It was the motivation for Shor's factoring algorithm.

(3) Shor's quantum algorithms for integer factorization and discrete logarithms (see [41, 42]). These algorithms have a great impact on the development of quantum algorithms.

(4) Hallgren's quantum algorithms for Pell's equations, principal ideal problem, and other algebraic number-theoretic problems such as unit group, class group and class number (see [14, 23–25]).

(5) The quantum phase estimation algorithm for estimating the eigenphase of an eigenvector of a unitary gate, given access to a quantum state proportional to the eigenvector and a procedure to implement the unitary conditionally. It is a quantum algorithm that finds many applications as a subroutine in other algorithms [28], including Shor's algorithms for integer factorization and discrete logarithms [41].

(6) Algorithm for solving the hidden subgroup problem [33]. The abelian hidden subgroup problem is a generalization of many problems that can be solved by a quantum computer, such as Simon's problem, solving Pell's equation, testing the principal ideal of a ring, integer factorization and discrete logarithms.

(7) Algorithm for solving the Boson sampling problem (see [34, 38]). This problem is to produce a fair sample of the probability distribution of the output which is dependent on the input arrangement of bosons and the unitarity. Traditionally, solving this problem with a classical algorithm requires computing the permanent of the unitary transform matrix, which may be either impossible or take too long time.

(8) Algorithm for estimating Gauss sums [48]. The best known classical algorithm for estimating Gauss sums runs in exponential-time. It is interesting to note that the discrete logarithm problem reduces to Gauss sum estimation, so an efficient classical algorithm for estimating Gauss sums would imply an efficient classical algorithm for computing discrete logarithms. At present, both problems cannot be solved in polynomial-time by classical algorithms, however, they all can be solved efficiently in polynomial-time by quantum algorithms (see [41, 48]).

2. Use quantum walk algorithm to solve:

(1) The element distinctness problem (determining whether all the elements of a list are distinct) [2].

(2) The triangle-finding problem (determining whether a graph is triangle-free or not) [36].

(3) Formula evaluation (evaluating, e.g., the Boolean formulas and solving the systems of linear equations) [3].
(4) Group commutativity (determining if a black-box group, given by k generators, is commutative) [35, 37].

A quantum walk is the quantum analogue of a classical random walk, which can be described by a probability distribution over some states. A quantum walk can be described by a quantum superposition over states. Quantum walks are known to give exponential speedup for some black-box problems. They also provide polynomial speedup for some other problems.

3. Use quantum mechanical idea to perform exhaustive search of n items in $\sqrt{n}$ time, these include Grover's quantum mechanical search algorithm and its generalizations (see [19–21, 23]). These type of quantum algorithms are based on *amplitude amplification*, they usually do not offer exponential speedups over, but still significantly faster than classical search algorithms.

4. Use quantum mechanical idea to solve quantum physics problems, say, e.g., using quantum computers to speed up the simulations of quantum physics [16]. This part of the work is usually done by physicists. Note that this problem belongs to $\mathcal{BQP}$-Complete problem. Similar problems include e.g., computing knot invariants: the Chern-Simons Topological Quantum Field Theory (TQFT) can be solved in terms of Jones polynomials. A quantum computer can simulate a TQFT, and thereby approximate the Jones polynomial [1], which is hard to compute classically.

Surprisingly enough, there are not many quantum algorithms been found particularly since Shor's discovered his marvelous quantum algorithms for integer factorization and discrete logarithms, leading naturally to the question that there might be indeed not many quantum algorithms that have the ability of the exponential speedups over classical algorithms (see [43, 49]). But we are not sure about this. We are even not sure exactly what quantum computer can do and what quantum computer cannot do, as quantum computers may beyond the limit of Turing machines, but of course, they may also not.

More research needs to be done before we can say something useful for the computability, complexity, and applicability of quantum computers.

The struggle continues!

6.4 Chapter Notes and Further Reading

Although quantum algorithms for IFP, DLP and ECDLP are the main stream of research in quantum computing in general and quantum computational number theory in particular, there are some other types of quantum algorithms for various problems in number theory, algebra, topology, searching and physics. Generally speaking, there are not many quantum algorithms being found since Shor discovered in 1994 his quantum algorithms for IFP and DLP. In this chapter, we discussed quantum algorithms for solving problems in algebraic number theory and for verifying number-theoretic conjectures. We also give a perspective of quantum algorithms for many other problems. Apparently, more research needs to be done before we understand the power and the applications of quantum algorithms, and also before the construction of the practical quantum computers.

In the references below, we listed over 50 bibliographic items on various quantum algorithms, most of them represent new ideas and new developments in the fields, interested readers are suggested to consult the references and the references therein for more information about quantum computing in general and quantum computational number theory in particular.

References

1. D. Aharonov, V. Jones, Z. Landau, A polynomial quantum algorithm for approximating the Jones polynomial, in *Proceedings of the 38th Annual ACM symposium on Theory of Computing*, Seattle, 21–23 May 2006, pp. 427–436
2. A. Ambainis, Quantum walk algorithm for element distinctness. SIAM J. Comput. **37**(1), 210–239 (2007)
3. A. Ambainis, New developments in quantum algorithms, in *Proceedings of Mathematical Foundations of Computer Science 2010*. Lecture Notes in Computer Science, vol. 6281 (Springer, New York, 2010), pp. 1–11
4. E. Bombieri, *The Riemann hypothesis*, in The Millennium Prize Problems, cd. by J. Carlson, A. Jaffe, A. Wiles (Clay Mathematics Institute/American Mathematical Society, Providence, 2006), pp. 107–152
   [8]: The Millennium Prize Problem (Clay Mathematical Institute and American Mathematical Society, Cambridge, 2006), pp. 105–124
5. C. Breuil, B. Conrad, F. Diamond, R. Taylor, On the modularity of elliptic curves over $\mathbb{Q}$: wild 3-adic exercises. J. Am. Math. Soc. **14**(4), 843–939 (2001)
6. M.L. Brown, *Heegner Modules and Elliptic Curves*. Lecture Notes in Mathematics, vol. 1849 (Springer, New York, 2004)
7. J.A. Buchmann, H.C. Williams, A key-exchange system based on real quadratic fields (extended abstract), in *Advances in Cryptology–CRYPTO 1989*. Lecture Notes in Computer Science, vol. 435 (Springer, New York, 1990), pp. 335–343
8. J. Carlson, A. Jaffe, A. Wiles (eds.), *The Millennium Prize Problems* (Clay Mathematics Institute and American Mathematical Society, Cambridge, 2006)
9. J.R. Chen, On the representation of a large even integer as the sum of a prime and the product of at most two primes. Scientia Sinica **XVI**(2), 157–176 (1973)
10. R. Cleve, A. Ekert, C. Macchiavello, M. Mosca, Quantum algorithms revisited. Proc. R. Soc. Lond. A **454**(1969), 339–354 (1998)
11. J. Coates, A. Wiles, On the conjecture of Birch and Swinnerton-Dyer. Invent. Math. **39**(3), 223–251 (1977)
12. H. Cohen, *A Course in Computational Algebraic Number Theory*. Graduate Texts in Mathematics, vol. 138 (Springer, New York, 1993)
13. D. Deutsch, R. Jozsa, Rapid solutions of problems by quantum computation. Proc. R. Soc. Lond. A **439**(1907), 553–558 (1992)
14. K. Eisenträger, S. Hallgren, Computing the unit group, class group, and compact representations in algebraic function fields, in *The Open Book Series: Tenth Algorithmic Number Theory Symposium*, vol. 1 (2013), pp. 335–358

15. K. Eisenträger, A. Kitaev, F. Song, A quantum algorithm for computing the unit group of an arbitrary degree number field, in *Proceedings of the 46th Annual ACM Symposium on Theory of Computing*, New York, 31 May–4 June 2014, pp. 293–302
16. R. Feynman, Simulating physics with quantum computers. Int. J. Theor. Phys. **21**(6–7), 467–488 (1982)
17. B.H. Gross, D.B. Zagier, Heegner points and derivatives of L-series. Invent. Math. **84**(2), 225–320 (1986)
18. B. Gross, W. Kohnen, D. Zagier, Heegner points and derivatives of L-series, II. Math. Ann. **278**(1–4), 497–562 (1987)
19. L.K. Grover, A fast quantum mechanical algorithm for database search, in *Proceedings of 28th Annual ACM Symposium on the Theory of Computing*, Philadelphia, 22–24 May 1996, pp. 212–219
20. L.K. Grover, Quantum mechanics helps in searching for a needle in a haystack. Phys. Rev. Lett. **79**(2), 325–328 (1997)
21. L.K. Grover, From Schrödinger's equation to quantum search algorithm. Am. J. Phys. **69**(7), 769–777 (2001)
22. L.K. Grover, A.M. Sengupta, From coupled pendulum to quantum search, in *Mathematics of Quantum Computing* (Chapman & Hall/CRC, Boca Raton, 2002), pp. 119–134
23. S. Hallgren, Polynomial-time quantum algorithms for Pell's equation and the principal ideal problem, in *Proceedings of the 34th Annual ACM Symposium on Theory of Computing*, Montreal, 19–21 May 2002, pp. 653–658, ed. by R.K. Brylinski, G. Chen
24. S. Hallgren, Fast quantum algorithms for computing the unit group and class group of a number field, in *Proceedings of the 37th Annual ACM Symposium on Theory of Computing*, Baltimore, 21–24 May 2005, pp. 468–474
25. S. Hallgren, Polynomial-time quantum algorithms for Pell's equation and the principal ideal problem. J. ACM, **54**(1), Article 4, 19 (2007)
26. S. Jordan, Quantum algorithm zoo (2015). http://math.nist.gov/quantum/zoo/
27. R. Jozsa, Quantum computation in algebraic number theory: Hallgren's efficient quantum algorithm for solving Pell's equation. Ann. Phys. **306**(2), 241–279 (2003)
28. A.Y. Kitaev, Quantum measurements and the Abelian stabilizer problem (1995). arXiv:quant-ph/95110226v1
29. V. Kolyvagin, Finiteness of $E(\mathbb{Q})$ amd III$(E, \mathbb{Q})$ for a class of weil curves. Math. USSR Izvestija, **32**, 523–541 (1989)
30. H.W. Lenstra, Jr., Solving the Pell equation. Not. Am. Math. Soc. **49**(2), 182–192 (2002)
31. J. Latorre, G. Sierra, Quantum computing of prime number functions (2013). arXiv:1302.6245v3 [quant-ph]
32. J. Latorre, G. Sierra, There is Entanglement in the primes (2014). arXiv:1403.4765v2 [quant-ph]
33. C. Lomont, The hidden subgroup problem – review and open problems (2004). arXiv:quant-ph/0411037v1
34. A.P. Lund, A. Laing, S. Rahimi-Keshari, et al., Boson sampling from gaussian states. Phys. Rev. Lett. **113**(10), 100502, 1–5 (2014)
35. F. Magniez, A. Nayak, Quantum complexity of testing group commutativity. Algorithmica **48**(3), 221–232 (2007)
36. F. Magniez, M. Santha, M. Szegedy, Quantum algorithms for the triangle problem. SIAM J. Comput. **37**(2), 413–424 (2007)
37. I. Pak, Testing commutativity of a group and the power of randomization. LMS J. Comput. Math. **15**, 38–43 (2012)
38. T.C. Ralph, Boson sampling on a chip. Nat. Photonics **7**(7), 514–515 (2013)
39. D. Shanks, Class number, a theory of factorization, and genera, in *Proceedings of Symposia in Pure Mathematics*, vol. 20 (American Mathematical Society, Providence, 1971), pp. 415–440
40. A. Schmidt, U. Völlmer, Polynomial-time quantum algorithm for the computation of the unit group of a number field, in *Proceedings of 37th Annual ACM Symposium on Theory of Computing*, New York (2005), pp. 475–480

41. A. Wiles, *The Birch and Swinnerton-Dyer conjecture*, in The Millennium Prize Problems, ed. by J. Carlson, A. Jaffe, A. Wiles (Clay Mathematics Institute/American Mathematical Society, Providence, 2006), pp. 31–44

42. P. Shor, Polynomial-time algorithms for prime factorization and discrete logarithms on a quantum computer. SIAM J. Comput. **26**(5), 1484–1509 (1997)

43. P. Shor, Why haven't more quantum algorithms been found? J. ACM, **50**(1), 87–90 (2003)

44. D.R. Simon, On the power of quantum computation. SIAM J. Comput. **26**(5), 1474–1483 (1997)

45. R.D. Silverman, A perspective on computational number theory. Not. Am. Math. Soc. **38**(6), 562–568 (1991)

46. C. Thiel, *On the Complexity of Some Problems in Algorithmic Algebraic Number Theory*. Ph.D. Thesis, Universität des Saarlandes, Saarbrücken, 1995

47. W. van Dam, Quantum computing of zeroes of zeta functions (2004). arXiv:quant-ph/0405081v1

48. W. van Dam, G. Seroussi, Efficient quantum algorithms for estimating gauss sums (2002). arXiv:quant-ph/0207131v

49. P. Vitányi, The quantum computing challenge, in *Informatics: 10 Years Back, 10 Years Ahead*, Lecture Notes in Computer Science, vol. 2000 (Springer, New York, 2001), pp. 219–233

50. Wikipedia, Quantum algorithms. Wikipedia, the free encyclopedia (2015). https://en.wikipedia.org/wiki/Quantum_algorithm

51. A. Wiles, *The Birch and Swinnerton-Dyer conjecture*, in The Millennium Prize Problem ed. by J. Carlson, A. Jaffe, A. Wiles (Clay Mathematics Institute/American Mathematical Society, Providence, 2006), Cambridge, 2006), pp. 31–44

52. H.C. Williams, Solving the pell equation, in *Surveys in Number Theory: Papers from the Millennial Conference on Number Theory*, ed. by M.A. Bennett, B.C. Berndt, N. Boston, et al. (AK Peters, Natick, 2002), pp. 325–363

53. S.Y. Yan, *Number Theory for Computing*, 2nd edn. (Springer, New York, 2002)

About the Author

Song Y. Yan is currently the specially-appointed professorship at Wuhan University, China. He received a PhD in Number Theory from the Department of Mathematics at the University of York, England, and hold various posts at Universities of York, Cambridge, Aston, Coventry in the United Kingdom, and also various visiting posts at Universities of Rutgers, Columbia, Toronto, MIT and Harvard in the North America. His research interests include Computational Number Theory, Computational Complexity Theory, Design and Analysis of Algorithms, Cryptography and Information/Network Security. He published, among others, the following six well-received research monographs and advanced textbooks in the related fields:

[1] *Perfect, Amicable and Sociable Numbers: A Computational Approach*, World Scientific, 1996.
[2] *Number Theory for Computing*, Springer, First Edition, 2000; Second Edition, 2002; Polish Translation, 2006 (Polish Scientific Publishers PWN, Warsaw); Chinese Translation, 2007 (Tsinghua University Press, Beijing).

© Springer International Publishing Switzerland 2015
S.Y. Yan, *Quantum Computational Number Theory*,
DOI 10.1007/978-3-319-25823-2

[3] *Primality Testing and Integer Factorization in Public-Key Cryptography*, Springer, First Edition, 2004; Second Edition, 2009.

[4] *Cryptanalytic Attacks on RSA*, Springer, 2008. Russian Translation, 2010 (Russian Scientific Publishers, Moscow).

[5] *Computational Number Theory and Modern Cryptography*, Wiley, 2012.

[6] *Quantum Attacks on Public-Key Cryptosystems*, Springer, 2013.

Index

© Springer International Publishing Switzerland 2015
S.Y. Yan, *Quantum Computational Number Theory*,
DOI 10.1007/978-3-319-25823-2

Printed in the United States
By Bookmasters